Driving across Kansas

Driving across

Kansas

A Guide to I-70, Revised and Updated Edition

TED T. CABLE AND WAYNE A. MALEY

University Press of Kansas

Published by the University Press of Kansas
(Lawrence, Kansas 66045), which was organized
by the Kansas Board of Regents and is operated
and funded by Emporia State University,
Fort Hays State University, Kansas State University,
Pittsburg State University, the University of Kansas,
and Wichita State University.

Library of Congress Cataloging-in-Publication Data

Names: Cable, Ted T., author. | Maley, Wayne A., co-author.
Title: Driving across Kansas : a guide to I-70 / Ted T. Cable and Wayne A. Maley.
Description: Revised and updated edition. | Lawrence, Kansas : University Press of Kansas, 2017. | Includes bibliographical references and index.
Identifiers: LCCN 2017007055| ISBN 9780700624140 (paperback : alkaline paper) | ISBN 9780700624157 (ebook)
Subjects: LCSH: Kansas—Guidebooks. | Interstate 70—Guidebooks. | Automobile travel—Kansas—Guidebooks. | Kansas—History, Local. | BISAC: TRAVEL / United States / Midwest / West North Central (IA, KS, MN, MO, ND, NE, SD) | HISTORY / United States / State & Local / Midwest (IA, IL, IN, KS, MI, MN, MO, ND, NE, OH, SD, WI)
Classification: LCC F679.3 .C33 2017 | DDC 917.8104—dc23
LC record available at https://lccn.loc.gov/2017007055.

British Library Cataloguing-in-Publication Data is available.

Printed in the United States of America

10 9 8 7 6 5 4 3 2 1

The paper used in this publication is recycled and
contains 30 percent postconsumer waste. It is
acid free and meets the minimum requirements
of the American National Standard for Permanence
of Paper for Printed Library Materials Z39.48-1992.

Contents

Preface and Acknowledgments

> The true West differs from the East in one great, pervasive, influential, and awesome way: space. . . . It's that apparent emptiness which makes matter look alone, exiled, and unconnected. Those spaces diminish man and reduce his blindness to the immensity of the universe; they push him toward a greater reliance on himself, and, at the same time, to a greater awareness of others and what they do. But, as space diminishes man and his constructions in a material fashion, it also—paradoxically—makes them more noticeable. *Things show up out here.* No one, not even the sojourner can escape the expanses. You can't get away from them by rolling up the safety-glass and speeding through, because the terrible distances eat up the speed. . . . Still, drivers race along; but when you get down to it, they are people uneasy about space.
>
> —William Least Heat Moon, *Blue Highways*

So you are crossing Kansas on Interstate 70. Early pioneers heading west hesitated at the edge of the eastern forests, mustering their courage as if the prairies were a lonely ocean or dangerous desert to be conquered. You will soon experience the vastness of the Great Plains and seemingly endless open spaces as you proceed across the state.

Some travelers still find the prospect of crossing the Plains daunting, even in climate-controlled cars cruising along at 70 miles per hour. Today as in the past, for many travelers, the Plains are an obstacle to be overcome on the way to a *better* place—the Rocky Mountains or maybe California. For eastbound travelers, the great eastern cities or Atlantic beaches beckon. Perhaps hometowns with family and friends are the ultimate destination.

Least Heat Moon wrote of the "apparent emptiness" of the Plains and the "terrible distances that eat up speed." Ian Frazier, in his book *Great Plains,* noted that interstate highways seem designed to get people across the Plains "in the least time possible, as if this were an awkward point in a conversation."

This book's purpose is to guide travelers through the apparent emptiness, to interpret things that show up out here in Kansas, and to break the silence in the awkward conversation. Rather than having sojourners escaping the expanses and being uneasy about the space, our goal is to have travelers revel in the spaciousness; sail under spectacular skies; perceive the beauty in subtle, understated, earth-toned landscapes; appreciate the buried treasures of rich soils; and discover compassion and courage in the tales of others who crossed these lands. Our hope is that this book will make travel across the immense space of Kansas an enjoyable and enriching experience.

As you drive through Kansas using this guide, you will glimpse what the state was in days past and what it is today. You will be introduced to prehistoric animals; vast herds of bison and antelope; Native Americans, French trappers, and Spanish explorers; and European settlers—all of which have impacted the landscape and natural resources of Kansas. You will see that the Great Plains are more than they appear at first glance. These lands played a pivotal role in westward expansion and in shaping our American heritage. The vast open spaces not only influenced our past but also continue to affect the lives of Americans from coast to coast, particularly at the dinner table. As you travel across Kansas, you may come to agree with Ian Frazier, who wrote, “The beauty of the plains is not just in themselves but in the sky, in what you think when you look at them, and in what they are not.”

We wish to thank the many individuals we interviewed along the route of I-70; their names appear in the references. We also offer our thanks to the many anonymous people who so generously volunteered information about sites or provided us with directions. In addition, the following people offered valuable information or other assistance: Kelley Blankley, LuAnn Cadden, Mike Chaneske, Robin Grumm, Hank Ernst, Keith Lynch, Elaine Marshall, Mike Rader, Scott Seltman, Jeff Sheets, Joan Shull, and Kasey Windhorst. We are especially grateful to Lowell Johnson for allowing us to use his excellent bird photos.

Most of all, we would like to thank our wives, Marianne Maley and Diane Cable, who served as drivers and readers as we developed and road-tested this book.

Introduction

> The world is a book, and those who do not travel read only a page.
> —Saint Augustine

The state of Kansas was named after a tribe of Indians called Kansa or Kaw, meaning "People of the South Wind." This tribe arrived in what is now Kansas around 1720 and settled in temporary villages near the current cities of Leavenworth and Atchison. Later, to be closer to the best bison-hunting grounds, they established their principal village where the Big Blue River joins the Kansas River, near the present city of Manhattan.

From 1492 to 1845, land that became Kansas was at various times claimed by six different countries. The first European to see this land was the Spanish conquistador Francisco Vásquez de Coronado, who explored the area in search of the Seven Cities of Gold in 1541. French trappers and explorers came to this land in the late 1600s and early 1700s. The United States bought the land that is now Kansas from the French in 1803 as part of the Louisiana Purchase.

Although the state's name honors the Kaw people, the first explorers to this region found it occupied by the Indians of Quivira, most likely the Wichita tribe and the Pawnee people. However, the Wichita spent most of their time in what is now Oklahoma and Texas. In an era when Spain ruled much of North and South America, Kansas was commonly called Harahey. The people of Harahey were probably Pawnee. Native Americans played a prominent role in the history of Kansas: their heritage and influence will be apparent at many locations along I-70.

As you travel along I-70, you will also see the influence of the trails and rails that carried settlers, cattle, and supplies to the West. Moreover, you will see how the issue of whether Kansas would be a free state or a slave state resulted in the violent "Bleeding Kansas" period that shaped the history of the eastern portion of the state.

Kansas is not crowded. It ranks thirteenth among the states in size but only thirty-fourth in population. That leaves plenty of space for nature. In fact, the state is home to almost 800 kinds of vertebrates, including 141 species of fish, 32 kinds of amphibians, 14 types of turtles, 53 different reptiles, and 87 kinds of mammals. More than 475 different bird species have been seen in Kansas, and more than 2,000 kinds of plants grow wild here, including 200 types of grasses. You will no doubt notice many of these plants and animals along I-70.

Traveling I-70 will be a trip through time as well as a tour across bountiful and beautiful lands. You will be driving along an east-west transportation corridor that has existed since presettlement times. Early pioneers followed the major river systems westward from Kansas City because they provided water for people and livestock and because the river valleys were relatively flat compared with the surrounding hills. I-70 parallels one such trail—the Smoky Hill Trail, which was noteworthy as the quickest route to the Denver goldfields that were discovered in 1858. Nine years later, railroads expanded westward and followed these routes to be close to water and to the wood needed for the ties. You will be paralleling the Rock Island and Union Pacific Railroad lines, which were built in the late 1800s.

Federal highways were constructed along the railroad lines to link the towns that sprang up near the rails and rivers. From Kansas City west to Oakley, I-70 follows—and at some points *is*—historic US 40. From Colby to the Colorado line, I-70 follows old US 24, a federal highway linking Kansas City to Denver. Completed in 1926, US 40 was the nation's first federally funded coast-to-coast highway. Its original 3,022-mile route connected Atlantic City with San Francisco. Unlike the more famous Route 66, US 40 still is formally designated across the country. In the mid-1900s, interstates such as I-70 replaced many state and federal highways. In this case, beginning in 1956, some segments of US 40 were transferred to I-70.

So, you will notice on your map that lots of highways and railroads follow routes parallel to one another, often adjacent to rivers—and I-70 is no exception. As you drive along, you will be following trails used by Native Americans and pioneers, rails used by early settlers, and highways used by drivers of the first automobile generation in the early 1900s. You undoubtedly will be moving down the route faster and more comfortably than any of your traveling predecessors, and we hope you'll be enjoying the trip at least as much as they did. Horace Greeley, the New York newspaperman who encouraged westward travel with the exhortation "Go west young man," claimed, "I like Kansas . . . better than

I expected to." We think if you slow down and look closely, you, like Horace, will be pleasantly surprised by Kansas too.

THE KANSAS STATE FLAG

Kansas flag

The Kansas flag will be waving in the wind at points along the highway (we can almost guarantee the wind). In the center of the dark-blue flag is the state seal, which paints a picture of Kansas history. The thirty-four stars represent the fact that Kansas was the thirty-fourth state admitted to the Union. The rolling hills depict those rising near historic Fort Riley, hills you will see along I-70. Scenes on the seal—Native Americans hunting bison, wagon trains heading west, and steamships carrying supplies up the Kansas River—all represent important aspects of Kansas history that will be presented as you travel across the state. The farmer plowing fields near his cabin reflects the fact that agriculture has always dominated the Kansas economy and landscape. Agricultural stories dominate in this book as well. The state motto, *Ad astra per aspera,* meaning "To the stars through difficulties," is included in the state seal. We hope you won't experience any difficulties as you travel across Kansas.

Kansas state seal

USING THIS BOOK

In this guide, the I-70 mile markers identify the location of features being described. Of course, a mention of a sight may not come precisely at the mile marker listed. Rather, the intent is to encourage a look ahead. Thus, eastbound and westbound references for the same feature may be given at different mileposts. Moreover, because some stories are too long to read about in the short time it takes to speed by a given location, we have cross-referenced multiple stories about the same place. To help you find more information about a topic, we direct you using the mile marker number combined with an E or a W for the eastbound or westbound texts.

Miles on all interstate highways are measured from the westernmost or southernmost point in the state. At Kansas City, you enter Kansas on I-70 at mile marker 423, meaning you are 423 miles from the westernmost point of the highway, at the Colorado state line. Thus, when you are heading west, the green mileage marker signs will be decreasing as you proceed toward Colorado. For travelers driving east, the mile markers will be increasing as they indicate the number of miles you have traveled from the Colorado line. On a section of I-70 in eastern Kansas that is part of the Kansas tollway system, the green mile markers measure the distance from the Oklahoma line south of Wichita.

OF COWS AND CLOUDS

If you are traveling with young children, you might want to engage them in the fun activity of cow and cloud identification to make the trip more fun.

Cows

Not all cattle are cows. Cattle are cows only if they are adult females that have given birth. Ranchers and "cowboys" call males *bulls*. They call young females *heifers* until they have their first babies called *calves*. If a bull has been castrated it is called a *steer*. Technically all of these cow-like creatures are *bovines*. Dozens of varieties exist, but see if you can find these common bovines on your trip along I-70:

- **Angus** — All black; famous for producing high quality beef. Look for these in the Flint Hills.
- **Holsteins** — Black and white patches like the familiar Chick-Fil-A cows; produce milk and other dairy products.
- **Herefords** — Brown cattle with white faces; if crossed with Angus you can get "Black Baldies," black cattle with white faces.
- **Charolais** — All-white cattle raised for meat; originally from the area surrounding Charolles in Burgundy in eastern France.
- **Belted Galloways** — Black and white, but instead of patches they are black at both ends and white in the middle, like the pattern of an Oreo cookie.
- **Texas Longhorns** — Cattle with horns that can be almost seven feet across from tip to tip. Texas Longhorns are descendants of cattle first brought to the New World by Christopher Columbus and the Spanish colonists. They do well in dry, drought-prone climates like western Kansas.

Clouds

If counting cows is not your thing, you might turn your eyes skyward and enjoy the clouds that grace the wide Kansas skies. Clouds are made from tiny water droplets or, if it is cold enough, ice crystals. The air is colder at higher altitudes so ice crystals can exist within a cloud even in summer. If clouds have fuzzy edges they have ice crystals. If clouds have sharp edges they have water droplets. If these water droplets get too heavy they drop as rain. Although the Kansas state song "Home on the Range" speaks of "skies that are not cloudy all day," see if you can find these clouds as you travel across Kansas:

- **Cirrus** — High, (above 18,000 feet) wispy clouds. *Cirrus* comes from the Latin for lock of hair. Generally indicate fair weather for the next twenty-four hours. They can sail on the jet streams at more than 100 miles per hour.
- **Stratus** — Layer of clouds covering the whole sky. When stratus clouds are touching the earth we call them fog. When this blanket of clouds is very high in the sky, it is called cirrostratus. Usually the sun and moon can be seen through this thin layer of cirrostratus clouds.
- **Cumulus** — Pretty, fluffy clouds that look like cotton and are often thought of as fair weather "nice day" clouds. Their bottoms are flat and they grow upward from the top, sometimes looking like a head of cauliflower.
- **Cumulonimbus** — Majestic, powerful, tall storm clouds that produce lightning, thunder, and sometimes hail or tornados. If they have a green tint to them, it probably means the presence of hail. High winds can flatten the top into an anvil shape. These clouds travel at 30—40 miles per hour, usually in the direction that the anvil is pointing. Cumulonimbus thunderheads are awe-inspiring, and their lightning and tops can be seen up to 300 miles away!
- **Contrails** — White lines crisscrossing the sky made by the many jets flying over Kansas. These clouds form when the hot humid air from the jet engine enters the cold dry air at high altitudes causing the moisture in the exhaust to condense and form a cloud trail.

We hope cirrus and cumulus clouds float above you on your journey, dreary stratus clouds are seldom seen, and that cumulonimbus clouds are only seen from a safe distance.

Driving across Kansas

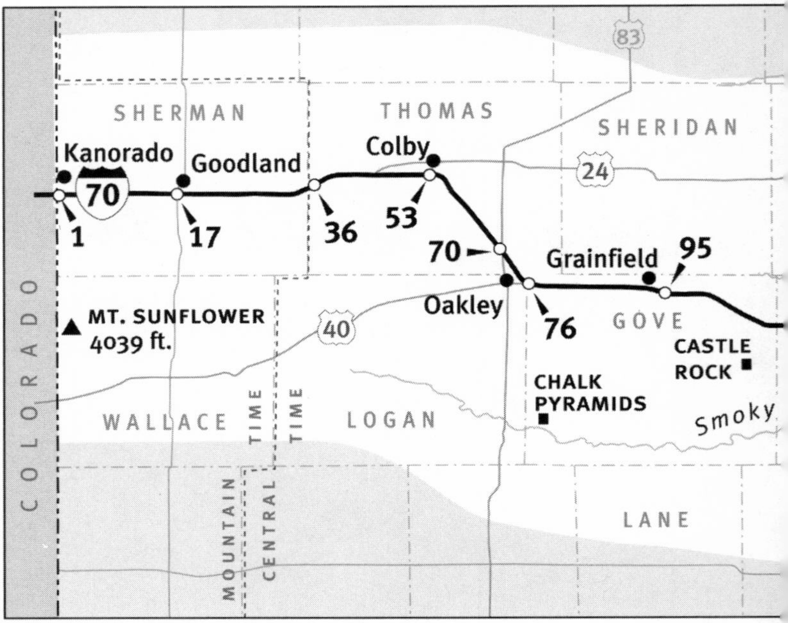

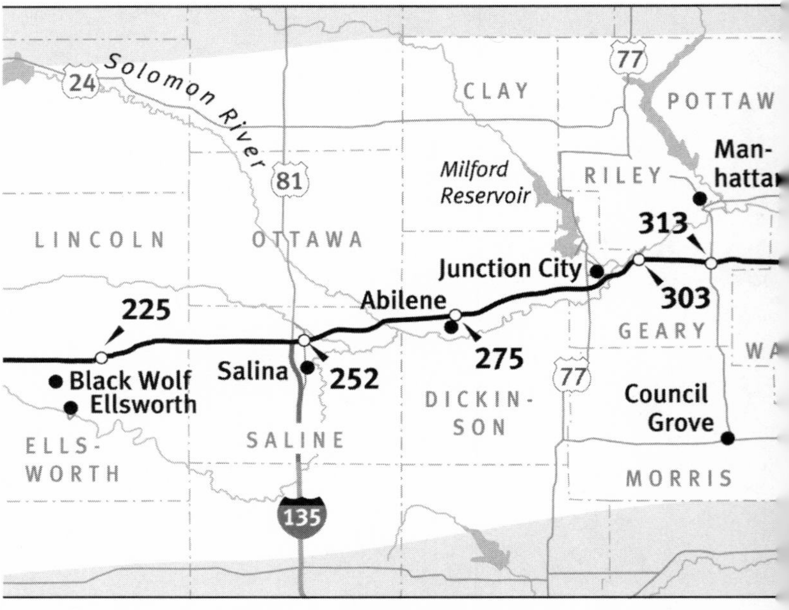

As I-70 crosses Kansas from Kansas City to Colorado, distance is posted on highway markers showing miles from the Colorado border. Where the route uses the Kansas Turnpike, distance is miles from Oklahoma.

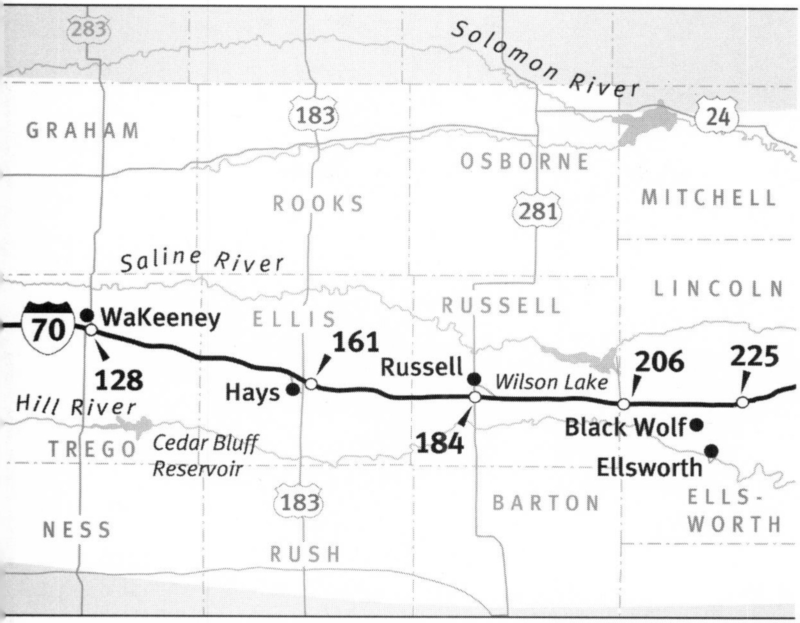
283
Solomon River
183
24
GRAHAM
OSBORNE
ROOKS
281
MITCHELL
Saline River
LINCOLN
70
WaKeeney
ELLIS
RUSSELL
161
Russell
206
225
128
Hays
Wilson Lake
Hill River
184
Black Wolf
TREGO
Cedar Bluff Reservoir
Ellsworth
183
BARTON
ELLS-WORTH
NESS
RUSH

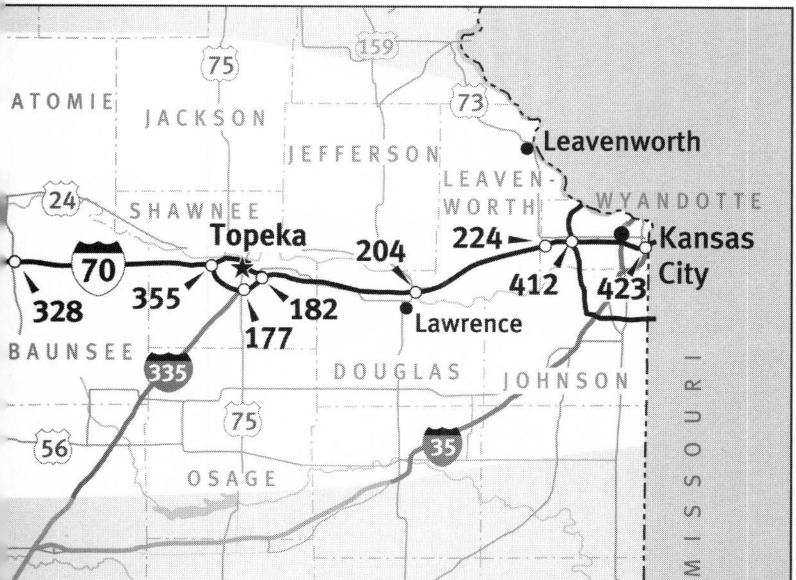
159
75
73
ATOMIE
JACKSON
Leavenworth
JEFFERSON
LEAVEN-WORTH
WYANDOTTE
24
SHAWNEE
Topeka
204
224
Kansas City
70
328
355
182
412
423
177
Lawrence
BAUNSEE
335
DOUGLAS
JOHNSON
MISSOURI
75
56
35
OSAGE

Westbound

KANSAS CITY – LAWRENCE AREA

423 Lowest Point of the Trip

Welcome to Kansas! This is the lowest elevation of your trip across the state. At the mouth of the Kansas River, where it joins the Missouri just to the north, the elevation is 760 feet above sea level. At its highest point, at mile 3.7, Interstate 70 will have climbed to an elevation of 3,910 feet. The elevation change between here and the Colorado line is so gradual that few people perceive the difference. However, I-70 will take you over hills and drop you into valleys along the way, and you will see that, in spite of what you may have heard, Kansas is not really flat.

If you drove in from Missouri, you crossed the Kansas River near its junction with the wide Missouri River. These two rivers have played a vital role in Kansas history ever since Meriwether Lewis and William Clark camped just north of the spot where you crossed, both on their famous exploration in 1804 and again on their return two years later.

422 Railroads

In 1802, Thomas Jefferson predicted, "The introduction of so powerful an agent as steam to a carriage on wheels will make a great change in the situation of man." Nowhere was his prediction more correct than in Kansas. Railroads changed everything there! The importance of railroads in determining the Kansas landscape becomes evident here at the beginning of your westbound I-70 trip. The extensive rail yards you see on the left mark the termination for the rail lines that fanned out to the west and southwest. Railroads moved people across Kansas and carried Kansas resources and products to distant markets. Today, building material, equipment, and supplies from industries in the East are taken across the state and beyond. Coming back from the West, trains are mostly transporting grain, that marvelous Kansas resource that is renewed every year.

Grain comes to Kansas City in gondola and hopper railcars to be unloaded at a trackside elevator, one of the tall structures visible across the valley; there, it is *elevated* by a conveyor to the top of the structure. The grain then flows by gravity into one of the tall round bins that are lined up side by side to form the grain elevator. As you travel westward, you will see many elevators where grain is stored in clusters of bins until it is moved to be processed into food.

The significance of the railroad cannot be overstated. For fifty years up until the 1920s, when autos and paved highways finally crossed the country, every facet of life was affected by the railroad. As you will see ahead, the location of the railroads determined which towns lived and which towns died. The rails stimulated commerce and brought people together.

420 Kansas City, Kansas

Although it is not easily identified, you are now in Kansas City, Kansas. This is not the biggest or most populated city in the state. In fact, it ranks third in population behind the cities of Wichita and Overland Park, a suburb south of this location. The reason most people think this is the largest city in Kansas is that they consider the whole metropolitan area, over half of which is actually in another state, comprising the *other* Kansas City—Kansas City, Missouri.

In August 1806, Lewis and Clark described the area where the Kansas and Missouri Rivers meet—the location of Kansas City. As they saw it, the river junction was a perfect place to construct a trading house or a fort. No immediate action was taken by the recipients of Lewis and Clark's news though. Indeed, it was not until 1868 that several businessmen organized the Kansas City, Kansas, Town Company. By 1885, the town was thriving, and it began to sprawl westward. Learn more about Kansas City at 412E (p. 243).

418 Wyandotte County

You are traveling in Wyandotte County, named for the Wyandot Indians. After the Wyandots ceded their Ohio lands to the US government, they moved to occupy land in the territory they thought the Shawnees had sold to them. But the Shawnees repudiated the agreement, and the Wyandots soon found themselves strangers in a strange land. They set up camp on a government-owned strip of land between the western boundary of the Missouri and Kansas Rivers—present-day Kansas City.

The Delaware Indians, distant relatives of the Wyandots who owned land on the north side of the Kansas River, came to the rescue and sold the Wyandots 36 square miles of land between the fork of the two rivers so they could have a home. The Wyandots liked their new homeland but soon encountered several difficulties. The story of how sickness and floodwaters reduced their numbers can be read at 415E (p. 244).

415 Grinter House and Ferry

Two miles south at Exit 414 is Grinter Place Historic Site. At this location, Moses Grinter traded with the Delaware Indians and maintained the first ferry to cross the Kansas River. For a time, it was the only ferry serving the important military road between Fort Leavenworth, just to the north, and Oklahoma.

Grinter began his operation in 1831. The ferry used a rope windlass to alter the angle of the hull into the current. This allowed the ferry to be pushed across the river by waterpower rather than hav-

Grinter Ferry (Kansas State Historical Society)

ing to be pulled manually. Grinter charged 50¢ per person or $2 per wagon to be taken across. Given inflation, that would be about $14 per person and more than $55 per wagon in today's currency—far more than the tolls you'd pay for driving your "wagon" over the entire Kansas Turnpike!

Grinter constructed a log cabin near the landing when he opened the ferry for business. However, he was a victim of the floods of 1844 and lost his ferry landing and home as a result of the high water. He rebuilt the ferry, put up a new cabin, and reestablished his business the following year. With no floods for the next several years and an increase in traffic due to all the settlers heading west, Grinter's business was again booming. As a result, he and his wife, Anne, a Delaware Indian, decided to construct a nicer home. The two-story red brick house, built in 1857, is still standing today—the oldest unaltered building in Wyandotte County—and is now a museum. Grinter is credited with being the first permanent white settler in the county and one of the earliest settlers in the state.

411 The Kansas Speedway

The large complex seen on the right is the Kansas Motor Speedway, which has been hosting NASCAR and Indy Racing League races, among others, since opening in June 2001. The stands seat about 64,000 people, a crowd larger than the population of all but six Kansas towns. Only Wichita, Overland Park, Kansas City, Olathe, Topeka, and Lawrence have more people than would fit into the grandstands at the speedway. In fact, the entire populations of most Kansas *counties* could watch a race together and not fill the stands.

At mile 410, you enter the Kansas Turnpike. The only indicator of this is that the mile markers have changed. You are now at mile 226, with the mile markers here reflecting the distance along the turnpike from the Oklahoma border. When I-70 leaves the turnpike near Topeka, the numbering once again indicates miles from the Colorado state line. Read about the history of the turnpike at 184E *(p. 233)*.

226 Fort Leavenworth

Fort Leavenworth and the town of Leavenworth lie about 15 miles north of I-70 on State Highway 7. The fort was established in 1827 as a starting point for westbound explorers, settlers, and military expeditions. Since it was located on the banks of the Missouri River, supplies and people found their way there by keelboats and shallow-water barges coming from St. Louis and the East. During the 1840s, thousands of wagons passed through the fort en route to California and Oregon. At 207E (p. 240), read about the history of Leavenworth, the fort, and the famous prison.

224 Marbles and Memories

If you've lost your marbles, you can replace them at Moon Marble Company south of Exit 224 in Bonner Springs. Moon Marble Company is one of the "8 Wonders of Kansas Commerce" because it is the only store in the country where you can both buy handmade marbles and watch them being made. Owner Bruce Breslow makes about a thousand marbles a year by hand. He also sells traditional old-fashioned toys that you might have played with as a child. Moon Marble Company offers tours and field trips where groups can learn how to play marbles. If you have memories of playing with shooters, bowlers, dobbers, bumblebees, cat eyes, peewees, or toebreakers, you might want to "knuckle down" (a marble shooting position) and visit Moon Marble Company.

223 Leavenworth County

Shortly ahead, you will enter Leavenworth County, established in 1855 as one of the first counties in Kansas. It was carved out of lands that belonged to the Delaware Indians and was named after Fort Leavenworth, the first fort west of the Missouri River. It is home to the famous federal prison that bears its name.

222 Beginning of Smoky Hill Trail

North of this location at Fort Leavenworth is where the Smoky Hill Trail began. The trail, which follows the Smoky Hill River through western Kansas, was the quickest route to the Denver goldfields, which were discovered in 1858. The Butterfield Overland Despatch (BOD) stagecoach line, owned by David Butterfield, traveled the Smoky Hill Trail to Denver from Atchison (north of here) three times a week. It took the BOD between eight and twelve days to

Butterfield's Overland Despatch coach leaves Atchison to follow the Smoky Hill Trail west. (Kansas State Historical Society)

make the trip to Denver, depending on weather conditions and delays. I-70 parallels this trail across much of Kansas; on this modern trail, you can almost but not quite travel the same route and distance in only eight hours!

Pioneers followed the major river systems westward from Kansas City because they provided water for both people and livestock, as well as trees for fuel, and because the river valleys were relatively flat compared with the surrounding hills. Railroads and then the early cross-country highways followed these routes for the same reasons—water and wood. You are the latest in a long history of travelers navigating this route across Kansas.

220 Kansas Farmstead Barn

One mile ahead, you will see a white barn at the Tate farm on the left. It is typical of barns that have served Kansas farmsteads for more than 100 years. The family farm needed a production center to house and care for livestock as well as storage for grain, so a design evolved that featured a high roof in the center of the barn and sheds on each side. You'll see other barns of this type as you travel across Kansas. Many will have a silo at the end to store chopped green stalks for the cattle.

The Tates built the center portion of this barn when they moved here in 1924. It has a high loft to store the hay needed to feed the horses and dairy cows. Later, a wing was attached to each side. One side was enclosed to become the milking barn that accommodated the expanding dairy herd. The other side had horse stalls and some pens for calves. Other buildings were added to the farmstead—a chicken house, a storage shed, and grain bins—but the classic barn was the focus for farm production.

Good barns are important because farm buildings are the farmer's factory. In them raw materials are converted into finished products. Feeds grown on the farm may be compared to the raw materials in manufacturing, and the milk, butter, cheese, beef, and pork to the finished products. Careful design and construction were given to the buildings so that the animals housed in them would be comfortable, enjoy good health, and receive the greatest possible benefit from the feeds given them; these structures are also designed with efficiency in mind, so that the least amount of time and labor would be required in caring for the livestock inside. For many years the Tate family grew corn and wheat on this farm, but today the land is leased to a neighbor for cropping.

218 Silo Collection

As you approach the tollbooths, you can see on the right a large group of grain storage bins. Bill Theno collects them to store 100,000 bushels of grain. His primary operation has been feeding hogs, and he stores enough grain to feed 7,000 to 8,000 of them per year. With shifting market conditions, you may be looking at a beef

Typical Kansas barn with silo

cattle feeding operation today. The long, horizontal buildings, 180 feet by 70 feet, can house 150 beef cows and calves.

The four tall blue silos are Harvestores. These glass-lined steel silos are filled from the top and have bottom unloaders, so the first grain loaded in is the first taken out. The thirteen other gray bins are connected to each other by conveyors. When grain is filled or moved, it is elevated to the top by the center column conveyor and then diverted by gravity through one of the "spiderweb" chutes to the desired bin.

The Theno farm has grown from the 40 acres that Bill's dad owned in 1956 to 3,000 acres of crop- and grassland. You will be driving along Theno acreage for several miles to the right of I-70. Fields near the highway may be planted to field corn, soybeans, or sorghum. Half of what is produced, about 135,000 bushels annually, is fed to the animals on the farm.

Besides erecting all that grain storage and housing for livestock, Bill built homes around an area where a one-room school he attended had once stood. He then bought and moved eight houses from the Kansas City Raceway property and added them to the community.

216 Nature's Sanitation Crew

When animals try to cross the interstate, they often don't make it, but an animal killed in nature does not go to waste. Something will eat it and return it to the food chain. Such are the cycles of nature.

If you are traveling during the months of April through September, you will notice large black birds soaring above the countryside with upraised wings. These amazing birds are turkey vultures, often called buzzards. By eating roadkills, vultures, which might be considered nature's sanitation crew, play a central ecological role in cleaning up and recycling dead animals. The turkey vulture's name reflects the fact that its bare, red head resembles the head of a turkey. The featherless head is an adaptation for the job; imagine the mess when the birds stick their heads into rotten carcasses if they had feathers on their heads. Vultures have strong, hooked beaks for tearing apart a carcass. Unlike hawks and eagles, however, they have weak feet because they do not need to kill their food.

Vultures are remarkable fliers. Watch them as they soar gracefully, rarely flapping their wings. They can be easily identified in flight because they soar with their wings in a V, their wing tips above the horizontal. In contrast, eagles hold their wings flat when soaring. Vultures need the updrafts, or thermals, to soar on, so don't expect to see flying vultures until after midmorning, when the sun has heated up the ground and atmosphere.

214 Ice Age Kansas

The gentle rolling hills and broad valleys indicate that you are traveling in the Glaciated Region of Kansas, which is bounded roughly by the Kansas River on the south and the Blue River (ahead near Manhattan, mile 313) on the west. Corn, soybeans, and hay are common crops on the productive farms.

This region differs greatly from the other parts of Kansas that you will cross ahead. Twice during past geologic ages an eleven-county area in the northeastern part of the state was covered by glaciers. These massive sheets of ice moved slowly, transforming the landscape. As the glaciers advanced south from Canada, they gouged out valleys in areas containing softer rocks. Soil and rocks were carried by the ice for hundreds of miles from their place of origin. When the glaciers began to melt, the debris that had been carried with them was deposited at the melting spot. The mixture of sand, rock, clay, and gravel that was left behind created a richer soil and interesting rock formations.

The elevation here averages 1,000 feet above sea level. Considerably more precipitation is received per year than in the other regions you will cross along I-70, averaging around 35 inches per year. In addition, more trees grow here than in the other regions, and they can be seen on the hilltops rather than only in the valleys, as you will see ahead in the Flint Hills. The growing season here is the longest in the state, averaging about 200 days. This factor plus adequate rainfall and fertile soil make the area good for agriculture.

212 Twisters

Ever since Dorothy and Toto were carried off from Kansas to the Land of Oz, this state has been associated with tornadoes. Although twisters have occurred in all fifty states, only Texas and Oklahoma have more than Kansas. However, Kansas has the distinction of having more F5 tornadoes (the most intense kind) than any other state because it's located where cold fronts coming down from the north meet hot, moist air from the south—ideal conditions for the formation of tornadoes. Almost every year between the months of April and July, tornadoes are seen somewhere along I-70 in Kansas.

Tornadoes are one of nature's most magical and menacing phenomena. They can be 2 miles across, with winds of 300 miles per hour. To see them from afar is awe inspiring. To witness them up close is terrifying. If you see a tornado along the highway, do not try to outrun it! Experts suggest leaving your vehicle and lying flat in a roadside ditch. Seeking shelter under an overpass may protect you from severe hail, but most overpasses offer little protection from a tornado. In spite of the threat of tornadoes, most Kansans believe, as Dorothy did, that there is no place like home. See mile 358E (p. 230) for a story of a tornado that hit Topeka.

211 Kansas Forests

You can see substantial forests along this stretch of highway. Less than 5 percent of Kansas is forested, but those 2.1 million acres of forests are important both ecologically and economically. Most forests are here in the eastern third of the state, with 83 percent of them adjacent to rivers or streams.

These riparian forests not only harbor wildlife, including endangered species, but also protect water quality in the streams by stabilizing the banks and filtering water running off from adjacent fields. Private individuals own 95 percent of all forestland in Kansas, mostly in tracts of less than 50 acres.

Kansas forest products—wood, lumber, paper—and related industries contributed $2.1 billion to the Kansas economy, support over 9,000 jobs, and are responsible for about $169 million in taxes each year. The state has more than fifty sawmills that harvest over 20 million board feet of timber annually, enough wood to construct an estimated 1,700 average-sized homes. However, most Kansas timber is not used for home construction but ends up as furniture, veneer, pallets, and gun stocks. In fact, much of the walnut harvested here goes into making gun stocks, establishing Kansas as a leading supplier for this industry. Black walnut accounts for most of the timber harvested. Other significant species are bur oak, red oak, and ash.

Although forests are scarce, they make a vital contribution to the quality of life in Kansas. As you drive west, you will see fewer and fewer trees.

207 Jayhawks

Looking ahead on the horizon, you can see the red-roofed buildings of the University of Kansas (KU), home of the Jayhawks. In 1866, a solitary building was erected overlooking Lawrence on Hogback Ridge to start the university. Since Hogback Ridge seemed to be an undignified name for the location of a dignified institution, the name was soon changed to Mount Oread, in reference to the mountain nymphs in Greek mythology. The new name seemed more appropriate for a place with such a grand hilltop view of Lawrence. Mount Oread also happened to be the name of a girl's seminary in Worcester, Massachusetts, home of one of Lawrence's founding fathers. Today, KU is a world-class university with more than 28,000 students from all fifty states and more than a hundred countries. Famous alumni include actors Paul Rudd and Mandy Patinkin and television personality Bill Kurtis.

Read more about KU and its mascot, the Jayhawk, at 200E (p. 237).

206 Douglas County

This county is named after Stephen A. Douglas, the Illinois senator who wrote the Kansas-Nebraska Bill that allowed the formation of Kansas and Nebraska and gave both territories the right to choose whether they would be free or proslavery states during the Civil War. Clashes between Free-Staters and proslavery forces dominated the establishment of Kansas and resulted in the state becoming known as Bleeding Kansas. For more of the Douglas County story, see 188E (p. 234).

The factory off to the left, beyond the trees and sand quarry lake, is a chemical plant that manufactures food-grade phosphates and phosphoric acids. That's correct, phosphoric acid—the effervescence that produces the fizz in a fountain soda and in colas and other soft drinks. There's more about phosphate and the plant at 204E (p. 239). Three generations of workers employed here continue the tradition of supplying products for processing food produced on Kansas farms.

205 New Grass

Ahead on the right, the Pine family farm produces sod that is rolled up from the fields at the right and delivered for new lawns. Bryan Pine says his most interesting delivery was made to the Kansas Motor Speedway to create the lawn areas around the grandstand and track. The farm also has supplied new grass surfaces for golf courses and soccer fields. From the sod-production fields on the right, the Pine farm can provide a homeowner with 1 square yard of replacement lawn or make an instant lawn for a major office complex. Sod is delivered to locations up to two hours away, from Kansas City to Manhattan.

The Pine family has been farming in the Kaw River valley since Will Pine moved here in 1868. Members of the sixth generation of the family now operate the farm. They also raise the traditional crops for this area—corn, soybeans, and potatoes. The total farm operation encompasses 4,000 acres. Sod growing is a recent niche opportunity. In the early 1970s, the first sod was sold as a way to stretch out the harvest season and to hedge against the weather-sensitive potato crop. Sod is now grown on 80 irrigated acres that can be seen from I-70. You'll pass by much more irrigated agriculture as you continue west; see 69W (p. 113) where you'll also find more about center-pivot irrigation machines like those watering the sod here.

Center-pivot irrigator

203 The Kaw

The Kansas River, also known as the Kaw, begins in Junction City (ahead near mile 298) at the confluence of the Republican and Smoky Hill Rivers. Its mouth is at the Missouri River in Kansas City. The Kansas River was an important means of transport for pioneers moving equipment and supplies into frontier Kansas. The river's water depth fluctuates wildly, and the many sandbars and other hazards made navigation difficult. Boat traffic declined with the development of the railroads and overland trails, and today, only canoes and small fishing boats ply the waters of the Kaw. A small hydroelectric dam downstream in Lawrence is the only one in the state.

202 Lawrence

Lawrence traces its roots back to Eli Thayer of Worcester, Massachusetts, who organized the New England Emigrant Aid Company to resist proslavery powers. Soon after the pioneers arrived in 1854, they adopted the name of Lawrence in honor of Amos Lawrence, a Massachusetts financier of the company. Interestingly, Lawrence deplored having the Kansas town named after him, for he feared that it would give the appearance of self-promotion and that it would lessen his influence for the good of the Free-State cause. Indeed, bloody conflicts were soon sparked when proslavery forces from Missouri attacked Lawrence. Read details of Quantrill's raid at 198E (p. 236).

Today, Lawrence is a thriving community supported by the University of Kansas and local industry. Crafts and antiques can be bought in the lively downtown area, and diverse restaurants cater to the eclectic appetite. Lawrence has a population of more than 90,000 and continues to grow.

200 Deer Crossing

Watch out for deer. They were eliminated from the state in the 1930s but have again become numerous. Deer have adapted to agriculture and even city life. In fact, many people now believe we have too many deer, which annoy farmers and gardeners by eating crops. More serious problems are caused when deer try to cross highways and tragic accidents result. About 10,000 deer-car accidents occur each year in Kansas!

You can see two different kinds of deer as you drive across the state. White-tailed deer are found throughout Kansas, whereas mule deer are found only in the western two-thirds of the state. Mule deer are generally larger and have big ears (hence their name). They have a white rump with a short, black-tipped tail. The more abundant white-tailed deer is reddish-brown, with a white tail that is especially noticeable when raised as a sign of warning or when the animal is running away from danger. Male mule deer antlers are distinguished by the Y-shaped forks, whereas the white-tailed deer has a large, curving antler beam with smaller unforked tines branching off it.

198 Lecompton: "Bald Eagle, KS"

North of I-70 at Exit 197 is Lecompton, founded in 1855. The town was originally named Bald Eagle for the birds that roosted in the trees along the river. "The great metropolis of Kansas" was the founder's optimistic forecast for the town located halfway between Topeka and Lawrence on the Kansas River.

Judge Samuel Lecompte presided over the town company that surveyed the 600-acre site. The town was later named Lecompton, after the judge. For three years, it fulfilled the expectations of its founders. Proslavery leaders made it their territorial capital, and workers began building the state capitol, as well as the governor's house. Soon, Lecompton had almost 5,000 residents. However, the victory of the Free-State forces in Kansas caused the booming town to go bust, and the capital was moved to Topeka. Along with the capital went the businesses of Lecompton.

During the 1850s, a ferry carried goods and people across the river in the Lecompton area. The ferry was actually a large dugout cottonwood trunk, not unlike the crude boats still used by indigenous people in Africa and South America. *The WPA Guide to 1930s Kansas* quoted William Simmons, the ferry operator, as saying to a hesitant traveler, "Don't feel skeery, mister, for she's as dry as a Missourian's throat and as safe as the American flag."

Lecompton is where President Dwight Eisenhower's parents met and were married while attending the now-defunct Lane University. Today, Lecompton is a small farming community with 600 residents. The eagles still roost along the Kansas River during winter, and they nest at Clinton Lake just south of here. Watch for eagles soaring overhead, especially during winter.

Bald eagle (Lowell Johnson)

196 Woodland Wildlife

Woodlands interspersed with farm fields and pastures provide ideal habitats for many kinds of wildlife. Deer and eastern turkey are especially easy to see from the interstate because they stand out in the fields. Bobcat and badger populations are increasing in the area. Red-tailed hawks are among the most conspicuous birds along I-70. Look for a white object in the trees—it will likely be the white breast of a red-tailed hawk.

You may spot coyotes in the fields along the interstate. Coyotes are most active at night, but you might be lucky and see one during the day, especially in the morning or evening. They are rather gangly, doglike animals, usually seen trotting alone across a field. They eat almost anything—plant or animal—and this versatility is one reason their numbers are increasing in Kansas and throughout the United States. Now, they can even be found in cities, howling at streetlights rather than the full moon!

195 The Oregon Trail

The ridge that parallels I-70 for the next several miles on the left was one route used by early traders and pioneers as they headed west. The wagon trains picked routes that minimized stream crossings and hills that had to be climbed. When highways were constructed for horseless carriages, it was natural for this route to be used. It became part of US 40, the first federally funded coast-to-coast highway.

If the pioneers were headed for Oregon, they called this the Oregon Trail. Those headed to California considered it the California Trail. Those who reached this point would probably have started in Independence, Missouri, the westernmost county seat in the United States at that time. Then, their trek to the northwest began, following ridges to watering stops like Big Springs, which is just ahead.

By 1849, spurred on by California's gold rush, more than 90,000 people had headed west on Kansas wagon trails. Today, the trails continue to provide a route across the state as the "I-70 trail." Tollway traffic records at this location count an average of more than 30,000 vehicles every day.

193 Clock House

Look among the trees on the left to see the Clock House. The clock over the front porch of this structure was taken from a courthouse and is a recent addition. The house itself, which was selected as the National Farmhouse of the Year in 1908, was built from a kit ordered from Sears, Roebuck. Learn more about the clock and the house at 192E (p. 235).

191 Big Springs

Two miles south of the interstate is the small farming community of Big Springs, the oldest settlement in Douglas County. When William Harper and John Chamberlain established Big Springs in 1854, it was already known as an excellent watering place along the Oregon Trail. As travelers emigrated west, the town became a prominent trading post.

Two noteworthy events occurred in the early history of Big Springs. One of the first blows against slavery in the Kansas Territory was struck at a Free-State convention of settlers who traveled to this town from all over Kansas on September 5, 1855. This meeting began the attempt to seize political power from proslavery sympathizers in the territory.

The other event was a strike against liquor. A Dr. Carter, the local physician, prescribed drugs and medicinal alcohol to the people of Big Springs. However, his practices came under scrutiny when a Missouri man delivered three barrels of whiskey to Carter's office, which the doctor used to start his own tavern. After the doctor's first night in business, thirty residents sent him a notice protesting his new operation. The doctor ignored the notice and kept the tavern open. The next night, forty angry residents marched into the bar, opened a barrel of whiskey, set a pile of wood shavings on fire, and burned down the tavern. After the fire, the citizens signed a temperance pledge abolishing alcohol in their town. This was one of the first recorded temperance meetings in Kansas, and it was the beginning of a crusade that led to prohibition laws.

189 Shawnee County

In 1830, pioneers began to settle in the Shawnee County area along Mission Creek, which you will cross west of Topeka (mile 351). The county, established in 1855, was named for the Shawnee Indians.

Award-winning Clock House

188 Trail Crossing

Here, your modern interstate trail crosses the historic Oregon Trail. The Oregon Trail continued toward the northwest, generally along ridgetops, to Topeka, where a ferry carried wagons across the Kansas River. The trail continued along the north side of the Kansas River toward the Platte valley and Fort Kearney in Nebraska Territory.

At Exit 362C ahead, you can celebrate another journey—a journey along the road to justice—at the Brown v. Board National Historic Site. Details about this inspirational place can be found at 362E (p. 231).

187 Roadside Gardens

Ralph Waldo Emerson declared, "The earth laughs in flowers." Over the next several miles and inside the cloverleaf at the next interchange (Exit 366, just past the tollbooths), notice how the land laughs in wildflowers in the summer months. Some areas are not mowed frequently so that you may enjoy the beauty of this wild garden. Because a variety of flowers grow here and because their blooming periods are short and varied, it is impossible to know what will be in bloom when you drive by, but some possibilities are pink prairie phlox, purple coneflower, prairie coneflower, black-eyed Susan, white and purple prairie clover, white and yellow evening primrose, chicory, gayfeather, mullein, goldenrod, milkweed, aster, coreopsis, and of course sunflower.

186 Woodlawn Farm and the Toll Plaza

When the toll plaza just ahead was constructed in 2001, much of the land came from Woodlawn Farm, which you will see on the right as you approach the tollbooths.

Woodlawn Farm is readily recognized by the white board fences that can be identified well before the buildings come into view. Gary Gilbert, the current owner, explained that even with reduced acreage, he is challenged to maintain the farm "to preserve the history of the dairy farm and keep the land in productive agriculture." You may see Hereford cattle in the pastures adjacent to the interstate. Beyond the pastures and farm buildings is cropland that produces corn, soybeans, and hay for the animals. These fields have the first soil conservation terraces in the region, built during a farm field day demonstration in the 1930s.

The barn was built in the 1920s based on plans from the magazine *Hoard's Dairyman* that encouraged a two-row arrangement of stanchions for the cows. It was argued that it would be cheaper to build and more convenient to have a wider barn than a longer one with a single-row arrangement. But then, the dairymen debated whether to face the cows away from or toward a center aisle. In this barn, the cows face a center feeding alley, making it more practical to distribute silage from the silo at the end of the barn. The turrets at the top of the barn are ventilators designed with flues to supply fresh air to the dairy cows.

The Tolbert family, who operated the dairy from 1926 through 1975, went to Wisconsin and brought back a railcar filled with Guernsey milk cows to get started. At first, Woodlawn sold cans of fresh milk in town. Then, the family started bottling the milk and delivering it door to door, using the slogan "From Moo to You." The Tolberts continued to upgrade the barn with coolers, a bottling room, and a pasteurizer (required by a Topeka ordinance passed after World War II).

The dairy was named after Woodlawn, Maryland, the birthplace of the first owner, John V. Abrahams. He and Tolbert had agreed to a farming arrangement in which they split profits and expenses fifty-fifty. Abrahams was responsible for providing materials to keep up the farm, and Tolbert supplied the labor. Cattle were owned equally. Tolbert did the field work to produce all the feed for the cattle, and Abrahams provided the seed for planting. By 1975, with milk with a high cream content no longer in demand, Woodlawn ceased operations.

Since the mid-1980s, Gary Gilbert has meticulously restored the farm buildings to their working condition. New field terraces and other erosion-control measures have been installed, along with the white board fences.

At mile 183, you leave the Kansas Turnpike. Beyond the tollbooths, I-70 mileage is once again measured from the farthest west point, the Colorado state line. Thus, Woodlawn Farm is 366 miles from Colorado and 183 miles from Oklahoma.

TOPEKA, THE STATE CAPITAL

366 Topeka: A "Capital" Place to Dig Potatoes

Just ahead is Topeka, the state's capital and fifth-largest city. On December 5, 1854, nine antislavery men met on the banks of the Kansas River at what is now Kansas Avenue and Crane Street and drew up plans for establishing Topeka. A ferry service had started there more than ten years earlier to take Oregon Trail wagons across the river. Colonel Cyrus K. Holliday, a Pennsylvania native who would become Topeka's first mayor and the founder of the Atchison, Topeka and Santa Fe Railroad, wanted to name the town Webster, after Daniel Webster. However, others wanted a more colorful local name. The word *Topeka* comes from three Indian words that have the same meaning among the Otoes, Omahas, Iowas, and Kaws. *To* means "wild potato" (or other edible root), *pe* means "good," and *okae* means "to dig." Thus, *Topeka* means "a good place to dig potatoes."

The town was incorporated in 1857 and became the state capital in November 1861. Railroad offices were established in Topeka, spawning its growth as a key railroad town.

364 The Capitol

You'll soon see the copper dome of the state capitol rising 286 feet above downtown Topeka. The capitol was constructed over a period of thirty-seven years, from 1866 to 1903, on land donated by Colonel Holliday. It was initially modeled after the Capitol in Washington, DC, but wings were added to the rotunda section in the shape of a cross, reflecting the strong role religion played in the state.

The capitol's rotunda features a series of murals illustrating the story of Kansas, painted by the native Kansan artist John Steuart Curry. One mural that depicts famed abolitionist John Brown is particularly impressive. Curry also painted the murals at the Wisconsin state capitol.

On top of the capitol dome is a 22-foot-tall statue of a Kansa Indian warrior with his arrow aimed at the stars. The statue, called *Ad Astra* (*To the Stars*), honors Kansas's Native American heritage and is based on the state motto *Ad Astra per Aspera* meaning "to the stars with difficulty." The two-ton sculpture was placed on the dome on October 10, 2002, and soon after, on November 4, Indians from five tribes took part in the dedication ceremony by singing prayers and blessings for the statue.

The capitol is considered the state's most significant architectural treasure. The Kansas Capitol Visitor Center has a gift shop and interpretive exhibits. Tours can be arranged, including dome tours that give a bird's-eye view of Topeka. See 352E (p. 228) to learn about some famous Topekans.

362 Twin Spires

You will see a prominent Topeka church as you come around the elevated 90-degree curve. The two spires adorn St. Joseph's German Catholic Church, a Romanesque-style building that was constructed in 1899 to serve the large German community in this area. For many years, the notably long sermons were preached in German. Travelers have commented that from a certain angle, the spires of the church appear to contain the faces of owls, with the clocks forming their eyes.

361 The River of Commerce

The Kansas River just to the right played a major role in the commercial life of Topeka as it brought people and goods to this loca-

Richard Bergen's Ad Astra *statue stands atop the Kansas capitol dome.*

tion. The French Canadian Pappan brothers married three Kanza Indian sisters and settled near this river. After they established a ferry over the river in 1842, wagon trains headed along the Oregon Trail made this their regular crossing.

Grain elevators along the river and railroad tracks will be familiar sights in the miles ahead. The elevators store wheat and other grains to support the food-processing industries here, and the trains allow shipment to the East and overseas.

Topeka's business sector includes food companies such as Frito-Lay, Hill's Pet Products, and the taco and tortilla bakery of Reser's Fine Foods. Other businesses include Goodyear Rubber and Tire, Burlington Northern Santa Fe Railway, Payless Shoes, and the Mars chocolate factory, which makes millions of candy products each year, among them Snickers and M&Ms.

360 Kanza Education and Science Park

This innovative outdoor education facility will be seen on the left. The local utility company partnered with the Topeka School District to create this park to teach students and families about renewable energy and to get kids interested in science and engineering careers. The site has a working substation that is color coded to teach about the different parts of the plant; it also features solar panels, a milking barn that has been converted into a learning center, a pavilion that serves as an outdoor classroom, and the 160-foot-tall wind turbine that you see poking above the trees.

358 Menninger and the Mansion

If the spire rising ahead looks familiar, it is because it is part of a replica of Independence Hall in Philadelphia. For many years, the building here was the home of the Menninger Foundation, a world-famous center for the study of psychological disorders that was founded by author and psychologist Karl Menninger.

To the right of Exit 357, back on top of that hill, is Cedar Crest, the Kansas governor's mansion. The land around the stately mansion is open as a public park and includes nature trails, exercise trails, and ponds for fishing and ice-skating.

357 Kansas Museum of History

The Kansas History Center, which includes the Kansas Museum of History and the Center for Historical Research, can be reached by

Menninger spire

taking Wanamaker Road, Exit 356. In the museum, you can view many objects related to the history presented in this book. The exhibits and artifacts make the experience of living in a log house or traveling in a covered wagon come to life. A nature trail provides an opportunity to stretch your legs in a relaxing and educational setting.

356 Kansas Symbols

As you leave the capital of Kansas, you might reflect on the official state symbols. Sunflowers were chosen as the state flower in 1903 because “the open frankness of the sunflower is indicative of the fearlessness with which Kansas meets her problems and solves them.” The cottonwood was named the state tree in 1937, and the buffalo (more correctly called bison) was adopted as the state animal in 1955. The western meadowlark is the state bird, the ornate box turtle is the state reptile, the barred tiger salamander is the state reptile, and the honeybee is the state insect. See if you can locate them all during the remainder of your trip. We’ll help by pointing them out in the pages ahead.

354 A Historic Highway

You are entering a historic stretch of highway—the very first section of the US interstate system to be completed. The 8-mile stretch of I-70 from the Topeka city limits to the Wabaunsee County line was opened on November 14, 1956, less than four months after President Eisenhower signed the Interstate Highway Act. This location marks the beginning of the nation's interstate system, the largest public works project in world history.

The interstate system was originally designed as a set of military highways to efficiently transport military equipment and personnel across the country and move thousands of people out of urban areas. Eisenhower's experiences in Europe during World War II, particularly his observations of Adolf Hitler's autobahn, had impressed upon him the importance of having highways to move military personnel and equipment as well as civilian populations. In fact, one of the goals of the Interstate Highway Act was to link all cities having a population greater than 50,000 to make quick evacuation possible in the event of an attack. Thus, the highways were born out of the fear of nuclear war, not with family vacations in mind. President Eisenhower apparently envisioned the ultimate "rush hour" of a mass evacuation, but he probably never imagined motorists dealing with twice-daily rush hours or today's intercity traffic. More details about this historic highway system are found at 346E (p. 227).

352 Healing Horses

Ahead 1 mile on the left are the Arrow H Stables. For more than twenty years, Lee Hart has trained horses and taught riding to young and old alike. He boards about fifteen horses for other folks and has an additional fifteen that he uses for training. The most rewarding aspect of his job is teaching young people to ride and through riding to build confidence, self-control, self-esteem, and healthy lifestyles. Horse therapy, which includes not only riding but also on-the-ground activities such as feeding, grooming, and leading the horses, has been used successfully in addressing mental health issues such as depression, attention deficit/hyperactivity disorder (ADHD), post-traumatic stress disorder (PTSD), eating disorders, and anxiety. It even has been used to treat children with Asperger's and autism. Clients call Lee "the horse whisperer" because he is so in tune with the needs of both the horse and the rider.

350 Tall Tower

The tall tower beyond the shorter cell phone towers on the left belongs to KTKA-TV. It is 1,440 feet high and supported by twenty-seven guy wires. Towers such as this take a toll on migrating birds: between 4 million and 10 million birds are killed each year by flying into communication towers. The tower warning lights, especially red ones, seem to confuse the birds on nights with low cloud ceilings and poor visibility. Birds often circle the tower and end up hitting the wires. Scientists studied this tower and found that about 1,000 birds representing 58 species were killed here between 1998 and 2000. The worst night was October 8, 1999, when 478 individuals of 35 species died. Scientists are studying the possibility that strobe lights or some combination of lights will reduce this mortality.

349 Wide Horizons

Ahead on the horizon, you can see Sleeping Buffalo Mound. You will drive over this hill at mile 339, about 10 miles ahead.

Speaking of seeing things on the horizon, over the next few miles you can see three smokestacks to the right. They are part of the Jeffrey Energy Center, the largest power plant in Kansas. This plant, more than 20 miles north of I-70, can produce 2,250 megawatts of electricity. It burns relatively clean coal brought in by rail from eastern Wyoming. Thousands of acres of land and lakes around the power plant have been designated as a wildlife refuge and the Oregon Trail Nature Park.

348 Kansas Crops

As you leave Topeka, you will enter a rural landscape that stretches for hundreds of miles. The crop production you're most likely to see here in eastern Kansas is hay or grains. Alfalfa is the leading crop cut for hay. During the growing season, it is cut and then baled for transport to barns and feedlots. You can recognize a field of alfalfa by its rich green color and the uniform distribution of plants across the field. The small, round leaves add to the look of complete ground cover as you drive by. Alfalfa may have blue or purplish flowers.

The grain crops include corn, soybeans, sorghum, and wheat. Corn and sorghum are grass crops, with long, wide leaves on a single stalk. Corn grows 8 to 10 feet tall, with ears on the stalk. By contrast, sorghum starts to produce a grain head at the top when the plant is about 10 inches tall. However, some grassy sorghums grown for silage will reach a height of 12 feet. You may see rows of soybeans growing here in eastern Kansas. The plants appear rather bushy until the beans are ripe and the rounded leaves fall off, leaving a 2-foot-high brown stalk with pods aligned in rows. Wheat covers the entire field rather than being planted in rows. Many Kansas farmers grow winter wheat, which is planted in the fall. It sprouts and creates a bright green cover that goes dormant in the winter. In the spring, it grows again and brightens to a golden color for harvest in early summer.

347 Rossville and Willard

Willard was once the site of Uniontown, a trading post for the Potawatomi Indians. Following two outbreaks of cholera, Uniontown was burned and abandoned in 1859. Rossville, just across the river from Willard, was named for William Ross, who came from Wisconsin in 1855 and later served as a Potawatomi Indian agent. William's brother Edmund G. Ross became a US senator in the 1860s and cast the deciding vote against convicting President Andrew Johnson after he had been impeached by the House of Representatives.

346 Wabaunsee County

This is one of the few Kansas counties whose name was taken from a Native American tribe or chief. It was originally known as Richardson County in honor of the man who introduced the Kansas-Nebraska Bill in the House of Representatives, the measure that created the territory. The county's name was changed to Wabaunsee in 1859.

Wabaunsee was a warrior chief of the Potawatomi tribe. He never lived in Kansas; he was born in Indiana in 1760 and died there in 1845. The Potawatomi term *Wah-banh-se* means "dawn of day" or "causer of paleness." Wabaunsee said that when he killed, the enemy would know him and call him Wae, then would turn pale and resemble the first light of day.

The earliest white settlers in the county were a band of outlaws known as the McDaniel Gang. Supposedly, they built a cabin near Harveyville, about 20 miles south of this area, near the Santa Fe Trail. There, they preyed on wagon trains. The gang was said to have buried a box containing $75,000 worth of gold under the cabin floor. Legend says that a "preacher-fisherman" came to the area, dug up the gold from beneath the ruins of the cabin, and left as mysteriously as he had arrived.

FLINT HILLS REGION

345 The Flint Hills

You have entered the grass-covered Flint Hills, the second landscape region of Kansas along I-70. The Flint Hills are characterized by flat tops and prominent valleys that in some places are 300 feet deep. It might be more accurate to call these the Flint Valleys because erosion has cut ever more deeply over the centuries, creating these "hills" from the flat terrain. The flint referenced in the name comes from the chert, or flint rock, that lies beneath the slopes.

The region averages only about 28 inches of precipitation annually, not enough to support the forests you saw back east of Topeka. As you drive through the Flint Hills, notice that there are few trees except in low spots or valleys. You are sailing across a sea of grass with islands of trees growing in low areas where they can get the additional moisture from rainfall running off the surrounding hilltops.

The Flint Hills stretch from Nebraska to Oklahoma across the entire width of Kansas. They create a picturesque landscape for I-70 travelers and indeed one of the most pleasant landscapes in the United States.

344 Hudson Ranch

The Flint Hills provide unexcelled pastureland for cattle, and prairie grasses flourish here on the Hudson Ranch. This ranch is more than 10,000 acres and extends for miles along both sides of the interstate. It is just one of the large ranches owned by the Hudson family in Kansas. The family home is perched high on a hill to the left of the interstate at mile 343. Read more about this ranch's operation at 341E (p. 225).

343 Gullies

The effects of erosion are visible in some pastures you see along I-70. The ongoing process of gullies cutting away at the dips and depressions in the pastures illustrates how the larger valleys have developed. When cattle remove the grass by eating and trampling it, the field becomes more susceptible to soil erosion. Banks form as water flows through depressions where plant roots had previously held soil in place. As cattle concentrate near water, they walk on these unstable banks, causing more soil to crumble and fall to the bottom of the gully. The next rain will then wash away this soil, and the process continues unless the banks and bottoms of these depressions are again stabilized with vegetation.

342 St. Marys

The town of St. Marys is located about 12 miles north of I-70 on what was the Oregon Trail. It was established as a Jesuit mission to the Potawatomi Indians. The mission evolved into a training school for the Indians and later became a school for Catholic children and a Jesuit seminary. The mission closed in the 1960s, and the grounds eventually were sold to a group of traditional Catholics who still conduct masses in Latin. During the time the Jesuits ministered to the Potawatomi, the Native Americans would come to a stone cabin to receive their government allotments. This cabin, built in the 1850s, still stands and is now the Pay Station Museum.

341 Sleeping Buffalo Mound

As noted several miles back, the hill that lies just ahead is referred to as Sleeping Buffalo Mound. As you go up the hill, notice the difference in vegetation on the north and south sides. Compare the area where vegetation is predominantly grass with the north side, which is mostly shrubs. The rancher on the south side burns the prairie annually to promote the growth of lush grass for grazing. Less frequent burning on the north side has allowed small patches of undesirable shrubs and trees to invade the grassland.

During the spring, you may look across the hills and see the prairies ablaze or blackened fields still smoldering. Or you may see hills that have become a bright "pool table green" with new growth after having been burned earlier. The lush green grass contrasts sharply with the brown vegetation in areas yet to be burned.

In 1866, a travel writer from Philadelphia witnessed the prairie fires in these Kansas Flint Hills and later wrote, with at least a touch of hyperbole, "I have seen the ancient light of Vesuvius by night, as it rose and fell in marvelous glory, but it did not impress me more deeply than did the long, wild sweep of the prairie fires of the West." You, too, may witness the glory of prairie fires if you travel through the Flint Hills in spring.

339 Rest Stop

The next rest stop features picnic shelters, a historical marker telling about the settlement and development of this region, and a memorial to highway workers killed on the job. It also offers native wildflower plantings and a woodland trail that leads to a sculpture on the hilltop and provides panoramic views of the Flint Hills.

338 Guard of the Plains

Try to spot the sculpture ahead, among the trees on top of the hill. Many local people believe that this work, titled *Guard of the Plains,* represents a howling coyote. A viewer who has a bit of imagination will see that, from any angle, it does resemble a coyote with its head thrown back, howling skyward. However, the sculptor, James Kirby Johnson, created the piece to symbolize a windmill and honor the important role windmills played in harnessing the wind for the good of humans on the Plains. You can hike the trail at the rest stop to get an up-close look at the sculpture.

337 Rails to Riches

To the right are the Union Pacific Railroad tracks, which veer off here but will be back alongside I-70 many times as both head west. After all, both the tracks and the highway, in their time, were built to move people, goods, and resources through this corridor across Kansas.

It's impossible to overstate the importance and lasting impact railroads have had in Kansas. Railroads determined land values

Guard of the Plains *sculpture*

and town locations. The steam engines' need for water determined the spacing of towns along the route. Maintaining and equipping the railroads determined which towns would survive.

In the late 1800s, the railroad provided a means of transportation for people and freight traveling west. People then took stagecoaches north or south to settlements not serviced by rail. Goods would be either stored in towns along the tracks or loaded into ox-drawn wagons to continue their journey, usually no more than a couple of hours' drive from a town. In trains heading back east, railroads transported wool, hides, cattle, and ore to eastern markets. Today, it is mostly grain that is shipped out to eastern states and ports.

Besides their geographic and economic impacts, railroads had a profound effect on the psyche of American society. Belching, noisy, and powerful steam engines traveling thousands of miles of tracks symbolized progress and caused Americans to view themselves for the first time as the world's technological and industrial leaders. Walt Whitman, traveling across Kansas by train in the fall of 1879, remarked that the railroad was America's furthest "advance beyond primitive barbarism." The railroad expansion in the late 1800s was met with an enthusiasm that rivaled the nation's response to the expansion of space travel a century later.

335 Paxico

Paxico (Exit 333 or 335) thrives on antiques. When Hollywood came to Paxico to film movies and television shows, the town's antique stores and florists supplied props and flowers. Scenes for the soap opera *Sunset Beach* were filmed here, as was the movie *Cross of Fire,* starring Patty Duke. The television miniseries *Sara Plain and Tall,* filmed in eastern Kansas, used antiques found here. In addition, pottery made in Paxico has been featured in the magazines *Country Living, Midwest Living,* and *Country Sampler.*

Paxico got its name from a Potawatomi medicine man, Pashqua. The land in this area was part of the Potawatomi Indian Reservation. In 1868, the federal government sold some of the land to the Atchison, Topeka and Santa Fe Railroad. At mile 332E (p. 224), read about the impact of the Rock Island line after the company bought the land in 1886.

334 Wine Country

At Exit 333 ahead, you will see an outlet of Wildwood Cellars Winery, the largest licensed winery in Kansas. This is one of more than two dozen wineries with tasting rooms in the state. Its signature wine is elderberry. The dark-purple berry was considered a noxious weed that grew wild on the family farm. In 1988, in an effort to make the farm more profitable, the brother and sister team of Dr. John Brewer and Merry Bauman began producing and commercializing elderberry wine, jelly, and a concentrate that can be added to drinks and other products.

Wildwood Cellars continues a long tradition of wine making in Kansas. The Kansa Indians were growing grapes in the area at least as early as 1794. In 1865, the community of Doniphan started vineyards along the Missouri River and made wines to offset the loss of trade with riverboaters, whose boats were being replaced by the railroads. However, the wine-making business was cut short when the state enacted a prohibition law in 1880.

333 Mill Creek

You just crossed Mill Creek, one of fourteen Mill Creeks in Kansas! This name indicates that the stream provided waterpower to a gristmill. Water was diverted to flow over a power wheel that turned a grinding stone to crush grain into grist. A coarse grind was used for animal feed; finer grinding produced flour for home cooking.

For the next 2 miles, you will be passing through flat floodplain, surrounded by hills. Deep, rich soil has been deposited over these bottomlands from thousands of years of Mill Creek flooding. Farmers take advantage of these rich bottomland soils for crop production. During the remainder of your trip, notice how crops such as corn and soybeans are grown in the flat bottomlands, whereas the steeper, rocky hills remain as native grasslands and are used for grazing cattle.

332 Silos

Ahead on the right, you will see a cement silo. Tall silos are part of the skyline throughout cattle country. The cylindrical structures store feed for cattle at both beef and dairy farms. They vary from 30 to 100 feet in height and from 20 to 40 feet in diameter. Two prominent types of silo construction may be seen along I-70—gray concrete silos with silver-colored aluminum dome tops, like the one here, and deep-blue steel silos popularly called by their trade name, Harvestores.

Silos are filled in late summer and fall with feed for cattle to eat during the winter and the dry months of late summer. Chopped grass crops are cut from fields; when packed in airtight silos, the grass cures somewhat like sauerkraut to become haylage, a delectable cattle feed.

In early fall, corn or a grain sorghum that has partially dried stalks may be chopped into fodder (a coarse feed). When placed in a silo, this fodder ensiles, or cures, into traditional silage. Silos may also be filled with high-moisture corn that has been harvested by combines early in the fall.

Concrete silos are unloaded from a mechanism at the top that throws the feed down a chute along the side of the silo to wagons or conveyors. The domed top covers the unloader. The first feed this type of unloader takes out is the very last that was put in. Harvestores, which have nearly flat roofs, are unloaded from the bottom, so that the first feed put in is also the first taken out.

Concrete silo

330 Weigh Station

You may have noticed an odd-looking pole hanging over the road near this location. The pole is used to signal the weigh station (or chicken coop, as some truckers might call it) at mile 330. Such poles also send signals to a box in the trucks to let truckers know if they must stop at the weigh station or if they can continue down the highway. Several things are checked at these stops: the weight and distribution of the truck's loads, driver safety issues, and whether appropriate taxes have been paid. On Kansas interstate highways, the weight limit per truck is 80,000 pounds, with no more than 20,000 pounds on a single axle or 34,000 pounds on a tandem axle. The size limits for a truck are 8.5 feet wide, 14 feet high, and 65 feet long for a truck-trailer combination. Most trailers are between 40 feet and 53 feet long, with "53 footers" becoming most common nowadays. Trailers pulled in tandem can be only 28.5 feet long each, and oversized loads require a special permit. These rules protect the pavement, bridges, and overpasses from damage. Agriculture's pivotal role in Kansas is reflected in easy-to-obtain special use permits for farm trucks during harvest season. Learn more about trucks at 243 (p. 58) and 57E (p. 152).

329 Wamego

Exit 328 ahead leads to the town of Wamego, where a Dutch windmill rises above the quaint city park. In 1879, a Dutch settler built the mill so windpower could be used to grind grain. The windmill was moved to the park, stone by stone, and reassembled in 1923. Wamego's Oz Museum contains one of the largest private collections of *Wizard of Oz* memorabilia. You can follow the yellow brick road and see over 100 years of Oz history, including original MGM movie production notes from 1939 and props from the Broadway musical *Wicked*.

Wamego is the birthplace of Walter Chrysler of automotive-manufacturing fame. You might be driving one of his cars right now! Read about Wamego's historic Columbian Theater, Plumlee Buffalo Ranch (ahead on the left), and the town of Alma at 326E (p. 221).

328 Wings over the Prairies

More than 475 kinds of birds have been seen in Kansas. If you are traveling across the Flint Hills during the summer months, you will spot interesting species that are rare in other parts of the country. Summer birds include the upland sandpiper, a long-legged, long-necked, pale brown bird that you might observe standing alertly on a fence post or flying with quivering wings over the grass.

Another conspicuous prairie bird of summer is the nighthawk; this is not a real hawk but a member of the so-called goatsucker family. The name *goatsucker* comes from a legend that contends these birds suck milk from goats at night. During the summer, you will see nighthawks flying erratically, fluttering and flopping over the prairie as they catch insects in midair. Although the nighthawk will appear, overall, as a sleek brown bird with long, slender, pointed wings, you may notice the bold white patch near its wing tips.

Throughout the year, the fences along I-70 are adorned with western meadowlarks. This meadowlark is the state bird of Kansas and five other states as well. If this bird is facing the road, you may see its yellow breast marked with a black. V-shaped band; when it is facing away, the meadowlark appears to be a chunky brown bird.

Upland sandpiper (Lowell Johnson)

In flight, it uses rapid wing beats and then glides. You may see the white outer feathers on its short, stubby tail.

326 Grandma Hoerner's

From the visitor's gallery in the red building seen on the right at Exit 324, you can watch the applesauce-canning process in action. The applesauce Grandma Hoerner became famous for, using big slices of apples, goes back a century, to her early years on a Kansas farm. She learned from her grandmother how to use the apples that were picked fresh on the farm to make apple butter and extra chunky applesauce. Grandma Hoerner loved to cook and became known for her mastery in the kitchen.

Now, Grandma Hoerner's whole-fruit products are again available through the efforts of her grandson, who started producing them in 1987. You can watch the kitchen workers as they combine apples with other fruits to create eight different flavors of applesauce and a dozen spreads and toppings, all available fresh from the processing line at the factory store.

Just past Exit 324, take a look at the wooden skeet tower on the hill. Read about this shooting sport at 323E (p. 220).

325 Beecher Bible and Rifle Church

Wabaunsee Road leads north 6 miles from Exit 324 to the Beecher Bible and Rifle Church. The church's story began in the spring of 1856, when a group of sixty people from New Haven, Connecticut, prepared to move to Kansas to cast their votes with the Free-Staters. Henry Ward Beecher addressed them with an eloquent antislavery speech and promised to donate twenty-five rifles, together with some Bibles, if the audience would provide twenty-five more. When the group left Connecticut, the rifles were packed in boxes labeled "Bibles" in an effort to smuggle them past proslavery settlers and into Kansas. The group set up camp at Wabaunsee. Some formed the Prairie Guard to fight against proslavery forces using the "Bible rifles," as explained at 324E (p. 220).

323 Riley County

You will soon enter Riley County. This county was established in 1855 and took its name from the military post that you will be passing in about 20 miles.

Beecher Bible and Rifle Church (Library of Congress)

322 An OK Corral

Just over the crest of the hill, the fencing and structures on the right side of the interstate make up a corral. Corrals were made famous in cowboy movies and are still an important part of ranching. The corral is where cattle are herded together to be treated if they are sick or loaded onto trucks if they are to be moved. The newest corrals can be identified by their curving alleys and solid panels that help calm the cattle. Designs are created to direct the livestock into different pens and sort them safely and efficiently. Attention is given to providing smooth surfaces and control gates in order to protect animals from injury. The corrals include features that make it practical for one cowboy to manage a herd alone when necessary.

321 Growing Beef

The tallgrass prairie that remains here in the Flint Hills supports thousands of cattle. The soil is too shallow and rocky to be plowed up, so it cannot be converted to cropland as was done in Illinois, Iowa, and other prairie states. The many thousands of buffalo that originally roamed here have been replaced by cattle, but the tallgrasses remain.

The Flint Hills are covered with big bluestem, one of the best grasses for grazing whether the animal happens to be a buffalo or a cow; it is even more nutritious than Kentucky bluegrass. Cattle are shipped into the Flint Hills each year from Oklahoma and Texas to graze upon the rich grasses as they are grown for market. During some periods, the grass eaten by a single cow is converted into 2 pounds of beef per day. If you multiply that by the hundreds of thousands of cattle in the region, you can see that the Flint Hills area produces many tons of hamburgers and steaks on a daily basis.

320 Distant Views

You might be able to make out cell towers and buildings on the horizon from this vantage point. Those structures are actually 6 miles ahead at mile 314. That hill on the horizon is I-70's highest point as it crosses the Flint Hills region—clearly, this part of Kansas is not flat!

319 St. George

In the Kansas River valley visible to the north lies the town of St. George. The founding of this town was accidental. In April 1855, a group of immigrants—George W. Gillespie and family, J. George Gillespie, and George Chapman and family—headed west from St. Joseph, Missouri. The families planned to go to California to look for gold. But after several hard days on the road, Mrs. Gillespie declared that she had traveled far enough and refused to go any farther. The group decided to camp there on the banks of the Kansas River, and the next day, they decided to homestead in Kansas Territory instead of going on to California. According to Daniel Fitzgerald in *Ghost Towns of Kansas,* they chose the name St. George because three men in the group were named George and they were "saintly" in that they accommodated the wishes of their wives.

318 Flint Hills Streams

North of the interstate is a stream that runs parallel to the road. You may be able to see the clear, silt-free water. The bed of this river, like that of many Flint Hills streams and rivers, is covered with limestone. Because the water drains off of grassy pastures, which hold the soil in place, rather than cultivated fields, these streams tend to run very clear.

317 Council Grove

The historic town of Council Grove is about 30 miles south of Exit 313. It is home to several sites of historical interest because it was a key location on the Santa Fe Trail. The trail was used by Native Americans, fur traders, and explorers when Santa Fe was the capital of Spain's province of Nuevo Mexico. William Becknell took the first wagons down the trail to Santa Fe in 1821, the same year that Mexico won its independence. Council Grove became a prominent stop along the trail. It was on the Neosho River, surrounded by abundant forests and grasslands, where horses, cattle, and oxen could be fattened on lush grasses and allowed to rest and drink before heading out on the long journey to Santa Fe. Since large trees of any kind were scarce west of Council Grove, timber to be used for replacing axles was gathered here and carried on wagons headed west. Read details about Becknell's journeys and famous Council Grove settlers at 312E (p. 216).

316 The Little Apple

Exit 313 north leads to the town of Manhattan, home to the Flint Hills Prairie Discovery Center—a fun, interactive, and educational place for children and adults to learn more about the Flint Hills area. Kansas State University (KSU) is also located here.

The town calls itself The Little Apple to avoid confusion with the *other* Manhattan. This Manhattan was formed in 1856 when a riverboat chartered by an antislavery group known as the Cincinnati Kansas Association got stuck on a sandbar in the Kansas River. The stranded travelers were 20 miles short of their destination, the junction of the Republican and Smoky Hill Rivers (mile 300 ahead). They were welcomed by a group of New Englanders who had already settled here as part of the effort to make Kansas a free state in the battle over slavery. A clause in the Ohio Company's constitution required the new town to be named Manhattan.

Kansas State University serves more than 24,000 students from all fifty states and more than a hundred countries. KSU's agricultural teaching and research programs are internationally recognized; its student livestock- and crop-judging teams have won numerous national championships and are consistently among the best in the nation, and its College of Veterinary Science performs more rabies testing than any other lab facility in the world. Because of these strengths, KSU will soon be home to the National Bio and Agro-defense Facility (NBAF), a government-run research facility that will replace the 1950s-era Plum Island Animal Disease Center in New York. NBAF will be operated under the authority of the US Department of Agriculture and the US Department of Homeland Security because it will focus on studying and developing countermeasures to combat dangerous biological threats involving diseases that can be transmitted from animals to humans, as well as on foreign animal diseases that could affect our nation's food supply.

KSU's Colbert Hills Golf Course was developed by KSU alum and PGA golfer Jim Colbert. This innovative course integrates nature conservation, economic development, and university education. Other well-known alumni include Eric Stonestreet, Emmy-winning star of *Modern Family*; actress Kirstie Alley; and Erin Brockovich, the environmental activist whose story was featured in a movie starring Julia Roberts.

312 Sea Bottom

Over the next 8 miles on both sides of I-70, you see limestone layers exposed during construction of the highway. Crews cut into the hills to level out some of the ups and downs of the terrain, revealing the rocky limestone layers.

Limestone is a sedimentary rock, composed of sediments that settle to the bottom of bodies of water. The layers here are mostly remains of sea animals, such as mollusks and corals, that died and fell to the bottom of the ancient sea that once covered this part of North America. At the top of the cuts, you also will see that the soil is very shallow. It is no wonder that these prairies have never been converted to cropland.

311 Konza Prairie

The Konza Prairie is located on the right side of the interstate. Scientists from Kansas State University and around the world come here to conduct studies on this 8,616-acre ecological research site.

The name Konza comes from one of more than 100 variations of the term used for the Kansa Indian tribe; this is also the source of the name Kansas. Much of the land here was a ranch owned by Chicagoan John Dewey, who grew wealthy by buying up real estate after the Great Chicago Fire. Between 1971 and 1979, tracts were purchased by The Nature Conservancy, a national organization dedicated to preserving significant natural areas. The group leases the land to Kansas State University.

The Konza Prairie is part of the tallgrass prairie that once extended from Texas to Canada and from the Dakotas through Iowa to Illinois and Indiana. Enormous herds of grazing animals such as bison, elk, and pronghorn antelope were important parts of the vast tallgrass ecosystem before European settlement. Today, cattle have replaced these native grazers.

Nearly 600 different species of plants have been found on the Konza Prairie, including 86 kinds of grasses. Typical grasses are big bluestem, switchgrass, Indian grass, and prairie cordgrass. Several types reach more than 6 feet in height, and two species, prairie cordgrass and Indian grass, have been known to grow 8 feet tall. More than 200 kinds of birds have been seen on the Konza. A herd of about 250 bison live alongside almost 40 other kinds of mammals and 34 kinds of amphibians and reptiles, including 15 species of snakes!

The prairie ecosystem involves complicated interactions between plants, animals, soil, climate, and fire. If any of these things changes, the entire prairie system changes. Kansas State University scientists study the plants and animals that live here, as well as the effects of cattle and bison grazing and prairie fires on the prairie ecosystem. Even the National Aeronautics and Space Administration (NASA) has been involved in research here.

308 Prairie Chickens

Prairie chickens thrive here in the Flint Hills. The destruction of prairies throughout the United States eliminated prairie chickens from most of their former range. In fact, one type of these birds, the heath hen, is now extinct.

Prairie chickens were an important food for Native Americans and especially for the settlers who came along later, who had fewer options and less knowledge about eating off the land. Kansas hunters still hunt prairie chickens, which William A. Quayle described as tasting "as wild as its prairie flight. Its tang is caught from the wayward prairies, a wild flavor as strange as bison flesh, the prairies become sapid."

People who spend time on the prairies receive benefits from

Prairie chicken (US Fish and Wildlife Service)

prairie chickens beyond their culinary value. These birds add animation and sound to the prairie landscape. Along I-70, you may see the fast-flying brown birds as they zoom across the landscape like feathered cannonballs shot low across the fields. Quayle wrote that they "whir away, brown-blown rags against a gray sky, . . . as if the brown prairie had found wings."

During the spring, groups of males perform amazing dances —jumping up and down, stomping their feet, spinning around, and inflating bright yellow sacks on the sides of their necks—all to attract a female mate. While dancing, they make unearthly hoots and "booms," some of which resemble the sound made by blowing across the top of a soda bottle. One or more females typically stand off to the side of the lek, or booming ground (the avian equivalent of a dance floor), and watch the males perform, seemingly unimpressed and aloof—all in all, not so different from what happens with humans in nightclubs and dance halls across the country.

People come from all over the world to see and photograph this incredible creature from blinds set up on the booming grounds. Kansans are indeed fortunate to share the grasslands with these extraordinary birds.

305 Hawks

As you drive along, you will see large hawks sitting on fences or trees near the highway. Most will be red-tailed hawks, which are common year-round wherever there are trees. Red-tails are attracted to the interstate because the grassy medians and right-of-ways provide ideal habitat for their favorite food—mice and other small mammals. Although some people call these birds chicken hawks, they do not bother chickens. In fact, red-tailed hawks are valuable to farmers because they eat rodents that otherwise would consume the farmer's grain. To spot a red-tail, look for a mostly white breast and short, fan-shaped tail, which may be brown or rusty-red depending on the age of the bird.

Between April and September, you may also see Swainson's hawks, particularly as you go farther west. These hawks have a dark upper breast, like a bib, and a distinct dark-and-light pattern under the wings when they soar. Sometimes, they migrate in huge flocks from their winter grounds in Argentina, and you may see them following tractors to eat the rodents and insects stirred up in the fields. In the winter, while the Swainson's hawks are in South America, rough-legged hawks come down from the Arctic. They have varying degrees of black and white coloring, with some forms being almost all black. Usually, you can see a wide black band across the belly; when the bird is flying, you might notice the black patches on the underside of the wing where it bends. The tail is usually whitish, with a large black band. You may see these rough-legs hovering—beating their wings rapidly in place—as they look for prey on the ground below.

303 Marshall Field—Atomic Cannon

Over the next hill is Fort Riley's Marshall Airfield, home to the 1st Infantry Division's Combat Aviation Brigade. The Brigade consists of 2,200 soldiers and Black Hawk, Apache, and Chinook helicopters. Many vehicles and helicopters stored here were used in Iraq. The vehicles were painted tan, rather than the usual army green, to blend in with the desert sands. Hap Arnold, the first commander of the US Air Force, got his start in aviation by flying biplanes from this field in 1912.

On top of the ridge on the left you can see one of only three atomic cannons in the world. This cannon was designed during the Cold War to shoot a nuclear warhead. It could hit a target more than 20 miles away.

Red-tailed hawk (Lowell Johnson)

302 First Capitol

Exit 301 also takes you to the first territorial capital of Kansas, in what was then a settlement called Pawnee. Work began on the capitol building in the spring of 1855. The legislature convened on July 2 as planned in spite of the shortcomings of the hastily built structure. Just days later, legislators passed a bill transferring the seat of government from this location to Shawnee Mission, near Kansas City, to be closer to their homes. The governor vetoed the bill, but his veto was overridden. Read about Pawnee's five hectic days as the capital of Kansas at 298E (p. 212).

301 Fort Riley

Built in 1853, Fort Riley encompasses 157 square miles. Its name honors Major General Bennett C. Riley, who led the first military escort along the Santa Fe Trail in 1827. Soldiers from Fort Riley provided protection for travelers on the Santa Fe and Oregon Trails, as well as for railroad builders and passengers. They also "policed" the territory during clashes between proslavery and antislavery factions.

Fort Riley's cavalry school, which trained horse soldiers until 1950, was the only one in the United States. You can visit the Cavalry Museum on the base to see the progression of equipment and uniforms of American cavalry through time, along with original artworks of Frederick Remington and memorabilia from military heroes. Military leaders who served at Fort Riley include George Custer, Philip Sheridan, Jeb Stuart, Robert E. Lee, and George Patton. Read more about Fort Riley at 295E (p. 211).

JUNCTION CITY – FORT RILEY

300 Head of the Kaw

In a short distance, the interstate crosses the Smoky Hill River. By this point, the river has flowed all the way from Colorado through a shallow valley you will see to the left of I-70 as you drive west. About 2 miles to the right, it joins the Republican River. Together, they form the Kansas River, which you have followed from its mouth in Kansas City to its source here.

The explorer Captain John C. Frémont camped near this spot on a trip west in 1843. "The Pathfinder," as Frémont was nicknamed, reported great numbers of elk, antelope, and friendly Indians in this area. Elk are once again roaming here: a herd has been reestablished at Fort Riley.

Several attempts were made to create a town where the Republican and Smoky Hill Rivers join. In 1855, settlers tried to reach this spot by steamboat traveling up the Kansas River, but as mentioned back at Manhattan, they got stuck and decided they had traveled far enough. Junction City was finally established in 1858. Today, looking at the shallow, silty, sandbar-strewn river, it is hard to imagine that steamboats would even attempt the trip from Kansas City. Early residents here called the area the Garden of Eden because the Smoky Hill, Saline, Solomon, and Republican Rivers all come together nearby and because the area matched the description of the garden in the book of Genesis.

Junction City is the seat of Geary County, which originally was named Davis County after Jefferson Davis, secretary of war from 1853 to 1857. During the Civil War, residents of Davis County became outraged that while Kansas men were fighting and dying for the North, their county was named after the Confederate president. Twice during the war, legislators tried to get the county name changed but failed. In 1889, long after the war was over, the legislature finally changed the name to honor Kansas's third territorial governor, John W. Geary. Geary went on to be mayor of San Francisco, where the famous Geary Street is also named for him.

297 Kansas's Largest Lake

Exit 295 will lead you north to Milford Lake, where you'll find more than 16,000 acres of water surface and 163 miles of shoreline for recreation. The lake was created by damming the Republican River. The primary purpose of the dam is to control flooding downstream on the Republican and Kansas Rivers. Although Kansas is not often thought of as a water recreation state, about twenty-five large reservoirs and dozens of smaller lakes make it one of the top states for sailing, waterskiing, fishing, and other water-based activities.

Below the dam are an interesting nature center and a fish hatchery. These facilities are open to the public and offer nature trails, exhibits, and educational tours.

296 Sausage Factory

The white factory visible on the right produces all types of smoked sausage and packaged pork products. It is a plant of Smithfield Foods, the world's largest pork processor and hog producer, and it operates as Armour-Eckrich, a part of the John Morrell Food Group.

You have probably purchased an Eckrich or Armour package of sausage produced here. This location for the plant was selected in 1995 after an extensive search and evaluation of locations in more than 1,300 counties across the Midwest. Key factors in selecting Junction City included the local population's strong work ethic and the availability of capable workers.

The four companies mentioned here have a long association with the meat industry. Armour began packing hogs in Chicago in 1867. John Morrell took over leadership of his father's thriving ham company in England, and by 1864, he had established operations in Ireland and the United States. Peter Eckrich opened a meat market in Fort Wayne, Indiana, in 1894. Smithfield Foods can be traced back to the opening of the Smithfield Packing Company in 1936 in Smithfield, Virginia, by Joseph Luter and his son Joseph Luter, Jr. Since 1981, Smithfield Foods has acquired some forty companies. Today, it is the leading integrated producer of prepared meat products such as smoked sausage, salami, pepperoni, hot dogs, cold cuts, ham, bacon, and deli meats for retail and food service markets.

292 Redcedars

The evergreen trees you see scattered in the grasslands ahead on both sides of the road are eastern redcedars. You will see these trees in Kansas windbreaks because of their heat and drought tolerance and because their dense foliage blocks the wind and snow. Redcedars are not really cedars but instead are members of the juniper family. They grow in open and sunny places, often encroaching into grasslands unless they are burned. Although ranchers do not like them because they compete with the grass, redcedars have many positive attributes. Because of its color, fragrance, and presumed ability to repel moths, redcedar wood is used for chests, wardrobes, and closet linings. Cedarwood oil is used for making many other fragrances. Woodenware and many of the wooden novelties sold at tourist attractions are made from redcedar. At one time, most wooden pencils also were made from redcedar, and the tree was known as pencil cedar; now, though, only about 10 percent of pencils are made from this tree. Redcedars are among the top five trees used for Christmas trees.

Redcedars benefit wildlife by providing year-round shelter from enemies and the elements. Birds use them for nest sites, and the trees' berries are eaten not only by many kinds of birds but also by raccoons, skunks, foxes, rabbits, and other mammals. Although most redcedars in Kansas eventually fall victim to fire or cutting, one tree on an undisturbed rocky bluff in Missouri is well over 1,000 years old!

290 Dickinson County

You are entering Dickinson County, established in 1857. This county was named for Daniel S. Dickinson, a US senator from New York who introduced legislation that helped create the Kansas Territory.

287 Chapman

Chapman, located on the north bank of the Smoky Hill River, is called Little Ireland because it was settled by Irish immigrants in the 1880s. Chapman is home to the first county high school in the United States.

One of our nation's premier pilots and astronauts is from Chapman. Joe Engle has spent more than 10,000 hours aloft, piloting more than 130 types of aircraft. His test flight on the X-15 to a height of 280,000 feet made him the youngest US Air Force officer to wear astronaut wings. He was part of the support crew for *Apollo 10* and the backup lunar module pilot for *Apollo 14*. In 1981, he was the commander of the second flight of the space shuttle *Columbia*. Astronaut Engle maintains close ties with family and friends in Chapman.

285 Serious Skies

Weather can affect Kansas travel, especially in winter. Kansas playwright William Inge noted that people on the prairie are

> more dependent upon and influenced by the sky and its constant maneuverings than in other regions. Men here look at the sky each morning as soon as they get out of bed, to see what kind of a day is indicated. Life and prosperity depend upon the sky, which can destroy a season's crops in a few hours, by hail or blizzards or tornados or a relentless burning sun that can desiccate the land like an Old Testament curse.

As you travel across Kansas, you, too, need to be aware of the sky. Regardless of the season, if skies look threatening, listen for weather reports. Nature can express its majesty and power not only in ways that can destroy crops but also in ways that can take a deadly toll on travelers.

283 Enterprise

Enterprising settlers founded the town of Enterprise in 1873 along the south bank of the Smoky Hill River about 2 miles south of this location. The town quickly became a milling center for locally grown wheat. By the 1880s, several flour mills had been established there.

In the early 1900s, famed ax-wielding prohibitionist Carrie Nation came to town and demolished a saloon with her ax. She had some women supporters, but according to an account in the *WPA Guide to 1930s Kansas,* her female opponents thought her behavior was "unladylike," and in true ladylike fashion, they ran her out of town under a barrage of rotten eggs.

281 Power Highways

Along I-70, we have crossed trails used by Native Americans and settlers, railroads that carry farm products to market, and roads for trucks and cars. Other "trails" transport electricity.

Power lines that will cross the interstate at miles 280 and 276 are constructed to carry different amounts of electricity. One determination of the amount of power is voltage, or the pressure that moves current through the lines. To move electricity through your home takes 120 or 240 volts. About 6,900 volts are used to move power through lines along city streets or out to farms. To connect eastern and western Kansas, the electric line here is designed for 345,000 volts. It connects with the Jeffrey Energy Center (see 320E,

p. 219), to wind turbine farms ahead, and to Salina and south to Hutchinson.

The three widely separated lines indicate a three-phase transmission. A single-wire neutral line at the top of the poles is a grounding neutral. You can tell the line carries high voltage by the wide spacing between cables and the long insulator hangers used to attach the cables to the tower frames. In your home wiring, a single layer of insulating tape can keep electricity from sparking off. As the voltage increases, greater separation is required. So when you see an electric line, note how the cables are separated; the greater the distance, the higher the voltage. In addition to longer, heavier insulators, it takes bigger cables to carry more power.

279 Historic Abilene

Approaching Abilene, you will see a grain elevator rising 143 feet to signal the city ahead. There are seventy-two bins here that store wheat for processing to produce bulgur. At 273E (p. 205), read about this rare facility and the importance of bulgur wheat as emergency food.

Abilene was founded by Timothy Hersey in 1858. Mrs. Hersey chose the name for the town by allowing her Bible to fall open and picking a name from that page. Her Bible opened to the third chapter of the book of Luke, which includes the name Abilene in the first verse. Appropriately enough, the word means "city of the plains."

Abilene was one of the first cattle boomtowns, receiving herds of longhorn cattle driven up the Chisholm Trail from Texas. James Butler "Wild Bill" Hickok served for a brief stint as the town marshal in the early days of Abilene.

Abilene was also the boyhood home of General Dwight D. "Ike" Eisenhower, president of the United States from 1953 to 1961. His presidential library, the Eisenhower Museum, and his boyhood home are all open to the public. President Eisenhower is buried in a chapel on the museum grounds, together with his wife, Mamie, and one of their two sons.

Abilene is known as the greyhound capital of the world (dogs, not buses!). The Greyhound Association Headquarters and Greyhound Hall of Fame are located here, and many kennels for the sleek racing dogs can be found in the area (see 86E, p. 158). The Hall of Fame bills itself as "offering a tribute to Man's Best and Fastest Friend." The museum honors racing dogs (some clocked at 45 miles per hour) and offers stories about the 4,000-year history of greyhounds and greyhound racing.

The Museum of Independent Telephony, featuring unique telephones, also is in Abilene. It has on display a silver-dollar pay phone, candlestick phones, a little pink "Princess" phone, and even a "mother-in-law" phone. You can be a "Hello Girl" at the manual switchboard and touch many pieces of telecommunications gear. Abilene was home to the founder of the independent Brown Telephone Company of Abilene, which later became Sprint.

The story of C. W. Parker, who became known as the "Amusement King," began in Abilene in the 1880s when he built a shooting gallery. He went on to construct his first carousels in Abilene, along with all kinds of carnival and amusement devices. You can ride one of his early carousels, operated by its original steam engine, at the Dickinson County Historical Society Museum. It is a track-operated machine with twenty-four horses, each mounted on a rocking mechanism instead of on a pole as in later designs. Parker horses have become highly collectible and valuable.

At Exit 275 on the right, the historic Brookville Hotel is recreated. It is open in the evening for the famous chicken dinners described at mile 240 ahead.

274 Chocolate Factory

You can see the Russell Stover candy factory ahead on the left. The company founder, Russell Stover, was born in a sod house in western Kansas in 1888. In 1921, he and a partner invented the world's first chocolate-dipped ice cream bar. At a dinner party. Russell's

Brookville Hotel

wife suggested calling it an Eskimo Pie. Increasing competition quickly drove Russell out of the ice cream business, but not before he made quite a fortune. His wife, Clara, started making candy in Denver in 1923 in a small bungalow. By the end of the first year, five stores selling "Mrs. Stover's Bungalow Candies" had opened in Denver, and in 1924, Clara opened stores in Omaha, Lincoln, Kansas City, and St. Louis. By 1943, the company headquarters were moved to Kansas City, and the name was changed to Russell Stover. Today, Russell Stover, Inc., which includes the Whitman and Pangburn brands, is the world's largest producer of boxed chocolates and the third-biggest producer of chocolate in the United States, behind only Hershey and Mars. Stover's produces about 100 million pounds of chocolate annually.

At this plant, employees make and package 90,000 pounds of candy each day! The layout of this 401,500-square-foot facility is highly efficient. Raw materials are stored in separate silos, designated for bulk sugar, corn syrup, milk, and cream. In-process storerooms hold nuts, chocolate, bag sugar, cocoa, fruit centers, and other ingredients. Separate production areas are designated for candy forming, chocolate melting, nut processing, caramel and fudge cooling, and hand dipping. Finished candy is stored in a 44,000-square-foot freezer maintained at subzero temperatures. This facility also has a box-making plant, a laboratory for in-process testing, and its own wastewater plant. Take Exit 272 to visit the factory outlet store.

271 End of the Chisholm Trail

Read about rail shipment of Texas cattle from Abilene to Chicago; about Abilene's reputation as the wildest town in the West; and about the town's famous sheriff, Wild Bill Hickok, at 275E (p. 206).

270 Sand Dunes

Over the last several miles, you may have noticed that the landscape here is sculptured differently from the terrain you have seen thus far. This is because there are sand dunes under the blanket of grass in this area. These dunes formed over many thousands of years as sand blew up from the Smoky Hill River valley. The coarse sand particles piled up, leaving these uneven surfaces on which grass took root.

As you would expect in this open country, the wind moves a lot of soil. Soils are classified by textures that range from very fine clay to loam to coarse sand. The finer soils are deposited in more rolling patterns than sand. The general region is loess plains. Loess (rhymes with *fuss*) soil is a loamy, windblown deposit that leaves a productive topsoil. Soil texture plays a significant role in the soil's ability to hold water and support plant growth.

269 Solomon

The next exit (Exit 266) takes you to the town of Solomon, which sits along the Solomon River and was named after it in 1894. Solomon had large salt deposits, and by the 1870s, salt producers were filling about 10,000 barrels a year.

268 Hedgerows

Exactly to the right of marker 267 is a hedgerow. Also to the right and throughout this area, you will see many fields bordered by hedgerows—single rows of rather short, rounded trees. The trees are Osage orange, often called hedge or hedge apple. Before the days of barbed wire fences, hedgerows were planted to serve as natural fences. Osage orange is a dense, bushy tree with thorns on the branches. When planted close together, these trees make an impenetrable fence touted as being "horse-high, bull-strong, and pig-tight." Although native only to Texas, hedgerows were already a common sight as far away as New England even before the Civil War.

The wood of the Osage orange is so hard and strong that it was used to make wagon wheels. Now, it is used in making fence posts, crossties, and archery bows. The hedge apple, or hedgeball, is a nonedible, softball-sized, yellow-green fruit that is lumpy and contains a sticky, milky juice. Hedgeballs are sold at farmers' markets to people who believe they repel insects and spiders from homes and other buildings.

266 Solomon River

Ahead along the Solomon River, the rest area provides a modern oasis in a setting like those the leaders of wagon trains must have searched out as they headed west. The spot would have had trees for firewood and wagon repairs, as well as grassy areas to feed the animals. A historical marker at the rest area introduces the story of wheat in Kansas.

You cross the Solomon River near mile 264. Explorers witnessed this stream being drunk dry by an enormous herd of buffalo. The river flows into the Smoky Hill River 2 miles south of the bridge.

The Solomon River was not named for the Old Testament biblical king; rather, French fur trappers called it Salmon, for a leader of the Louisiana Territory. Explorer Zebulon Pike crossed this river in 1806 on his way to what is now Pikes Peak and modified the name to Solomon's Fork.

264 Saline County—Saltwater in Kansas

The first European to visit the Saline County area was Coronado, the Spanish explorer. In 1541, he led the expedition searching for the Seven Cities of Gold, but instead he must have found salty water. When explorer Zebulon Pike camped near here in 1806, he tasted the stream water. It was salty or "saline." He reported to the government that the region was "The Saline River Country." Hence the name Saline County was adopted when the county was organized in 1859.

263 Winter Wheat

You are in the area where winter wheat was first planted in Kansas. T. C. Henry, mayor of Abilene in 1870, secretly planted a five-acre patch of winter wheat and proved that if seeds were sown in the fall, the young plants would be protected by winter snows and would then produce grain for harvest before the hot, dry summer scorched the plants. He unveiled his success in 1871 and transformed the high, dry plains of western Kansas into the nation's breadbasket. Today, Kansas produces almost a fifth of the US wheat crop. Depending on when you are traveling through, you will experience wheat fields differently. Just as forests change color with the seasons, wheat fields will be dark brown in the late summer and fall when they are being planted, light green in late fall and winter, and bright green in early spring. Then, in June and July when the crop is ready to harvest, they will become the "golden waves of grain" that we sing about. You'll pass many miles of wheat fields on the road ahead.

262 Iron Mound

To the left of the interstate in the far distance, you can see Iron Mound, which has an elevation of 1,497 feet. Iron Mound is a clay and gravel hill capped with Dakota sandstone. The flat-topped mound is the result of erosion caused by heavy rains. Because the sandstone is less prone to erosion, the mound area has remained while the surrounding soil eroded.

261 New Cambria

New Cambria is located at Exit 261. S. P. Donmyer, a settler born in Cambria County, Pennsylvania, founded this town in 1872. The name honors both his Pennsylvania birthplace and his Welsh heritage.

260 Alfalfa

Alfalfa also was first introduced to Kansas here in Saline County. *The WPA Guide* explained how Dr. E. R. Switzer planted alfalfa seed here in 1874. That year, a grasshopper plague and drought seemed to destroy the new crop, but September rains brought it back to life. Switzer thought that the crop would be just the thing for a place like Kansas.

Alfalfa is valuable for its ability to restore nitrogen to the soil as well as its ability to grow back every year, even after a cold winter. You'll see the purple or bluish blossoms on alfalfa fields in the spring. Throughout the summer and fall, there will be fields where the crop is being cut, dried, and baled. It grows back after cutting and can be cut again. Depending on the amount of rain in a given season, farmers can take three or four cuttings of alfalfa from a single field each year. There's more about this important Kansas crop at 261E (p. 202).

258 Motherly Love

Mary Ann "Mother" Bickerdyke, the famous Civil War field nurse, lived in Saline County. Many Civil War veterans settled in Kansas. In fact, Kansas had more Grand Army of the Republic members per capita than any other state, leading it to be nicknamed "the Soldier State." Mother Bickerdyke alone was responsible for bringing over 300 families into Saline County after the war. She provided care for veterans and their families throughout Kansas's days as the Soldier State. Forty-six Kansas counties are named for Civil War soldiers, most of whom died in battle.

SALINA: CROSSING THE CENTER OF THE STATE

257 Salina

Ahead, you see the buildings of Salina. This city was founded by William Phillips, a lawyer and writer for the *New York Tribune* who wrote articles about the slavery issue in Kansas. He was a colonel in the Civil War and later became a Kansas congressman. In 1858, Phillips and several other men established the town site of Salina near the confluence of the Saline and Smoky Hill Rivers. One of the men, A. C. Spillman, is given credit for picking the name. The name was first pronounced "Salēna," but because the group feared that would suggest salty stock water, they changed the pronunciation to "Salīna."

The Union Pacific Railroad tracks extended to Salina in 1867. J. G. McCoy, a livestock dealer from Illinois, visited Salina and proposed that it be the end of the Chisholm Trail. Fearing the violence and vices of a cow town, the people rejected McCoy's offer. Instead, Abilene gained the distinction of being the end of the Chisholm Trail and became the cow town that Salina feared and rejected.

Native Americans believed Salina was safe from tornadoes because it was at the confluence of two rivers; this belief is just one of many Indian legends about tornadoes. Maybe they were right, though. As Kansas towns go, Salina has been relatively fortunate in never being in the path of killer tornadoes.

255 Aviators

Several prominent people in the world of aviation have come from Salina. These include Glen Martin, who in 1908 flew the first flight of an aircraft that took off under its own power. Martin also invented the first parachute and the first bomber and founded Martin Aircraft in California. Two other famous aviators from Salina were Tom Braniff, the founder of the now-defunct Braniff Airlines, and Steve Hawley, a NASA astronaut who flew on the maiden voyage of the space shuttle *Discovery.*

In 2005, seventy years after Kansan Amelia Earhart attempted to fly solo around the world, adventurer Steve Fossett—the first person to circumnavigate the globe solo in a balloon—took off on the first solo, nonstop flight around the world from Salina's airport. In just over sixty-seven hours and without refueling, he landed back

The Global Flyer piloted by Steve Fossett lands at the Salina airport. (Jim Turner, Turner Photography, courtesy of the Salina Airport Authority)

here in Salina. The city was chosen because the airport, the former Shilling Air Force Base, has a runway that is more than 2 miles long. The 25,000-mile flight was financed by Virgin Atlantic Airlines chief Richard Branson. The British billionaire said, "Virgin Atlantic is delighted to be launching this historic record attempt from Salina, Kansas, and I hope that we can add Salina to the roll call of sites like Kitty Hawk which have been the setting for milestones in aviation history."

253 Blue Beacon

The very first Blue Beacon truck wash is at this exit on the right. The concept of a fast multibay truck wash was started here in 1973. There were other truck washes at that time, but drivers commonly had to wait in long lines, and the wash could take forty-five minutes. Blue Beacon introduced high-pressure sprays that made it possible to wash a truck in ten minutes; the company also emphasized attentive care of its customers. Blue Beacon now has a nationwide network of about 100 locations, many with three bays to maintain its short-line, fast-wash reputation.

252 The Wheat State

The first railroad car full of wheat traveled from Saline County to New York City in 1870. Within a decade, Salina had three flour mills and six grain elevators. More than 120 years later, wheat still plays a major role in Salina's economy, as evidenced by the enormous Cargill-Salina grain elevator seen on the left. This elevator has a 32-million-bushel capacity. The 140 bins are 150 feet tall and from 25 to 35 feet in diameter. Not as visible are six flat storage buildings, each one big enough to house two football fields.

An elevator is a cluster of bins with a single mechanism to take the grain to the top. It received its name because grain is "elevated" to the top of the tall storage bins. In one type of elevator, buckets attached to a moving belt scoop the grain and carry it to the top. From there, the grain is discharged to one of several chutes, where it flows by gravity down into one of a number of storage bins. Most Kansas towns have elevators to store grain from the surrounding area. The size of elevators and the huge number of them indicate the tremendous volume of food resources that come from our farms year after year.

Grain purchased at the Cargill-Salina elevator is carried in by truck from farms within a 30-mile radius. Sixty percent of the storage is used for hard red winter wheat. Bins are also filled with sorghum, corn, and soybeans. Grain is shipped out in hundred-car trains, with 85 percent of the wheat destined for export. Trains go to Texas and Louisiana seaports to load ships that take the grain to other parts of the world.

As much as 50 percent of the US wheat production is exported. Some top customers have been China, the former Soviet Union, Japan, Korea, and Egypt. According to the Wheat Foods Council, the average American consumes about 150 pounds of wheat flour products every year. But even though China is traditionally thought of as a rice-eating nation, the Chinese consume 180 pounds of wheat flour products per person per year, mostly in the form of noodles. Other high-consumption nations include France (241 pounds), Egypt (384 pounds), and Algeria (441 pounds).

Among the six classes of wheat, there are differences in the color of the kernels and the hardness of the grain. But the only difference in nutrients is the protein content, which is nutritionally insignificant but makes a big difference for baking. Hard red winter wheat like that grown here has 10 to 15 percent protein, which is good for breads and all-purpose flour. The soft red winter wheats range from 8 to 11 percent protein and are used in cakes, cookies, pastries, and crackers. Hard spring wheat, with 12 to 18 percent protein, is used for yeast breads. Durum, the hardest wheat, averages 14 to 16 percent protein and is used for pastas.

That's a lot about wheat! In the miles ahead, it will become even more evident why Kansas is called the Wheat State.

248 Bombs Away!

The small, flat-topped hill seen on the far left horizon, first appearing to the left of the white elevator, is called Soldier Cap. From this distance, the landscape seems pastoral and peaceful, but looks are deceiving. That hill is located on the Smoky Hill Air National Guard Range, where jets from McConnell Air Force Base in Wichita and other bases conduct target practice. This practice range was particularly important during World War II, when it was a training base for B-29 bomber crews.

Can you estimate the distance to where those bomb runs were made at Soldier Cap? That particular hill is actually 11 miles off. You can see a long way here on the Plains.

247 A World of Wildlife

A section of Kansas prairie south of Exit 244 has been transformed into a beautifully landscaped zoological park. The Rolling Hills Zoo, a 95-acre prairie oasis, is dedicated to conserving and propagating rare and endangered wildlife. You can see a rare white camel, an Indian rhino, and more than a hundred kinds of animals, ranging from aardvarks to orangutans. A 64,000-square-foot museum has wildlife dioramas representing habitats in Africa, Asia, the Arctic, and four other regions. Some of these exhibits have robotic human figures that speak to visitors, allowing them to experience the wide world of wildlife.

246 Farm Ponds

Small farm ponds such as those you'll see on the right and over the next 50 miles provide great fishing. State records for eight kinds of fish have come from farm ponds, including the state record largemouth bass, weighing in at 11 pounds, 12 ounces. The Kansas Department of Wildlife and Parks will stock ponds with channel catfish and largemouth bass at no cost if the landowner agrees to allow public access.

Farm ponds store water for livestock but are most frequently constructed as water- and sediment-control basins near the top of a watershed. Such ponds are created by constructing a compacted earth embankment, forming a small dam to hold back the water. According to agricultural engineering design standards, a pond should be able to "control runoff from a 10-year frequency, 24-hour storm without overtopping."

244 Sunflowers

Fields in this area are sometimes planted to sunflowers. During the summer, you'll see many different varieties of these yellow flowers, but they all have one thing in common. When sunflowers are blooming, all their heads are turned in the same direction. Throughout the day, they follow the sun across the sky as if commanded to look up to it in unison.

This is wild sunflower country, as indicated by its designation as the state flower. But farmers grow a commercial variety of sunflower, an important crop in Kansas. Sunflowers are used to make oils, birdseed, and of course the sunflower seeds you can buy at convenience stores to munch on during your travels. You will see commercial sunflower operations at miles 57 and 13 ahead. Read more about this crop at those locations and also at 241E (p. 196).

243 Get to Know Your Semis

Freightliner is the top-selling brand of semitruck, accounting for about a third of the 190,000 new semis sold annually. The second most popular brand is Navistar International, followed by PACCAR, which owns the Peterbilt and Kenworth brands. Volvo, which also owns the well-known Mack Trucks brand, is fourth. See if your observations along I-70 bear all this out.

The top three trucking companies by revenue are UPS, FedEx, and J. B. Hunt. You'll also pass Old Dominion (OD), Schneider, and C. R. England trucks. Each represents an American success story.

FedEx—The name is the shortened version of Federal Express, the original company name. Look for the hidden arrow pointing to the right inside the clever FedEx logo.

UPS—In 1907, two Seattle teenagers founded the precursor to UPS. Their first delivery car was a Model T Ford. In 1937, when the company changed its name to United Parcel Service, it selected the now-famous Pullman brown color for its vehicles and uniforms. Originally, founder James E. Casey wanted the trucks to be yellow, but one of his partners said that they would be impossible to keep clean, and that Pullman railroad cars were brown for that reason. Now, the company tagline is "What can Brown do for you?"

J. B. Hunt—Johnnie Bryan Hunt founded his company in Arkansas in 1961. He started with 5 trucks and 7 refrigerated trailers to transport rice hulls. Now, the company employs over 16,000 people, operates more than 12,000 trucks, and has over 47,000 trailers and containers.

Old Dominion—OD began in 1934 with a single truck running a 94-mile route between Richmond and Norfolk, Virginia. During World War II, it grew considerably as it transported materials between military bases in those two cities. Today, it employs nearly 20,000 people.

C. R. England—In 1920, Chester Rodney England bought a Model T truck to provide farm-to-market service for farmers in and around Weber County, Utah. He then began hauling milk for Weber Dairy. During World War II, Chester began buying Mexican bananas entering the United States at El Paso, Texas. He would transport the bananas to Utah and then return to Texas with Idaho potatoes. C. R. England is now the largest refrigerated-controlled carrier in the world, and it is still family owned after four generations.

Schneider—In 1935, A. J. "Al" Schneider used the money from the sale of his family car to buy his first truck. Today, the business he started has grown into a $4 billion company and is still based out of Schneider's hometown of Green Bay, Wisconsin. Schneider's 10,120 pumpkin-orange trucks collectively drive 8.2 million miles each day—equivalent to 329 trips around the globe!

See how many of these moving success stories you can spot rolling down the highway and learn more about semitrucks, including how they got that name, at 57E (p. 152).

240 Brookville

Brookville, about 5 miles south of the interstate, once bustled with 2,000 residents. This is the same town famous for the Brookville Hotel and its chicken dinners that you read about at 279W (p. 48). Business flourished after the arrival of the Union Pacific Railroad in the 1870s. There were two lumber yards, a general merchandise store, flour and feed stores, and a second hotel. Because this was a division point for the railroad, train crews lived here and took the trains a specified distance in either direction, where they would turn the train over to the next crew. They would then work on another train for the return trip to Brookville.

Brookville's economy suffered a blow when, around the turn of the twentieth century, the Union Pacific moved its division farther west. Businesses left town and moved to Ellsworth and Salina. Residents went off to find jobs in larger towns, and Brookville became a quiet country community.

The Brookville Hotel remained, though, and its reputation grew. During World War II, the military personnel at the nearby Smoky Hill Army Air Base patronized the hotel by the hundreds. People came from miles around for dinner, and notable guests came to stay. Originally known as the Cowtown Café and then the Central Hotel, the Brookville Hotel has had notable guests such as Buffalo Bill Cody, J. C. Penney, and Henry Chrysler, whose son Walter founded the Chrysler Corporation.

SMOKY HILLS REGION

238 Entering the Smoky Hills

The Smoky Hills, so named because in the summer the hills are obscured by a smoky-looking heat haze when viewed from a distance, are the third region through which I-70 passes.

You have climbed to over 1,500 feet from the 760-foot low point at Kansas City. The elevation will change another 1,000 feet as you travel the next 60 miles to the western edge of the Smoky Hills region. Considerable ruggedness is evident over short distances, particularly where rivers have eroded their channels. Along the Saline River, just north of the interstate, the river has cut canyons that are 300 feet deep in places. You will notice interesting rock formations exposed on eroded slopes. The area only gets about 24 inches of precipitation annually, so trees are confined to the edges of streams and ponds—mostly cottonwoods and willows, with green ash and hackberry sometimes present.

Streamside bottomlands, with their deep, rich soils, will be in cultivation. The uplands, with poorer, shallower soils, will still be in prairie grasses: buffalo and grama grass interspersed with taller grasses such as bluestems. You will cross Elkhorn Creek ahead, which reminds us that elk once roamed these lands along with herds of buffalo, grizzly bears, and wolves. Today, watch for coyotes, wild turkey, and deer.

The Smoky Hills region is the heart of the state's oil production. Natural gas and salt are taken from underground. On the surface, rich soils produce sorghum, wheat, soybeans, hay, and new varieties of drought-resistant corn.

236 A Land of Lincoln

You will be passing through Lincoln County, established in 1867 and named after Abraham Lincoln, who had been killed only two years earlier. President Lincoln was a hero here because Kansas was an antislavery state and remained with the Union throughout the Civil War. After George Washington's name, Lincoln's is the most popular choice among political place-names in the United States. There are, for instance, twenty-two Lincoln Counties in the nation!

235 Bison

Just to the left, you will notice a ranch with a tall flagpole; it often has buffalo, more accurately called bison. In earlier times, bison numbered in the millions in this region. However, the coming of the white settlers and the railroad quickly eliminated them from Kansas. At first, settlers killed bison only for their meat and hides,

Shooting buffalo on the line of the Kansas Pacific Railroad in 1871. (Library of Congress)

but soon after the railroads arrived, bison were killed from trains by sport hunters, and their carcasses were often left to rot. Within a few years, the bison were gone. This mindless slaughter not only eliminated a fuel and food source for settlers but also helped to seal the fate of the Plains Indians, who depended on bison herds for survival; in fact, this was the motivation of some buffalo hunters: to wipe out a key source of food for the Indians. In 2016, President Barack Obama signed the National Bison Legacy Act, which made the American bison the US National Mammal. Our national mammal can be seen up-close at Frontier Park across from Fort Hays State Historic Site (Exit 159).

234 Wind Farm

For the next 25 miles, you will be driving through a wind farm owned by Enel Green Power North America, Inc., the world's largest producer of renewable energy. At the top of each of the towers (which are 80 meters, or 265 feet, tall) is an electricity-generating turbine. Each turbine is capable of producing 1.5 megawatts. At typical efficiencies, this is enough energy to supply the needs of 332 homes. This "farm" has 155 towers, meaning that, collectively, it could serve the needs of more than 50,000 households. As you observe the wind farm, some blades may not be turning because the winds are not sufficient or because they are turned off for maintenance.

The turbines seen here are three-bladed, upwind, horizontal-axis wind turbines with rotational diameters of 72 meters (240 feet). The blades are 35 meters (115 feet) long, with yaw control to keep the rotor pointed into the wind. They are designed with an active blade pitch control to regulate the turbine motor speed as wind force changes. The horizontal shaft is geared to produce a high-speed drive for an electromagnetic generator. A wind speed of 6 miles per hour will start the turbine turning, and the unit will shut down if the wind speed exceeds 50 miles per hour.

Enel Green Power leases land from the farms where the towers are located. The contract allows for access roads to be built during construction as well as easements for maintenance. Contracts vary, but in general, the farm's land continues to be used for crops or grazing. The towers are connected via underground electric cables that continue to the Midwest Energy Post Rock 230-kilovolt substation. From the substation, electricity is fed into the grid for distribution to factories, farms, and homes.

231 Post Rock

Over the next 50 miles or so, you'll see stone fence posts being used with barbed wire to section off farm fields. You have entered the heart of "Post Rock Country." When pioneers arrived, few trees grew here, so there was no wood for fence posts, corrals, or homes. Everything had to be made from stone, including fence posts. Indeed, fence posts created from limestone have been used so extensively that they are an identifying feature of this landscape. The Post Rock Country is from 10 to 40 miles wide and stretches about 200 miles from the Nebraska border south to Dodge City. The next rest area (mile 224) is a good place to get an up-close look at examples of post rock fences. Details about the history of post rock use are provided ahead at mile 190W (p. 74).

230 Spite Fence

On both sides of the road, you will see two post rock fences running parallel up the hill, just a few feet apart. These "spite fences" have been built where there was a dispute or at least some confusion be-

Spite fence

tween landowners about the exact location of their property lines. More commonly, disagreements about fair and equal maintenance of fences placed directly on a property line caused a landowner to build the fence well inside his or her own boundary. The space between the fences, called the devil's lane, often is filled with woody vegetation because livestock cannot graze between the fences.

229 Living Snow Fence

The redcedars planted in dense rows form a living snow fence. They block the wind and blowing snow from reaching the highway. Other snow fences can be seen along I-70, including a large one at mile 15. Ahead, you will begin noticing such windbreaks around farmsteads.

228 Cheyenne Bottoms

About 30 miles south of Exit 225 lies Cheyenne Bottoms, the "Jewel of the Prairie." Cheyenne Bottoms is the largest inland marsh in the United States. It is a critical migration point for North American shorebirds and waterfowl, making it a world-class bird-watching destination. More than 25 kinds of ducks and geese have been seen at the Bottoms, and at times, they have numbered in excess of 600,000 birds. Besides the large numbers of waterbirds, Cheyenne Bottoms is an important rest stop for the endangered whooping crane. In all, at least 330 species of birds have been identified here.

Cheyenne Bottoms is a threatened ecosystem plagued by a lack of water inflow due to increased irrigation in the Arkansas River watershed. In some years, you might find it mostly dry. But even in its tenuous condition, this is a wonder-filled wetland to visit, as bird-watchers from around the world will attest.

226 Fort Harker

Fort Harker, located south of this location, provided a safe haven for settlers headed to western Kansas. The fort, named to honor Captain Charles Harker, who had been killed during the Civil War at the Battle of Kennesaw Mountain, could accommodate about 700 soldiers and 1,400 civilians. Distinguished generals who visited the fort included Ulysses S. Grant, Philip Sheridan, William T. Sherman, and the infamous George Custer.

Fort Harker provided protection for the Butterfield Overland Despatch during its short (eighteen-month) existence. The fort was called Home and Eating Station Number 6. After Fort Harker was abandoned in 1880, families dug homes into the sides of nearby bluffs and lived in caverns like cave dwellers. Carvings and petroglyphs created by Native Americans and early settlers can be seen on the walls of caves in this area. The Fort Harker Museum in Kanopolis contains artifacts and war memorabilia displayed in one of the fort's original buildings.

Read about the oldest continually operating salt mine in the United States and the small town of Kanopolis, which was designed for 150,000 people and promoted by land developers as "the Capital Metropolis" or "Kansas Metropolis," at 223E (p. 190).

224 Ellsworth

You entered Ellsworth County a few miles back. Both the county and the town of Ellsworth are named after 2nd Lieutenant Allen Ellsworth of Company H, Seventh Iowa Cavalry. He established a small fort in 1864 along the Smoky Hill River. Two years later, it was moved a mile or so and became Fort Harker, which you just read about at 226W. During its short history, Fort Ellsworth was attacked twice by Indians; on one occasion, a raiding party drove off fifty horses and five mules. No deaths were reported from these attacks.

South of Exit 219 is the town of Ellsworth. This town prospered from the cattle trade. It was the end of one branch of the Chisholm Trail, which split into two branches just south of the Kansas border with the Oklahoma Territory. The other branch ran to Abilene, as you read at 279W (p. 48).

Rumors that Ellsworth would be the end of the line for the Union Pacific Railroad helped it thrive by attracting speculators. The first railroad cars arrived in Ellsworth on July 5, 1867, bringing merchants, lawyers, doctors, gamblers, gunmen, laborers, and thieves. They all played different roles in shaping the newest important cow town on the Texas cattle trail.

Along with these people came drinking, gambling, prostitution, and all sorts of trouble. Gunfights occurred regularly, including the killing of Sheriff Chauncey B. Whitney. Another dispute resulted in a vigilante group hanging two men. A local newspaper reported the story and stated: "As we go to press, hell is in session in Ellsworth."

The town's role in the cattle industry was over almost as soon as it started. By 1875, the cattle business left Ellsworth as the railroad extended west and people moved on with it.

222 Pioneer Problems

Kansas farmers still face hardships, but they are much less severe than those faced by the original pioneers. See the description of the challenges presented by the harsh environment, conflicts with local Indians, and especially the grasshopper invasion of 1874 at 230E (p. 192).

220 So This Is a Farmstead?

The cluster of buildings in back of the service station at Exit 219 looks like a business center. It is. It's the center of the Helvey Farm's 6,000-acre operation. Forget the image of a self-contained farmstead complete with home and garden, livestock barns, and barnyard. The farmstead of the 1900s has given way to this machinery repair and parking center with fuel and chemical supply tanks.

The farm originally was on the 80 acres near the exit. The first Helveys moved here from Illinois. For five generations, the family has produced food, mostly wheat and soybeans, on this land. But to

Helvey Farms

keep up with farming trends and costs, it is now necessary to grow more crops and market new varieties. The family's land is spread from Ellsworth to Lincoln and Mitchell Counties as insurance against damage from extreme weather. David Helvey explained, "With the cheap food policy of the United States, farmers are forced to continually produce more for less." When he started farming in the 1950s, you could sell a bushel of wheat for three dollars. Today, you still get about the same price for that bushel, but the cost of seed, fuel, and fertilizer has gone up 300 percent.

We asked him why he stays, given the situation today. "To meet the challenge," Helvey said. He now grows corn, sorghum, and sunflowers in addition to wheat. Crop rotations conserve soil and moisture. New techniques fight insects, and machines ease the heavy labor. "This is a great place to live. We can trust people," he stated. "Here a person's word is a person's bond. We're staying."

215 Dog Soldiers

During Indian raids in this region, the most feared of all roving war parties were the "Dog Soldiers." These Kiowa and Cheyenne warriors were driven by the single purpose of killing white settlers who were encroaching on their traditional lands. What made the Dog Soldiers so dangerous was their independence. They were members of a blood brotherhood who chose their own leaders and did not submit to the tribal chiefs established through family lineage. They did not honor peace treaties made by other Indian leaders and continued to attack settlers even in times of truce.

214 The Lighted Cross Church

Dwarfed by the wind turbines, the quaint white Excelsior Lutheran Church on the left is known as the Lighted Cross Church. The cornerstone for this church was laid in 1908. The adjacent cemetery has markers for people born in the early to mid-1800s, pioneers who came to farm these hills and now rest in them.

The church's cross is 65 feet tall. It is lined with forty-eight lights that are lit from dusk to dawn, making it conspicuous from the interstate in an otherwise dark stretch of road. The cross arm is a circle of lights 16 feet in diameter, arranged so that the arm appears in perfect proportion from any direction. A fund has been established to ensure that the lights will continue to shine even if the continually diminishing congregation no longer exists. The landmark is so

Lighted Cross Church

prominent that gifts from travelers have been delivered when only a "Wilson, Kansas 67490" address is used.

213 The Big Bales

The big, round bales you will see rolled up in the fields or stacked near a feed yard are likely alfalfa hay that will be used to feed cattle in the winter. Some may be straw that was baled after wheat harvest, to be used as livestock bedding. These bales, which look like giant shredded wheat biscuits, often weigh 2,000 pounds.

These big bales have their roots here in Kansas. When Wes Buchele grew up on a Kansas farm, hay was gathered loose and pitched to the cattle with a fork. In high school, he ran a crew that went from farm to farm to compact hay into 60-pound bales, thus making it easier to stack and transport. But handling those bales required a lot of backbreaking labor, and the compacting plunger that was used injured many farmers.

After receiving engineering degrees at Kansas State University, Buchele continued to think about ways to mechanize the handling of hay. In 1968, by now a teacher at Iowa State University, Professor Buchele suggested that one of his graduate students should try to design an economical hay package that would reduce the number of bales to be handled and be safer to operate. Together, they created a machine to make big, round, rolled-up bales that completely eliminated the need for hand labor, all for a reasonable investment in equipment and twine. The result of the agricultural engineers' design has been the creation of a new industry to manufacture the balers and related handling equipment that reduce the drudgery of farming. Their work innovations made it possible for fewer workers to supply our food at a lower cost.

211 Pioneer Immigrants

Another cemetery lies just to the right of the interstate here, amid the cluster of redcedar and elm trees. Grave markers carry the names and dates of people who were among the first settlers of the region and who died in the 1880s. Family names include Peterka, Hanzlicek, and Dolezal, reflecting the Czech influence in this area. See 207W (p. 70) ahead.

210 Black Wolf

The town of Black Wolf, 5 miles south, was named after an Indian chief who was well liked in the area. For many years, this spot was famous for the following sign, which was posted south of town:

Black Wolf, Kansas
Population 41
Speed Limit, 101 Miles Per Hour
Fords, Do Your Damnedest

209 The Post Rock Scenic Byway

At Exit 206, you can take the Post Rock Scenic Byway north to the Garden of Eden. The byway traverses beautiful rolling hills covered with lush grasses and dotted with lines of post rock fences. Lucas is home to the Grassroots Art Center, which is devoted to exhibiting folk art.

In Lucas, you also will see an unforgettable example of folk art—the Garden of Eden. This site, which is listed on the National Register of Historic Places, was built by Civil War veteran Samuel Perry Dinsmoor and includes an eleven-room limestone-and-concrete "log" cabin and 150 amazing concrete sculptures depicting Bible stories and making Populist political statements. An interesting side note to the Garden of Eden story is that at the age of eighty-one, Dinsmoor married a twenty-year-old woman and fathered a son and daughter who, as of 2002, were the only living children of a Civil War veteran. Dinsmoor died in 1932; his body lies in a glass casket in the concrete mausoleum he built to display his remains.

208 Wilson Lake

Wilson Lake, about 5 miles north of this point, was created in 1964 when the Army Corps of Engineers dammed the Saline River as a flood-control measure. Grasslands above the lake hold the soil in place when it rains, making this one of the clearest lakes in Kansas and thus a popular fishing spot. The lake is noted for its walleye, striped bass, and smallmouth bass. With over 9,000 surface acres of water and more than 100 miles of shoreline, Wilson Lake attracts people who come to water-ski, windsurf, hang glide, picnic, and camp.

207 Czech Capital

Exit 206 leads to Wilson, also known as the Czech capital of Kansas, and the Kansas Originals Market. The market displays the works and products of 1,200 Kansas artists, craftspeople, and cooks. The cooperative association behind this market has been featured in the magazine *Midwest Living* and has sold Kansas products to people in all fifty states and more than a hundred countries, bringing in more than $2 million to the artists and craftspeople.

In 1865, Wilson Creek was a watering stop for horses on the Butterfield Overland Despatch stagecoach line. An early name for the settlement was Bosland, as cows were envisioned to be an important part of the town: the settlers used *Bos* from the Latin term for "cow" or "oxen." But few cows were actually shipped from the town, and in 1874, the name was changed to Wilson. The town was promoted by a Czechoslovakian named Francis Swehla. Wilson still reflects the original Czech culture. Traditional foods and handicraft are available here, and during special events, descendants wear authentic Czech costumes.

The town's Midland Hotel was used in the movie *Paper Moon*. In addition, Alaska's first state governor, William A. Egan, married Neva McKittrick, a Wilson resident. So the very first First Lady of Alaska was from Wilson, Kansas.

205 Russell County

This county and the town of Russell (mile 187) were named after Avra P. Russell, a captain in Company K, Second Kansas Cavalry, who fought in the Civil War and died of battle wounds in 1862. The county was established on February 26, 1867.

Russell County's economy is largely supported by oil. Ahead, you will see many oil wells and storage tanks along the interstate.

204 Abandoned Homes

Over the last 20 miles, you may have noticed several abandoned homesites. Many of these vacant, ramshackle dwellings mark the end of efforts to make a living from this land. Each house once held a family and tells a story of their struggles. The dust bowl years drove many residents to California. Others left because of harsh winters, the unreliable water supply, or homesickness for places back east. Sometimes, all that remains of a family's dream home is a shade tree that they had planted and nurtured. In fact, in western Kansas, where trees are naturally scarce, a good way to locate an old homestead is to look for a tree out in the middle of a field. Often, it provides shade only to a crumbling foundation, the remnants of what was once someone's pride and joy.

The abandoned square, yellowish limestone farmhouse on the right side of the interstate just before marker 201 was built sometime before 1910 and abandoned in the late 1950s when the last residents moved to Wichita. The house reminds us of what Ian Frazier noted in his book *Great Plains*:

> You can find all kinds of ruins on the Great Plains; in dry regions things last a long time. When an enterprise fails on the plains, people usually just walk away and leave it. With empty land all around, there is not much reason to tear down and rebuild on the same site. In the rest of America, you are usually within the range of the sound of hammers. A building comes down, another goes up, and soon it is hard to remember what used to be there.

200 Dorrance

Home of the hoops! For many years, National Basketball Association (NBA) basketball rims and backboards were made here in Dorrance, and other equipment used by NBA teams is still made here. At 197E (p. 183), read about how backboard designs were changed because of a Dorrance firm's influence. Like many Kansas towns, Dorrance is named after a railroad man. In this case, O. B. Dorrance was the Union Pacific Railroad superintendent when the town was founded.

198 Wind Power

Windmills, such as the one on the right at this location, have been used by Kansas farmers and ranchers since the late 1800s. Windmills harness an ever-present Kansas resource, the wind. In the Smoky Hills, the average wind speed is 13 miles per hour, with gusts of 40 to 60 miles per hour. Windmills attached to pumps are a natural way to lift water from wells for livestock, for crop irrigation, and (when combined with an elevated storage tank) for household needs. As you have seen, modern wind farms are sprouting up around the state to put the Kansas wind to work, but settlers did this 150 years ago and their descendants still do.

196 Why Are Barns Red?

You will see several red barns in the area ahead. Red was the color of choice for painting barns for many years, probably because the ingredients for red paint were inexpensive and easy to mix. Iron oxide powder was often used to give a deep red color. Mixed in linseed oil, it could be spread easily on barn boards. When a little casein (as in white glue) was added, the protective coating had a longer life. Casein adhesive is a constituent of skimmed milk, which was always available on the farm. To produce a more red-orange color, lead oxide powder was used. With today's technology for formulating ready-to-use paint, white and other colors have become popular for painting barns.

194 Bunker Hill

The next town is Bunker Hill. A stagecoach station on the Butterfield Overland Despatch was located here in 1865, and the Union Pacific Railroad went through in 1867. A colony of settlers from Ohio arrived in Bunker Hill in May 1871. The settlers named it after a town in Ohio with the same name.

193 Chief Spotted Horse

At the east end of the Bunker Hill Cemetery is the grave of a young Pawnee chief named Spotted Horse, who died of typhoid fever in 1874 near Bunker Hill. His father, a Pawnee chief who had converted to Christianity, requested a Christian burial for his son in the whites' cemetery. As a result, Spotted Horse's grave lies among the graves of Civil War veterans and early settlers.

192 Tower No. 4

That slim tower off to the left is 110 feet tall but only 10 feet in diameter. It holds 60,000 gallons of water and provides water pressure for the Post Rock Rural Water District. In many areas, water is distributed to small towns and farms through rural water districts like this one. In this district, water for the system is pumped from Kanopolis Lake, downstream from Fort Harker on the Smoky Hill River (226W, p. 64). After purification, the water is pumped to a series of towers stretching across much of the area through which you've been traveling. This Tower No. 4 provides pressure to serve customers ahead in Ellis County, as far as 15 miles away in Walker.

This rural water district started signing up subscribers in 1974. Ten years later, since enough users had agreed to support the system, Tower No. 4 was erected. The water purity has never been a concern, but customers can detect seasonal differences in flavor that result from lake water changes. Today, nearly 1,200 customers in eight counties are assured of a reliable supply of healthful water,

Chief Spotted Horse's grave

something that was not always possible when they depended on individual wells.

Throughout history, the quality and quantity of water have been determining factors in where communities have been located and the types of commerce that have developed. Managing water is complicated here because there is a limited supply. In Kansas, over twenty governmental agencies address water-related issues. This tangled web requires vigilance and cooperative efforts to optimize the value of the water resource.

190 Still More Post Rocks

You will see more post rock fences ahead. The early settlers were British, Scandinavian, German, and Czech, and some were skilled in masonry and stonecutting. As the saying goes, "Necessity is the mother of invention." In a land without trees to supply wood, these folks saw the potential of the area's limestone and used it in place of wood for fence posts and buildings.

The original idea of using stone for fence posts supposedly was conceived by C. F. Sawyer, who lived near this location. Sawyer was a stoneworker in Illinois before moving to Kansas, and he recognized the possibility of using limestone for posts. According to one of his sons, Sawyer built the first stone post fence in December 1878. Today, more than 40,000 miles of stone post fences remain in this region of Kansas!

Limestone is unique in that while the stone is covered with earth and protected from the air, it remains soft enough to be cut with a handsaw (although most post rock was split off using hammers and wedges). Upon exposure to the air, however, chemical changes take place that turn the stone hard. The limestone here is in thin, 6- to 8-inch layers and lies near the surface, making excavation convenient. Horses would drag the 400-pound cut rock posts to their final locations.

Each group of people who inhabited the Post Rock Country used the easily accessible limestone. Native Americans used broken pieces for burial mounds and crude weapons. Explorers and trappers used the stone as markers. Surveyors made stone pillars for landmarks. Early horse traders and cattlemen placed upended slabs side by side along ravine walls to form corrals. Settlers built churches, schools, bridges, water towers, and even silos from this amazing stone. Some of it was shipped by rail for building construction as far east as New York. Grace Muilenburg and Ada Swineford, in *Land of the Post Rock,* described how important limestone was to settlers in this region: "Throughout the area, remains of old self-sufficient homesteads may include a stone dwelling, a cave or cellar with a stone entrance, a stone barn, two or three other stone outbuildings, a stone corral, stone clothesline poles, stone gate posts, a stone hitching post or two, flagstones for walks between buildings, stone well curbs, stone feeding floors and hollowed-out slabs for watering or feeding farm animals."

At the parking area ahead, you can get an up-close look at post rock. Although more cost-effective types of construction are used today, limestone is still available and specified when a particular architectural effect is desired.

187 Sober Senators

A group of seventy German settlers from Ripon, Wisconsin, established the town of Russell in the winter of 1871. Early accounts state that they were "good, sober, industrious people" who prohibited gambling and saloons. When *The WPA Guide* was written in the 1930s, the authors noted that the German Russian population

Post rock fence

was still made up of "good, sober, industrious people." Russell is now known for being the hometown of two influential US senators. Longtime Kansas senator and presidential candidate Bob Dole and Senator Arlen Specter of Pennsylvania both have good, sober, industrious roots here. Russell was once known as Fossil Station because of the rich fossil beds in the area.

186 The Coyote and the Doodlebug

The Oil Patch Museum in Russell tells the story of the area's oil industry. At Exit 184, you can see derricks and an outdoor collection of rotary drilling rigs, pump jacks, steam engine power units, and an oil storage tank that you can actually walk through.

The oil boom here has been credited, oddly enough, to a coyote and a "doodlebug." In the early 1920s, representatives from the firm of Sterns and Streeter were searching for oil when a coyote ran in front of their car. One of the men claimed they would find oil where the coyote had been. A contraption called a doodlebug, which supposedly indicated the presence of oil, "doodled" at the spot where the coyote had stood. Sure enough, there was oil there. A wooden derrick, Carrie Oswald No. 1, named after the landowner, was erected at that spot in June 1923.

184 Wonderful Wetlands

Small wetlands such as the marshy areas seen on the left and ahead on the right are more valuable than most people realize. Wetlands can take many forms, from damp meadows to forested swamps. Regardless of their appearance, they serve us all by serving as natural sponges to soak up floodwaters and act as nature's filters, removing pollutants. Wetlands also allow water to replenish the groundwater rather than running off, a valuable function out here on the Plains where people rely on the groundwater for nearly all their water needs. Wetland plants protect shorelines from wave erosion. In some places, wetlands are important for fisheries because they serve as nurseries for young fish. Indeed, wetlands provide habitat for hundreds of kinds of wildlife, including waterfowl that migrate across North America, as well as many endangered species. They also provide opportunities for recreational pursuits such as birdwatching, fishing, hunting, and photography. Moreover, they enhance the beauty of an area. Wetlands certainly are not wastelands.

182 Tanking the Crude

Notice the oil storage tanks scattered in the fields in this area. Where does the crude go after it is lifted from the ground? A network of pipes connect the oil wells with those storage tanks. The crude oil is then picked up by tanker trucks and transported to refineries. In some cases, it is piped directly to refineries near Wichita or as far away as Texas. There are both oil and gas wells in the fields you pass. You can see the "rocking horse–style" pump on oil wells. Gas accumulates under its own pressure, so no pump is needed on a gas well.

Something you will not see are tall oil derricks. At one time, every well had a derrick, but in the 1950s, a team of men from Texas came to Ellis County and quickly removed all of them. Witnesses said it was quite a sight to watch, as the men used their hands to "flip" each derrick up into the air so it would land on its top rather than just tipping it over. This prevented joints and beams from being bent on impact with the ground. Then, like a NASCAR pit crew, they feverishly dismantled the derrick and loaded it for shipment to Texas, where much of it was used for scrap metal.

180 Sinkhole

The pond on the left side right at mile 179 ahead is the result of a sinkhole. Note the dip in the road here. Over the next couple of miles, you will notice several such dips, which are also the result of sinkholes beneath the roadway. According to Rex Buchanan and James McCauley, authors of *Roadside Kansas,* I-70 was originally flat in this area. As they explained, these sinkholes form when water dissolves or washes out cavities in salt beds 1,300 to 1,600 feet below the surface. Some sinkholes here are caused by water dissolving the salt around abandoned oil wells. Occasionally, a sinkhole develops suddenly when a salt cavern is formed, and the overlaying rocks then cannot support the weight above and come crashing down. Everything above collapses, forming the sinkhole at the surface.

177 Water-Loving Willows

Ahead at mile 175, notice the willows growing along the stream. Willows and water go together. Old Testament prophets, Shakespeare, and a multitude of writers and artists have linked willows and water for centuries. Unlike some other literary linkages, this association is biologically accurate. Willows require an abundance of water and can survive long periods of flooding, attributes that make them the perfect shoreline tree. Willows serve a vital function in preventing the erosion of banks in ponds and streams; their roots form dense mats that hold the soil particles in place instead of being washed away by waves or flowing water.

Native Americans used willow wood and limber willow sprouts to make traps, tent poles and stakes, mats, baskets, drums, meat-drying racks, and many other objects. Today, willow wood is sometimes used for boxes, crates, and furniture parts. A specialty use of willow wood is for artificial limbs for amputees.

Willows were a living pharmacy for both Native Americans and European settlers. Virtually every potential health problem was treated with teas or pastes made from parts of the willow tree by some group of people on the Plains. Even "chew sticks," the precursor to toothbrushes, were often made with willow twigs. These sticks may have provided other dental health benefits as well due to the chemicals in the wood. Salicin, a painkiller used in modern pharmaceuticals, is found in willow bark and leaves.

175 Ellis County

Ellis County was settled primarily by Germans, but it is named for George Ellis, a Pennsylvania man who came to Kansas and enlisted in the Twelfth Kansas Infantry. He fought Quantrill's raiders at Lawrence in 1863 (see 198E, p. 236) and died at Jenkins Ferry, Arkansas, the following year. Kansas legislators honored Lieutenant Ellis by naming a county for him.

Ellis County has consistently been the best oil-producing county in Kansas. The Ellis Oil Field was discovered in 1943, and today, it produces more than 2.5 million barrels of oil each year.

174 St. Ann's Church

On the right, St. Ann's Church in Walker, with its towering steeple, is a prominent landmark. It was constructed using local limestone in 1904. St. Ann's small parish benefits from being close to a major cathedral because a priest is always available to minister to the congregation and to conduct services. One parishioner explained, "It is smaller, but it is friendlier to worship here."

St. Ann's Church

173 An Avenue Exit

In the more than 400 miles of I-70 running across Kansas, there are only two exits for avenues—the one for Walker Avenue, which you have just passed, and another for First Avenue in downtown Topeka, about 200 miles to the east. Having only two exits for avenues in more than 400 miles illustrates the rural character of your trip across Kansas.

172 Abandoned Air Base

The remains of the abandoned Walker Army Airfield can be seen rising among the trees on the horizon to the right. The base was built by the Army Air Corps in 1942 and served as a training center for the Boeing B-29 Superfortress until 1946. Thousands of troops were stationed here during World War II, but today, very little is left of the base. Because of the proximity of the aircraft industry near

Wichita, the wide-open spaces, and the generally clear weather, Kansas was home to sixteen army airfields and even two naval air stations during World War II! The primary mission of these bases was to train air combat crews. A large percentage of all World War II flight crews received at least part of their training in Kansas.

171 Cathedral of the Plains

On the left, the twin steeples that dominate the landscape identify the Basilica of St. Fidelis, known as the Cathedral of the Plains. Exit 168 ahead leads to this stunning Romanesque-style basilica with forty-eight historical stained-glass windows; the St. Fidelis cemetery just north of town has hauntingly beautiful iron cross grave markers. Read about these iron crosses, which were the subject of a PBS documentary, at 166E (p. 177).

Catholic settlers built three churches before constructing the current cathedral. The first church in Victoria was merely a 40-by-24-foot lean-to attached to the south side of a house. It could accommodate only half of the congregation. A 60-by-30-foot stone church was completed one year later, in 1878, with funds raised by the Honorable Walter C. Maxwell, a Catholic Englishman. The contributions he obtained included one for 100 pounds from the Duke of Norfolk in England.

Cathedral of the Plains

However, the community quickly outgrew this church, too. In 1878, Father Hyacinth Epp visited Victoria and convinced the Kansas Pacific Railway to donate 10 acres for a larger church. Parishioners spent four years building a new church that held 600 worshippers, completing it in 1884.

By the turn of the twentieth century, the people again found themselves in need of a larger structure. The present church was completed in 1911 using native fence post limestone, quarried south of Victoria. The stone was cut by hand and hauled to the building site, where masons dressed the stone blocks and placed them by hand. Each stone weighed between 50 and 100 pounds. The settlers hauled and dressed more than 125,000 cubic feet of rock to complete the church.

William Jennings Bryan visited Victoria in 1912 while campaigning as the Democratic Party nominee for president. He thought the church was a beautiful symbol of faith and called it the Cathedral of the Plains. The lovely sanctuary seats 1,700 people, and its spires rise 141 feet toward the heavens.

168 A British Colony

The town of Victoria was founded by Sir George Grant, who wanted to form an aristocratic British colony in the United States. In 1871, he bought land from the Union Pacific Railroad and named the settlement he envisioned after Queen Victoria. Two years later, he arrived with a group of wealthy young men who would be supported from home while the colony was established. Read about their escapades with a riverboat on the Plains at 167E (p. 178).

Volga Germans also formed a colony adjacent to Victoria. These people were well trained for conditions on the Plains. and unlike the young British men, they were skilled in agriculture. They prospered and eventually absorbed Victoria when the British abandoned it. You will read more about the Volga Germans who settled in this area ahead at 119W (p. 97).

HAYS

166 Fort Hays Historic Site

Mark Twain said, "A railroad is like a lie—you have to keep building it to make it stand." This observation was borne out in Kansas as the railroads kept being built across the Plains. As railroads moved west through this part of Kansas, so did the settlers. This encroachment into "Indian" territory sparked conflicts between settlers and Native Americans. To protect the settlers traveling the rails and trails, the I-70s of the 1800s, the federal government built military posts along the way. Forts provided some peace of mind for settlers and encouraged settlement. In 1867, Fort Hays was established and named to honor General Alexander Hays, a hero at Gettysburg who was killed at the Battle of the Wilderness.

Fort Hays was the headquarters for military campaigns into all of western Kansas and parts of Colorado. The fort also served as a supply depot for all military activity in the area, as well as for military operations farther west and southwest. It was never attacked. In its heyday, Fort Hays was home to about 210 soldiers. Notable military figures, including George A. Custer and Philip H. Sheridan, passed through the fort. Custer led many expeditions against the Indians, taking supplies and military support from Fort Hays.

As the railroad expanded farther west and more people settled in the area, the need for the fort dwindled. By the mid-1870s, commanders were recommending that the fort be abandoned. On November 8, 1889, the last garrison of troops left. The government donated the land to the state of Kansas to be used for a college, an agricultural experiment station, and a park. The college, now called Fort Hays State University, offers degrees in education, business and leadership, arts and sciences, and health and life sciences. It occupies 4,160 acres of land that once was part of the fort. The agricultural research station, with its experimental cropland and pastureland, belongs to Kansas State University and comprises 6,100 acres of former fort property. A city park called Frontier Park, across the road from the fort's entrance, has a small buffalo herd, providing a close-up look at these powerful creatures.

Four of the original buildings remain at the site of Fort Hays, including the stone blockhouse that served as post headquarters.

The fort was featured in the movie *Dances with Wolves*. You can get to the fort from Exits 157 or 159.

163 Hays City

In 1867, soon after the new fort was constructed to protect travelers along the trails, Hays City was staked out 1 mile to the east. When the railroad arrived in the fall of the same year, Hays City and Fort Hays in essence became one. Hays grew quickly and became another wild frontier town filled with saloons and dance halls. The excitement enticed Wild Bill Hickok to serve as special marshal for four months in 1869. Hickok left Hays after a brawl with some troopers from the fort.

Rome wasn't built in a day, but Buffalo Bill Cody built Rome, Kansas, very quickly. Read about the boom and bust of this settlement at 154E (p. 174).

162 Sternberg Museum of Natural History

Ahead on the left is the domed roof of Fort Hays State University's Sternberg Museum of Natural History. If you or your children get excited about fossils and dinosaurs, then this is a great place to stretch your legs. Here, you can see the famous "fish-within-a-fish" fossil and walk among spectacular, life-size automated models of dinosaurs in their natural environment. Children can get hands-on experiences with specimens in the Discovery Room. The museum is namd to honor two generations of the Sternberg family that col-

Fort Hays headquarters

lected spectacular fossils. George F. Sternberg joined the university in 1927. He established the fossil collection and played a major role in the study of North American fossil vertebrates and the science of paleontology. The museum's collections include 3.7 million specimens, among them the third-largest collection of flying reptiles in the world and some of the most complete dinosaur fossils found anywhere. If you want some fresh Kansas air, you can walk the Dr. Howard Reynolds Nature Trail, which winds through upland prairie, over a stream, and under the shade of trees. More than 200 species of plants and plenty of wildlife can be seen along the trail. Follow the signs from Exit 159 to visit this fine museum.

160 Boot Hill

Hays is the home of the original Boot Hill Cemetery, where men were buried with their boots on. This cemetery was the final resting place of many an overzealous cowboy or unwary pioneer in Hays. Some people think Dodge City had the first Boot Hill, but when Dodge City was founded in 1872, the Hays City Boot Hill was already filling up. Hays's brief status as a lawless frontier town helped create the need for such a monument to violence. Estimates of the number of people buried at Boot Hill vary from thirty-seven to over a hundred, but the most reliable estimate is that there were about eighty graves. When homes were built at the site, some bodies were moved to Mount Allen Cemetery, but records on those relocated to the new cemetery were incomplete, and the whereabouts of those buried and moved are lost for all time.

158 Big Batteries/Stone House

Just beyond the overpass on the left is the 352,000-square-foot EnerSys battery factory. The company makes big, stationary batteries to provide backup electric power when regular service shuts down; it sells them to businesses such as telecommunications companies, medical facilities, public utilities, and a host of others requiring uninterrupted power. Batteries from this plant are shipped to customers in fifty-five countries.

EnerSys maintains the small limestone house near the highway on the left. It was built in 1866 by Joseph and Mary Roth. The Roths, along with their six sons and two daughters, migrated to Hays by way of Brazil after leaving Germany and living for a time in Russia. They were wheat farmers and probably lived on the land for many

Roth stone block house

years before claiming ownership. The first records at the Register of Deeds office show that Joseph Roth filed a homestead claim for the farm in 1897. He purchased an adjacent 320 acres in 1904, and this land was farmed until it was sold for the adjacent warehouse/ factory. The house was restored in 1975, using the original stone blocks. At that time, one of the Roths' daughters, who had lived in the house for her first fifteen years, explained that a kitchen had been attached to the stone house and added that her brothers slept in a loft just under the roof. The little two-room house on the buffalo grass prairie is a good reminder of how modestly the early settlers lived.

156 Yocemento

Behind the grain elevator at Yocemento on the left, notice the bluff known as the hogback. This town got its name from the words *Yost* and *cement*. In 1906, I. M. Yost and Professor Erasmus Haworth met in Hays and decided to build a cement plant at the hogback. You can still see where the quarries operated along the ridge, now much reduced by the mining activity that ensued.

Haworth, a professor in the Department of Geology at the University of Kansas and director of the Kansas Geological Survey, was revising geologic maps and spoke to Ike Yost, a longtime Hays resident and mill owner, about the area's topography. After Haworth outlined the kind of information he needed, Yost drove him to an outcrop of rock along Big Creek. When he climbed the steep bank and looked at the site, Haworth commented that cement could be made there more cheaply than anywhere else in Kansas because of the availability of limestone and water in the area.

Yost was excited about such an enterprise, and the men began plans to start a mill. Yost thought they should set up a town and begin selling lots to builders, as well as selling stock in the mill. With the Union Pacific tracks being close by, passengers and freight would come and go from the town, along with the cement. The men sold stock to people in both the eastern and western United States, and construction began in July 1906.

Within two years, cement was being made at the US Portland Cement Company. Yocemento became a thriving town of 350 people, with a train depot, post office, hotel, company store, restaurant, town newspaper, and office building. Two hundred men were on the plant payroll. For several years, the mill made a small profit. Some of the cement was used in building Union Station in Kansas City in 1910 and 1911. Today, part of that station houses a science museum.

But the good times were short-lived. By 1912, the cost of getting coal from Wyoming to run the huge furnaces dug too deeply into profits. At the same time, competitors in southeast Kansas and Colorado started expanding their operations, thereby further reducing the profits of the Yocemento plant. After the company declared bankruptcy, a Colorado competitor, the Boettcher Cement Company, bought and dismantled the plant. Yocemento slipped into obscurity as most people moved to Hays to find work. However, the lives of the ambitious founders of Yocemento were not ruined by this failure. Yost went back to his thriving flour mill, and Haworth continued to serve as the state geologist until 1915.

151 Another Wind Farm

The wind turbines seen to the right are part of the Buckeye Wind Energy Center's 200-megawatt project, which covers more than 28,000 acres in Ellis County. The 112 turbines have the capacity to produce enough energy to power 104,000 homes. Invenergy, based in Chicago, developed this site along with sixty-seven other wind farm projects in the United States, Canada, and Europe.

150 White Roads

Notice how white the county roads are in this location. This is because they are surfaced with crushed limestone, a particularly white rock that is found in this area. Along the interstate, road cuts clearly reveal limestone layers similar to those that provide the road-surfacing rock. You may recall that these layers were formed at the bottom of a warm, ancient sea.

ENTERING THE HIGH PLAINS

149 The High Plains

You have entered the High Plains region—the largest, highest, and driest region in Kansas, covering the western third of the state. Elevation ranges from about 4,000 feet above sea level along the Colorado-Kansas border to 2,000 feet here on the eastern edge of the region. The climate is becoming drier as you travel west. This region receives less than 20 inches of precipitation per year. The High Plains have a reputation for having strong winds and extreme temperatures (both hot and cold) that can fluctuate wildly, sometimes changing by 60 degrees in less than twenty-four hours.

148 Three Museums

Ellis, ahead on the left, boasts three small museums. The Ellis Railroad Museum focuses on Union Pacific Railroad history and offers a 2.5-mile miniature train ride. The Bukovina Society of the Americas Museum honors the immigrants to this area of Kansas from the province that was once part of the Austrian Empire and now is divided between Ukraine and Romania. As you can imagine given its location on the eastern slopes of Eastern Europe's Carpathian Mountains, Bukovina and its people were deeply affected by both world wars in the last century. As a multiethnic province, the name Bukovina has several spellings, but all mean "Land of the Beech Trees." The Bukovina Society of the Americas welcomes everyone with an interest in the history and culture of this land to visit the museum.

The Walter P. Chrysler Boyhood Home and Museum marks Ellis as the town where inventor and automobile manufacturer Walter Chrysler grew up during the 1880s as the son of a railroad worker. You may recall he was born back in Wamego. He moved here at the age of three as his father followed the railroad work west. Walter learned about engines by working on the railroad himself. His first job as an apprentice paid 5 cents an hour. Before long, he was forging steel to make his own tools. Because of the quickness and quality of his work, he was soon a master mechanic.

Chrysler's boyhood home contains his personal memorabilia. The museum also displays a Chrysler car from 1924, the first year of production. Maybe you are driving a car that bears his name. Every day, Chryslers pass Chrysler's hometown.

Other notables who spent time in Ellis include Wyatt Earp and Buffalo Bill Cody. Walt Disney's grandfather and father both lived in Ellis as well.

144 Field Windbreaks

On the right, you will notice a row of trees along a field. These "field windbreaks" have several purposes: they prevent the wind from blowing the soil from fields; they help crops conserve moisture by reducing evaporation; they protect livestock, birds, and other wildlife from winter winds; and they are used as snow fences to prevent snow from drifting across roads (see 16W, p. 131). Research has also shown them to be an important recreational resource, especially for hunters, and an aesthetically pleasing visual addition to the landscape.

Many field windbreaks were planted after the dust bowl disaster, which is described vividly at 50W (p. 119). With the United States reeling from the dust bowl and the Great Depression, the US Department of Agriculture developed an ambitious plan to plant trees in 100-foot-wide strips, not more than a mile apart, in a band from Canada to the Gulf of Mexico. During this project, 18,599 miles of windbreaks containing more than 223 million trees were planted.

According to the Kansas Forest Service (KFS), the state now has almost 270,000 acres of windbreaks. However, the KFS also has reported that 43 percent of these windbreaks need to be rehabilitated due to a lack of care as the trees age. The KFS concluded, "Not

Chrysler home

enough field windbreaks are planted or maintained to protect our soil and crops."

143 Trego County

This county was established in February 1867 and named in honor of Captain Edward P. Trego of Company H of the Eighth Infantry. Captain Trego was killed in September 1863 at the Battle of Chickamauga.

Several Trego County residents died during the "dirty thirties" from "dust pneumonia," which was caused by blowing soil. Herman Elriches, a prominent Collyer Township farmer, suffocated during a dust storm on February 21, 1935. The storm hit at about 3:30 in the afternoon and darkened the sky so that people had to turn on lights in homes and businesses. The fine silt swirling in the air made breathing difficult. Herman attempted to drive home from Collyer in near-total darkness at the peak of the dust storm, but he ran off the road and into a ditch. He tried to walk home; his body was found about a mile from his car. Read more about the dust bowl days ahead at mile 50W (p. 119).

142 Riga Road

The town on the left was named by the Volga Germans. *Riga* means "ridge of sand." The town's grain elevator, like many others in western Kansas, is located along the Union Pacific Railroad tracks to facilitate the shipping of grain.

141 Kansas Skies

Montana officially calls itself Big Sky Country, but its state motto would apply to Kansas as well for it, too, has impressive skies. Kansas playwright William Inge wrote, "One is always aware of the sky in these states, because one sees so much more of it than in the mountainous regions where the horizons are blocked and the heavens are trimmed down like a painting, to fit a smaller frame." Other states may claim more spectacular landforms, but Kansas has spectacularly spacious skies. And they are usually clear. Typically for 300 days each year, the sun shines brightly, and the night sky teems with brilliant stars. But clouds also add beauty, interest, and inspiration. In summer, majestic, anvil-shaped thunderheads (some containing as much energy as a nuclear bomb) build before your eyes. Sweeping across the horizon, they often drag a curtain of blue-gray rain beneath them. Slivers of lightning tear through the dark pedestal of the thunderhead. Throughout the year, fair-weather cumuli push their shadows across the landscape, beckoning wayfarers to join them. Sunrises and sunsets hang like stage backdrops over our subtle and understated landscapes.

Walt Whitman described such sunsets on the Plains in the poem "Prairie Sunset," from *Leaves of Grass*:

> Shot gold, maroon, and violet,
> dazzling silver, emerald, fawn,
> The earth's whole amplitude and
> Nature's multiform power consign'd
> for once to colors;
> The light, the general air possess'd by
> them—colors till now
> unknown,
> No limit, confine—not the Western
> sky alone—the high meridian—
> North, South all,
> Pure luminous color fighting the
> silent shadows to the last.

138 Lifeline

As you cross over the Union Pacific Railroad tracks ahead, imagine Buffalo Bill Cody galloping along them. This stretch of railroad was completed in 1868 as part of the line that connected Kansas City to Denver. Buffalo Bill came here to supply the railroad construction workers with buffalo meat during those years. He claimed to have killed 4,280 buffalo around this area in only eighteen months!

Consider how the railroad affected every facet of life on the Plains for more than fifty years, until roads like US Highway 40 were built across Kansas in the 1920s. All sorts of people came and went on the railroad—poor immigrants, wealthy speculators, soldiers, criminals running from the law—the same range of people who use I-70 today. Food, furniture, fuel, and other freight arrived by train, a lifeline from the East. In return, buffalo skins, grain, cattle, and stories of romance and rowdiness on the range traveled eastward. Today, the railroad is still a lifeline, as grain from the small towns hugging the tracks is sold and shipped to markets across the globe.

136 Ogallah

Cedar Bluff Reservoir is 13 miles south of Ogallah on State Route 147, part of the 60-mile-long Smoky Valley Scenic Byway. Cedar Bluff has over 20 miles of shoreline and over 14,000 acres of land and water for recreation. Within the lake's Wildlife Area is Threshing Machine Canyon. Located along the Butterfield Overland Despatch (BOD) trail, the canyon is the site of a Native American attack on a wagon train that was transporting a threshing machine to Brigham Young in Salt Lake City. The travelers were killed, and the threshing machine was set on fire. Old burned-out remains of the machine could be seen in the canyon for many years after the attack. This canyon has rock carvings going back to the mid-1800s, left by gold-seeking "Pikes' Peakers" and US cavalrymen who traveled along the BOD.

The name Ogallah, originally spelled Oglala, was taken from a tribe called the Oglala Sioux, a division of the Teton Sioux who lived in South Dakota. Experts disagree over the exact meaning of the word *Ogallah*. Some say it means "to scatter one's own," whereas others claim it means "she poured out her own."

Read about Ogallah being home to the state's first tree nursery at 138E (p. 171).

135 Grain for the World

At the elevator on the right are four Cargill grain storage bins, each with a capacity of 110,000 bushels. Operated with the elevator in WaKeeney, ahead, wheat and milo begin their integration into the Cargill Grain & Oilseed Supply Chain, which consists of eleven businesses that operate on a coordinated global basis.

Sitting along the Union Pacific Railroad tracks, this location becomes a busy shipping center at harvest time. Trucks bring grain from as far as 50 miles west and 40 miles east. Grain is also received from 40 miles south and 60 miles north.

Trains of 100 cars are loaded three or four times per week during the harvest. You often see a line of railcars on the siding, ready to move under the filling chute. Cargill officials explained that they have developed significant expertise in preserving the identity of products such as those shipped from this location. The differentiated products sustain their distinctiveness in numerous overseas markets.

133 Rest Area

Most of the trees at this rest stop are Austrian pine, a species native to Europe. Kansas has the distinction of being the only state other than Hawaii that has no native species of pine. In other words, until settlers planted them, there were no pines growing in Kansas for at least several thousand years. All the pines you see in Kansas today are native to other lands.

132 Corn

As you travel across the High Plains, you will be driving past miles and miles of cornfields. Whether it is used to make corn dogs, to produce corn oil, to turn out corn-based biodegradable plastics, or merely to be eaten straight off the cob, corn is America's number one crop. The US Department of Agriculture (USDA) has reported that corn leads all other crops in acreage planted, bushels harvested, and dollar value. Corn is a vital component of the Kansas agricultural economy. The 2012 USDA Census of Agriculture ranked Kansas ninth among the states in volume of corn production. In recent years, more than 11,000 Kansas farms planted 4.9 million acres to corn. In good-weather years, a half billion bushels are grown. Most Kansas corn is "field corn," which is used for feed and other products rather than for human consumption.

About 60 percent of the US corn crop is fed to livestock. Each bushel of corn fed to livestock produces 5.6 pounds of retail beef, 13 pounds of pork, 19.6 pounds of chicken, or 28 pounds of catfish. Export markets and other uses are vital to the corn industry. Over 3,500 supermarket products contain corn or corn by-products. The average American consumes 3 pounds of corn every day through food and nonfood products.

A bushel of corn can yield 32 pounds of cornstarch, 2.5 gallons of ethanol auto fuel, or 33 pounds of corn sweetener, enough to sweeten more than 400 cans of soda. After one of these products is extracted, that bushel will also produce 1.6 pounds of corn oil, 11.4 pounds of 21 percent protein gluten feed, and 3 pounds of 60 percent gluten meal.

Corn is a North American grain. Fossilized pollen from corn plants found in Mexico is believed to be 60,000 years old. Europe knew nothing about corn before Columbus returned home with samples. But Native Americans from Canada through South America raised corn with red, blue, pink, and black kernels, as well as the familiar yellow kernels.

129 WaKeeney

You are welcomed to WaKeeney by a World War II Iwo Jima memorial at the first exit, an A-14 Tomcat navy fighter jet in Eisenhower Park along I-70 at the second exit, and flags at the Kansas Veterans Cemetery just at the north edge of town. As a local travel and tourism council member explained, "It's a patriotism thing with us."

WaKeeney has been a town since 1878. That same year, people from throughout Trego County fled to WaKeeney for protection from a group of Cheyenne Indians. The next year, they chose the town as the county seat.

"Beautiful location and surrounded for scores of miles by the most fertile agricultural land in the world"—this is how settlers saw WaKeeney, Kansas, which was named after John F. Keeney, a Chicago real estate developer, and his friend Albert Warren. The men chose this spot along the route of the Union Pacific Railroad, halfway between Kansas City and Denver. A stone post at the downtown railroad underpass points on one side to Kansas City, 322 miles, and on the other to Denver, 322 miles.

In 1974, the Trego County Courthouse was used to film several scenes for the movie *Paper Moon.*

128 Merry Christmas

Since 1950, WaKeeney has been known as the “Christmas City of the High Plains.” It claims to have the largest Christmas tree and lighting display between Kansas City and Denver. Prior to Thanksgiving each year, the residents build a 35-foot Christmas tree made of 2,300 pounds of fresh evergreen branches, 1,100 yards of hand-tied greenery garlands, and over 6,800 lightbulbs.

127 Plows

As you drive through western Kansas, you will observe many kinds of farm implements. Before these machines were developed, the settlers had to cultivate the land using horse- and ox-drawn plows. The original tilling of Kansas soil was tough work because the ground had a dense network of roots that resisted usual techniques and equipment. Special plows had to be created that were up to the task. Oxen were the favored animals for plowing up this tough sod because they could maintain their energy by eating range grass, whereas horses needed supplemental feed. The pioneers rarely had extra feed for horses, so they used oxen. Nowadays, farmers pull plows with powerful tractors complete with air-conditioned cabs and guidance from computers, lasers, and even satellite positioning data to ensure crops are planted in straight rows that are precisely spaced without overlap.

125 Terraces

Here on the left and ahead on the right, note how farmers are using not only contour plowing (plowing and planting rows of crops across the slope) but also terracing to slow the runoff from rain and melting snow. Mounds or ridges of soil are plowed to curve along a slope, making level areas to hold the moisture so it will soak into the soil for crop production. To grow crops successfully in the same field on a sustained basis, water and topsoil must be saved. When water runoff is slowed, less soil is carried away, which preserves the topsoil and reduces erosion. You will see more of this widespread and valuable farming practice on steeper slopes as you travel across Kansas.

Standards for terrace design have been established by the American Society of Agricultural and Biological Engineers. It encourages the use of parallel terraces so that an equal number of crop rows can be planted, thus making it easier to operate tractors, combines, and tillage tools. The design standard suggests that terraces be spaced 9 meters (30 feet) apart to accommodate the rows for most crops. Long, gentle curves aid in making terraces farmable using commercial farm equipment.

Several types of terraces channel water into grass waterway outlets. The design engineer calculates water runoff from weather and soil data. An outlet is then constructed at a slope so no erosion will occur. You will see many terraces ahead. At mile 121, you will see terraces with concrete channels directing water into the roadway ditch.

Just building the terrace does not assure erosion control. Every year, farmers must maintain the terrace shape and restore ridge height.

123 Farms in the Forest

Notice how the farmsteads in this region are hidden among dense stands of trees. Ever since the first settlers arrived, trees have been precious commodities on the Plains. In fact, when settlers first arrived, it was rare to see even a single tree. Shade was scarce, and so was wood for building or burning, so any tree encountered was likely to be cut for wood. Settlers planted trees for shade, for windbreaks, and just because the treeless Plains seemed empty. Then, too, they missed the forests of their eastern homes, and so they planted trees around their buildings.

Today, people plant and maintain these shelterbelts for protection from the brutal winter winds and for shade during the harsh summers. Not only do they make life around the farm more comfortable, but by reducing the wind, they also reduce energy costs for heating and cooling. In addition, shelterbelts lower maintenance costs because the farmhouse and buildings need to be painted less frequently and generally hold up better in less severe conditions. These shelterbelts can reduce stress on livestock and prevent snow from piling up in the farmyard or on long driveways. For all these reasons, trees are a wise investment out here on the Plains. Eastern redcedar is the most common tree planted in the windbreaks because it is one of the few trees that thrives in the abundant sunlight and dry conditions of western Kansas. Its dense foliage, which it keeps year-round, is an effective barrier to the winter winds.

Because of these tree-planting efforts and because wildfires are kept under control, many more trees grow in western Kansas now than during settlement days. Over the next 50 miles, you will see that most farmsteads are located in the heart of their own small forests.

121 Rocks on Their Way

Here, you can see the concrete outlets of terraces, which direct water runoff into the roadside ditch. Because soil is made up of particles that have been weathered and worn from rocks and because erosion by wind and water is a universal natural phenomenon, it has been said that "soil is rocks on their way to the sea." Although the movement of soil into the sea is inevitable, farmers try to slow the trip. They are now using more environmentally friendly techniques that conserve topsoil, moisture, and nutrients, such as leaving residue plant material from previous planting seasons, contour plowing making furrows across the slope, and (as you saw back at mile 125) using raised terraces that catch rainwater and allow it to soak into the soil rather than run off and carry soil with it. All these strategies help hold soil particles in place and prevent them from moving toward the sea.

120 Homes on the Range

Cattle ranches are common throughout the High Plains. Most ranches are large compared with those farther east. It takes more acres to support each cow out here where grass is short and sparse. A herd that could live on a few acres in Missouri would need hundreds of acres to survive on the High Plains. The only plants that make it here are those that tolerate dry conditions, like cactus or yucca, and buffalo grass and blue grama that survive long, hot periods. These grasses are important both for holding the soil and for grazing livestock.

Ranches in this area raise more than beef cattle. Grama grass is a good source of food for jackrabbits and prairie dogs, which in turn are good food for hawks and coyotes. Finches, longspurs, and other birds eat the grama seeds. North America's closest relative to the antelope, the pronghorn, grazes these grasslands of western Kansas.

119 Volga Germans

Most original settlers here were Volga Germans, descendants of Germans who migrated to the Volga River region of Russia in the 1700s. Catherine the Great had enticed Germans to Russia by guaranteeing the colonists and their descendants free land, exemption from military service, freedom of religion, and local self-government. Catherine made these promises because she wanted to strengthen her empire by having southern Russia and the Ukraine settled. Her invitation appealed to the people of the southern provinces in Germany who had recently suffered great economic hardship as a result of the Seven Years' War. Yet even when they lived in Russia, they maintained their German language and customs.

Unfortunately, the resident Russians resented the special treatment Catherine the Great had given to the new immigrants, and this caused conflict. Catherine's promises lasted for about 100 years. However, in 1874, the Russian government passed a law requiring Germans living in Russia to serve in the armed forces or leave the country within ten years. Soon after this ultimatum, the Germans sent scouts to America to find a new home. Railroad land agents, town site developers, and state government officials lured them here with promotional efforts, some of which were less than honest in their portrayals of the climate and living conditions the immigrants would encounter. However, the Germans discovered the landscape and climate to be similar to those in Russia and suitable for their people.

The Germans adapted well here, having been hardened by living in Ukraine. They learned to use what nature provided, perhaps better than any other immigrant group. Though many other European pioneers moved on as the frontier shifted westward, the Volga Germans stayed to raise their families and crops. They persevered against the difficulties presented by the harsh High Plains environment. Many people in the small towns along I-70 still speak German.

117 Collyer

Ahead on the right is a town named for the Reverend Robert Collyer, who was president of an organization from Chicago that formed a soldiers' and sailors' colony here in 1878. This group was joined by a colony of Irish settlers and a Czech colony. Read more about Collyer and his colony at 114E (p. 164).

116 The Lipp Farmstead

The red barn on the left was the center of the Lipp farm operations for nearly a century. When Phillip Lipp arrived from Russia in 1907, he had only thirty dollars with which to start farming. His family settled at this location, built a house using blocks of sod, and started farming the surrounding 160 acres.

Ten years after his arrival, Lipp built this traditional barn to house fifteen milk cows and the horses needed to do the field work. The barn became his factory, where grain from the fields was converted into milk, cream, eggs, and meat. This barn was the warehouse for feed grain bins on the ground floor and had a center loft for hay forage.

Barns of this type were common across Kansas. Today, however, few barns have animals, and little grain or hay can be found in them. The barns no longer serve as centers of production, and many fall into disrepair. As tractors replaced horses, it became possible for one farmer to productively work many more acres of land. A great-grandson now operates the original Lipp family farm, which has expanded to 1,500 acres, but he no longer maintains the farmstead. See more about Kansas barns at 115E (p. 165).

114 Capturing an Iron Horse

In 1868, on the railroad track that parallels I-70 to the right, Indians tried to capture a locomotive "alive" by taking telegraph wire, doubling it back and forth several times, and stretching it across the track, with an Indian or two holding each end. Needless to say, the "iron horse," running at full steam tore through the snare like a rampaging buffalo tearing through a spiderweb. The stunning introduction of the railroad stimulated great changes in nineteenth-century cultures. A few years after the attempt to capture an iron horse, Thomas Curtis Clarke wrote, "The world of today differs from that of Napoleon more than his world differed from Julius Caesar; and this change has chiefly been made by railroads."

113 Gove County

You have just entered Gove County, which was created in 1868 and named in honor of Captain Grenville L. Gove, who had died four years earlier. The soldiers of Company G under Captain Gove's command had become so famous for being the best-drilled unit around that when they marched, people came to watch.

The first settlers did not arrive in Gove County until 1871. Immigration to the county began seven years later as Pennsylvania and Holland Dutch people arrived in the area. Before Gove County was settled, many had traveled through it and kept right on going. The discovery of gold near Pikes Peak in 1858 led to the development of the well-used Smoky Hill Trail along the Smoky Hill River. Like many westbound travelers on I-70, those travelers had their sights set on the mountains of Colorado.

112 Skyscrapers

Fred Atchison, a forester and poet, wrote this poem about the High Plains landscape:

Security
The vastness of the prairie would be
overwhelming
Were it not for a canopy of blue sky
pinned neatly along the horizon
by grain elevators.

As you drive along, note these rural white skyscrapers pinning the sky to the horizon—some visible from as far as 20 miles away. Plains people call them prairie cathedrals.

110 A Gambrel Roof

That barn on the right has a gambrel roof. You can recognize it by the two ridges added parallel to the peak ridge, making a steep slope on either side below the flatter upper slope. The design features a truss-type bracing that strengthens the roof, but the primary advantage of the gambrel roof is that it provides for a high, open loft that has a lot of room to stack loose hay. Of course, today, with the availability of big, round bales and tractors to move them, no one is putting loose hay into a hayloft anymore.

You will see other types of roofs at farmsteads along the way, including simple one-slope lean-tos, simple gable roofs, and two-slope roofs. A roof that slopes up from all four sides is called a hip roof if there is a single slope or a mansard if there is a double slope, similar to a gambrel on four sides.

Two blue Harvestore silos beside the barn you see here store chopped alfalfa or stalk corn, an indication that feeding cattle has been an important part of this farm operation.

109 Quinter

This town was founded by a group of Dunkards, also known as Baptist Brethren, in 1886. They named the town after Pennsylvania immigrant and church elder Reverand James Quinter. The town is home to Scott Huffman, a US pole vault record holder.

108 A Million Bushels

Ahead on the left, just past the Quinter exit, you will see unusual long, flat bunkers with plastic covers. They provide supplemental on-ground storage. Each bunker holds a million bushels of corn, an overflow for the Frontier Ag tall bins that you can see rising above the north side of town. In 1998, a particularly good harvest year for corn, "temporary storage" was needed until the grain could be shipped. The bunkers seem to have found a use every year since that time.

Frontier Ag is a full-service, member-owned agribusiness cooperative (called a co-op for short and generally spelled without the hyphen) offering grain, feed, agronomy, petroleum, shop, and transportation products and services to customers. Here at Quinter, the coop's services include the sale and maintenance of farm equipment. It even has twenty-four-hour emergency crews available. A cooperative consists of members who unite to economically purchase supplies and market their products more profitably. A basic code specifies democratic control, with each member having one vote and sharing in the profits in proportion to the amount of his or her patronage.

In the Quinter bunkers, grain arrives by truck and leaves by truck. Some corn is fed at cattle feedlots in the area, but most of it goes to millers for processing into corn products such as starch and sweeteners. In the miles ahead, you will see many Frontier Ag elevators built alongside the Union Pacific Railroad, where grain cars are loaded with crops destined for markets all over the world.

106 "A Dry and Thirsty Land"

Most of the cropland between here and Colorado is irrigated (see 69W, p. 113, and 19E, p. 142). Great civilizations such as the Babylonians, Assyrians, Sumerians, and others throughout history failed because their food production took place in dry regions requiring irrigation, and eventually, their irrigation systems became inefficient. These collapses in agricultural production led to scarce commodities, poverty, and even wars between nations. Even today, battles are fought at the state level in legal wars over water between Colorado, Nebraska, and Kansas. Water is the lifeblood of the Great Plains.

Irrigation alone accounts for 85 percent of all water used in Kansas, and 92 percent of all groundwater used is devoted to irrigation. In some areas, the aquifer is being depleted fourteen times faster than it is being recharged from rains. This "mining" of groundwater has caused some wells to go dry, which means that wells must be dug deeper at great expense or irrigation must be turned off. Because the region's economy is based on irrigated crops, many fear that when it becomes infeasible to continue mining this groundwater, the economic consequences will be disastrous. The High Plains could face the same fate as those ancient civilizations did.

104 Cottonwoods

Notice the groves of cottonwood trees on both sides of the interstate. On the High Plains, unless trees are watered by landowners, they will grow only in low areas where scarce water can collect over time. The cottonwood, the state tree of Kansas, gets its name from the soft, white, cottonlike hairs attached to its small seeds that

Cottonwood tree

allow them to drift gently on the breeze. Cottonwood trees grow quickly, but they produce light, brittle wood. Native Americans made a tea from cottonwood bark and also fed the bark to their horses. Ian Frazier, in *Great Plains,* observed how cottonwoods "lean at odd angles, like flowers in a vase." He also noted how the bison loved to rub against the cottonwood's bark, which is ribbed like a tractor tire. According to Frazier, "in the shedding season" in areas with cottonwoods, "the river bottoms would be ankle deep in buffalo hair."

101 Park

The white "prairie cathedrals" and the tall steeple of the beautiful Sacred Heart Church, built in 1898, mark the town of Park. Originally called Buffalo Park, this was a station on the Union Pacific Railroad. The town was named for the great herds of bison that roamed the area. These herds left their mark on the land in the form of buffalo wallows. During the spring calving season, when the weather got warm, the bison would wallow on the ground to try to rid themselves of their heavy winter hair. As a result, depressions formed in the soil, some 2 or 3 feet deep and spreading across several acres. These wallows became dust baths or water holes for the bison. If water was present, the animals would wallow in the water and carry the mud away, making the wallow deeper still. Even now, more than 120 years later, you can see different plants growing in buffalo wallows because of soil changes caused by the wallowing animals.

In the late 1800s, Gove County was a popular place to hunt buffalo. One early resident of Park was allowed to join an Omaha Indian buffalo hunt. The man's journal described how the specific posture of a scout on his horse would signal that buffalo were nearby. The arrows used by the Indians were grooved to identify the tepee the hunter came from. These grooves also allowed blood to flow out of a wound. The Indians used all parts of the buffalo: skins for shelter and warmth, meat for food, and sinews for sewing and bowstrings. Most of the meat was cut into 1-inch strips and dried in the sun.

99 Strong Sorghum, Mighty Milo

During the summer growing season, you can see fields of grain sorghum, especially during hotter and drier times. This sorghum is usually planted in rows, and it looks like corn early on but grows into a bushy plant about 3 or 4 feet tall. Sorghum's strong, stocky profile resists being toppled over by the wild winds of western Kansas. Anyone who has seen a cornfield after a severe thunderstorm will understand why farmers choose to plant this crop. In the fall, the seed heads create a pinkish carpet across the field. Originally from Africa, grain sorghum is also known as milo, to distinguish it from sweet sorghum, which is grown for syrup. The feed value of milo for livestock is nearly equal to that of corn. The grain has more protein and fat than corn, but it is lower in vitamin A. In the United States, milo is used primarily as a feed grain and for ethanol production. See more at 110E (p. 163).

98 Rest Area for the Birds

During spring and fall on the High Plains, areas such as this one provide a resting place for travelers other than humans—migrating birds. Rest areas, windbreaks, and the small towns scattered across the Plains are islands of trees in a sea of wheat and corn for these long-distance travelers. Some birds using this rest area may be on their way to or from South America or the Arctic. And you think you have a long trip ahead!

During summer at rest areas in western Kansas, you can see iridescent great-tailed grackles, with their huge and wedge-shaped tails, walking on the lawn. Or you may hear yellow-and-gray western kingbirds chattering from the treetops.

97 Grainfield

The next town on the right is Grainfield. In an area with many grainfields, this name was appropriate back in 1879 when a little girl riding down the trail in a wagon commented to a Union Pacific Railroad official, "Oh, what a pretty green field!" The man, who had been sent by the railroad to lay out the town site, recalled the girl's remark and decided to call the new town Grainfield. Now, more than 120 years later, wheat grows right up to the edges of town, making Grainfield the most obvious and appropriate town name along I-70.

An ornate opera house built here in 1887 is listed on the National Register of Historic Places. In the early days, stock companies would arrive by rail and put on plays or concerts for three to five nights and then move on to another town. Since local schools did not have auditoriums, dances, holiday celebrations, and graduations were also held in the opera house.

The Frontier Ag elevator, visible ahead, can store nearly two million bushels of grain. Wheat, corn, and some milo are purchased, and about 80 percent of these crops is shipped to markets in the United States. However, some is sent to ports on the Gulf of Mexico for shipment to China, and some is processed into feed for cattle at the surrounding farms. Railcars and trucks are loaded with grain of a specific quality. A state inspector certifies the grade and quality before a load leaves the property.

95 "A Newer Garden of Creation"

You have seen that this land is a bountiful garden of wheat and corn. In his poem "The Prairie States," Walt Whitman called the High Plains "a newer garden of creation." In another piece, written while he was traveling across these High Plains, he wrote the selection that follows. Maybe you, like Whitman, will find this landscape profoundly and positively engaging.

> My days and nights, as I travel here—what an exhilaration!—not the air alone, and the sense of vastness, but every local sight and feature. Everywhere something characteristic—the cactuses, pinks, buffalograss, wild sage—the receding perspective, and the far circle-line of the horizon all times of the day, especially forenoon—the clear, pure cool, rarefied nutriment for the lungs, . . . the prairie dogs and the herds of antelope—the curious "dry rivers"—occasionally a dug out or corral . . . ever the herds of cattle and the cowboys ("cowpunchers") to me a strangely interesting class, bright-eyed as hawks, with their swarthy complexions and their broad-brimm'd hats. . . .
>
> Then as to scenery (giving my own thought and feeling), while I know the standard claim is that Yosemite, Niagara Falls, and Upper Yellowstone and the like afford the greatest natural shows, I am not sure that the prairie and plains, while less stunning at first sight, last longer, fill the esthetic sense fuller, precede all the rest, and make North America's characteristic landscape.
>
> Indeed through the whole of this journey, with all its shows

and varieties, what impress'd me, and will longest remain with me, are these same prairies. Day after day, and night after night, o my eyes, to all my senses—the esthetic one most of all—they silently and broadly unfolded. Even their simplest statistics are sublime.

92 Don't Fence Me In

Fences have been installed at the side of the I-70 right-of-way to prevent livestock and wildlife from wandering onto the road. Typically for range fences, three or four strands of barbed wire are attached to posts spaced about 1 rod (16.5 feet or 5 meters) apart. Barbed wire is made of two strands of steel wire twisted together with thornlike barbs at about 6-inch intervals. The first patent for barbed wire was granted to Joseph F. Glidden of DeKalb, Illinois, in 1873. Once Glidden's fence proved it could restrain cattle, many different styles of barbed wire were developed. In fact, hundreds of patents have been granted for unique ways to make a fence that will more effectively hold animals.

Arguments raged over barbed wire fences. To deter their installation, cattlemen claimed the barbs seriously injured livestock. Those who wanted free access to the prairies did not agree with farmers who fenced off areas to grow crops. Barbed wire hastened the end of open-range grazing and encouraged crop farming by inexpensively controlling livestock and restricting their movements. Some historians say barbed wire settled the West.

90 The Dinosaur War

One of the most bitter duels that ever took place in Kansas was held in Gove County. It was not a gunfight in front of the saloon at high noon, though; instead, it took place between two scientists using pens rather than pistols to attack each other.

According to the book *Heartland History: Stories and Facts from Kansas,* it all started in 1868, when a 40-foot fossil was sent to Edward Drinker Cope of the Philadelphia Academy of Natural Sciences. Cope, a renowned paleontologist who had been educated at Harvard, was asked to identify the fossil. He reconstructed the figure but could not determine its identity. He named the long-necked skeleton *Elasmosaurus,* or "ribbon reptile."

However, another famous paleontologist, Othniel Marsh, disagreed with Cope's reconstruction of the *Elasmosaurus,* and as a newly appointed professor at his wealthy Uncle George Peabody's Museum of Natural History at Yale University, he didn't mind pointing it out to the rest of the scientific community. This, of course, made Cope angry, and he directed his anger, bitterness, and resentment at Marsh. This disagreement set the stage for a lifelong feud, which was not merely a scholarly competition between professors; at times, it resembled a full-fledged, knock-down, drag-out fight.

After reviewing the specimen, the men wondered how many more unidentified and unique fossils existed in Kansas. Because Cope received the first skeleton from western Kansas and had other workers sending him fossils, he claimed western Kansas as his own research grounds. But Marsh was tenacious, and he knew the chalk beds in Gove County were in the public domain and could be a gold mine of fossils.

Instead of a gold rush, this was a fossil rush, as both men raced to Kansas to unearth, reconstruct, and name as many of the fossilized skeletons as they could. In the process, they extracted the largest collections of dinosaur fossils ever amassed at the time.

In 1870, Marsh, accompanied by Buffalo Bill Cody, trekked back across Kansas to uncover more fossils. As luck would have it, he discovered a previously unknown flying reptile with wings over 20 feet long. He named it a *Pterosaur.*

The rift between Cope and Marsh continued to widen as they gathered fossils from the same area. Each scientist sent spies to the other's camps in Kansas, which often resulted in brawls. The scientists verbally attacked one another at professional meetings and in scientific journals. They even diverted shipments of each other's fossils.

Marsh returned to the Kansas chalk beds in the Smoky Hill River valley in 1871 and claimed to find a fossil of a huge, flightless bird and other fossils. Whether he actually discovered them was a matter of great dispute. Nevertheless, he took them back to the Peabody Museum and claimed them as his own.

As soon as Marsh left Kansas to study his new finds, Cope moved back into the state and frantically tried to increase his own collection of important fossils. The autumn and winter of 1871 saw many papers feverishly produced by both men, each claiming new specimens while criticizing the work of the other. Both scientists had sympathizers in the profession and in the newspapers, so their feud expanded into a national conflict.

The two scientists obtained many of the same fossils. The first to have his report printed would be recognized as the person who discovered the fossil. Cope presented a paper to the American Philosophical Society on March 1, 1872, introducing his Kansas discoveries. But the *American Journal of Science,* housed at Marsh's institution, Yale University, announced that even though Cope's report was read on March 1, it was not printed for distribution until March 12, five days after Marsh's report. As a result, Marsh got official credit and naming rights.

For the next two years, both men delved deeply into the study of their relics while abusing each other both in print and in person. All this occurred because unique fossils were found near the terrain you are crossing today.

86 Grinnell: Home to Early Jerky

German farmers established the town on the right in 1870. Grinnell had two large sod buildings for drying buffalo meat. The air was so dry here that meat could be stripped off in layers and hung to dry. The dried meat would then be preserved, and it would not spoil. This was critical in the days before refrigerators. The people called this meat "jerked" because of the way it was torn from the buffalo's carcass. Today at convenience stores along I-70, you can buy similar jerked meat in the form of beef jerky.

85 Dryland Farming

Fields without irrigation rigs may indicate an area of dryland farming. When the prairies were first cultivated, irrigation water was not available, so farmers developed techniques for dryland farming. This type of farming helps conserve precious groundwater. To allow moisture to build up in the soil, dryland farmers often leave some fields unplanted for a year. These fallow fields are plowed to kill weeds and keep the soil loose enough to soak up what little rain they receive. During the second year, the land will have accumulated enough moisture for wheat or sorghum to grow successfully. Dryland farming allows two years of rain and snowmelt to accumulate in the soil, which may be just enough to grow one crop. Sometimes, farmers can get two crops before having to leave the ground fallow once again.

Improved varieties of crops developed specifically for dry areas are resulting in dryland yields unheard of just a few years ago. You may notice these cultivated but unplanted fields as you drive through western Kansas.

84 Frozen Cattle Pools

The Smoky Hill Cattle Pool was formed in Gove County in 1883. Ranchers established cattle pools to allow cattle with different brands to graze and mix together throughout the year. The cattle were rounded up annually and sorted. Unfortunately, the pool ended in 1886 after an estimated 10,000 cattle died as a result of a severe blizzard.

It may be hard to believe if you are driving through on a hot summer day, but blizzards still kill cattle on the western Kansas range. Imagine how the winter's winds blow snow across this open landscape and how, without shelter, cattle are exposed to the fierce elements. After some blizzards, hay is airlifted to the cattle. dropped from helicopters and airplanes to keep the animals from starving. You probably have noticed the "Road Closed" signs and gates at exits over the past 100 miles. This stretch of I-70 is sometimes closed because of blowing snow. If you are traveling during winter, don't get caught in the open like cattle. Listen for weather reports, and stay close to the shelter of local motels.

82 Hellendale Ranch

At the Hellendale Ranch on the right, you will see Holstein dairy cattle with those familiar black-on-white patches. There could be as many as 1,200 animals in the ranch's pens. New heifer calves are added every six to eight weeks, and as they grow, they are moved from small pens to the larger lots.

Farm manager Cheryl Madison grows most of the feed for the cattle on the ranch, which extends for 3 miles along I-70. Alfalfa is produced with the help of a center-pivot irrigation system. Haylage (fermented alfalfa hay used for feed) is produced in the bunkers along the highway on the right. Wheat and corn also are important feeds.

Only female (heifer) calves are bought from area dairies. They live in private, individual hutches (like big dog houses) for about eight weeks. Madison explained that the most difficult part of raising calves is preventing them from getting wet and cold, for they may develop pneumonia if exposed to the elements. As they mature, heifers are artificially inseminated. At one year of age, they are sold to dairy farms to begin their milk-making "careers."

81 Renewable Fuel Plant of Western Plains Energy

The plant to the right began with a simple idea to expand the market for local farmers to sell their grain crops. It has turned into a tremendous economic boon for northwest Kansas. The Western Plains Energy plant has expanded since it opened in 2004 to become the complex of structures you see on the right, just ahead at Exit 79. Here, corn and milo (grain sorghum) are the primary feedstock for the production of 50 million gallons of ethanol each year. This biodegradable fuel is derived from the sugars, starches, and cellulosic matter found in renewable plant material. When grains are the feedstock, 30 percent of the kernels' weight is returned to feedlots as a high-value protein feed. Read more at 76E (p. 156).

80 Monument Rocks

Exit 70 takes you to Monument Rocks Natural National Landmark, located 25 miles south of Oakley. The rocks are impressive chalk bluffs and pyramids poking high out of the prairie. Native Americans used them as a lookout perch, and they were a landmark for travelers riding on the Butterfield Overland Despatch on their way to Denver. These rocks continue to be the source of many fossils.

79 Kansas Sharks

As you sail down the highway in your car, try to imagine you are sailing across a warm tropical sea. Geologists believe that if you had been here 80 million years ago, you would have found yourself adrift in water. Much of present-day Kansas was part of a large, shallow, shark-infested inland sea that teemed with life ranging from coral to sea turtles. Over time, wind and rain eroded the rocks and carried the eroded material into the water, covering the remains of dead creatures that had settled on the bottom of the sea. Over the ages, the winds and rains again laid bare the ancient ocean bottom, including the animals that died there.

Today, the only fins you'll see along I-70 are on the backs of vintage automobiles from the 1950s and 1960s. But at one time, shark fins sliced the surface of the sea here. Shark teeth are still commonly found in the area because the sharks were continually growing new teeth and replacing older ones, much like people losing their baby teeth but over and over again. The Fick Fossil Museum, at Exit 76, contains more than 11,000 shark teeth discovered by Earnest and Vi Fick from the Monument Rocks. The museum also holds fossils found locally by famed paleontologist George F. Sternberg (see 159E, p. 175).

77 Eliza, Not Annie

The town of Oakley, ahead, was founded in 1885. People assume that it was named for the famous female sharpshooter Annie Oakley, but it was actually named for Eliza Oakley Gardner-Hoag, the mother of David Hoag, who founded the town. This does not make for quite as good a story, but who can argue with a son honoring his mother?

Annie never made it to Oakley, although some of the West's most famous riders passed through this area. In 1868, William "Buffalo Bill" Cody and William Comstock, both scouts with the US Cavalry and Union Pacific Railroad, competed in a buffalo-shooting contest 3 miles west of town. It was after he won this contest that Cody began to be called Buffalo Bill.

Take Exit 70 south for 4 miles to visit the Buffalo Bill Cultural Center. There, you will learn about Cody and see an enormous, larger-than-life bronze statue of him on his favorite horse. Brigham. The center also is a gateway to the scenic and geologically rich Western Vistas Historic Byway. While there, you can visit a gift shop and enjoy a free cup of coffee.

76 Logan County

You will just clip the corner of Logan County, named after General John Alexander Logan, a Civil War veteran and US senator from Illinois from 1871 to 1877 and 1879 to 1886. The story of this county's name illustrates the rancor and divisiveness of the early politics on the Plains. Read more about it and about Governor John St. John at 74E (p. 156).

75 Yucca

Ahead over the next mile or so, yucca, or soapweed, can be seen growing along both sides of I-70. The plants on the right look like shrubs with spikes pointing out in all directions. During spring and early summer, yucca has a stem, going straight up, with large,

Buffalo Bill Cody, 1880

white flowers. The sharp, spiny leaves stay green even in winter. The name soapweed comes from the fact that the plant's roots can be made into soap. When mixed with water, the crushed roots form a shampoo that was used by Native Americans and marketed commercially in the late 1800s. The flower stalk can be cooked and eaten like asparagus, and the flower buds and seed pods were eaten by Native Americans. The leaves have been used to make cord and twine. Yucca is pollinated by a small, night-flying moth. Both the moth and the yucca are dependent on one another for their survival—a small example of the interrelatedness of all of nature.

74 Thomas County

You are now in Thomas County, which was established in 1873 and named for Civil War hero Brigadier General George H. Thomas. Thomas was known as the "Rock of Chickamauga" because he held his ground during that key battle while others retreated. Kansas infantrymen served under his command. In Colby (mile 51), streets such as Mission Ridge, Nashville, Franklin, and of course Chickamauga are named after battles fought by General Thomas.

73 Pole Towers

The double-pole construction of the electric transmission line on the right contrasts with the steel towers pointed out earlier (281W, p. 47). Electricity is routed along this line at a lower 115 kilovolts. Therefore, shorter and thus lighter-weight insulators are used to separate the cables from the support beams, allowing a somewhat simpler tower construction. This line connects the power plants in Colby, ahead, with plants in Great Bend to the south. At Colby, there are connections with the transmission lines carrying electricity between east and west Kansas. Watch for other lines operating at different voltages as they extend from the Colby plant.

71 Ring-Necked Pheasants

You may see pheasants along the roadside and in the fields. Kansas is consistently one of the top three states for pheasant hunting. As many as 800,000 of these birds have been harvested here during a single hunting season. Hunters from all over North America come to Kansas during the opening week of pheasant season in November.

Pheasants are not a native bird, having been introduced to the United States from China. In 1760, Ben Franklin's son-in-law tried unsuccessfully to introduce pheasants to his farm. But by the late 1800s, pheasants had been established in several parts of the country. They were first introduced in Kansas with the release of 3,000 birds in eighty-four counties in the spring of 1906.

Some strongly independent citizens from southwestern Kansas, southeastern Colorado, north Texas, and the panhandle of Oklahoma, being so far removed from their current state capitals, have sought to form a fifty-first state called Cimarron. At a recent convention, they voted to make the ring-necked pheasant their state bird. No doubt, this is in recognition of the bird's tremendous economic impact on the region. In Kansas, pheasant hunting annually contributes well over $75 million to the state's economy.

Ring-necked pheasant (US Fish and Wildlife Service)

69 Super Sprinklers

The irrigation systems you have seen mounted on wheels and stretching out above the crops are center-pivot rigs. These are not your typical lawn sprinklers! This type of sprinkler slowly sweeps around the field, pivoting from the center, where water enters. The water flows out through the long arm with sprinkler heads hanging from it. Deep well turbine pumps deliver water from wells, sometimes up to a mile away, to feed the arm. Electric motors drive the wheels very slowly so the arm makes one revolution in twenty-four hours or longer, sprinkling the crop within the circle. Most irrigation arms are a quarter-mile long and cover 130 acres, but some extend for a half mile, thereby watering 568 of the 640 acres in a square-mile field as they sweep above the crops.

Farmers are trying to be more efficient in their water use by switching to center-pivot irrigation from "flood irrigation" systems that allow water to flow in crop rows across the ground. Many farm managers also apply fertilizers, herbicides, insecticides, and fungicides through these irrigation systems. When properly adjusted according to standards established by the American Society of Agricultural and Biological Engineers, only the amount that the crop needs is applied, most frequently with nozzles directed at the plant roots so that evaporation loss is minimized. Center pivots create large green circles of crops on an otherwise brown landscape. It has been said that when you gaze out at western Kansas from an airplane, it looks as if you are flying over a pond with giant lily pads.

66 Pocket Gophers

The mounds of sandy soil seen along the roadway are made by Plains pocket gophers. Unlike ground squirrels or prairie dogs, these amazing creatures almost never come aboveground, instead remaining in underground tunnels and chambers. Pocket gophers are well designed for their subterranean life. They have small ears and eyes (not really needed in their world), and their front legs are short, thick, and muscular, with long claws for digging tunnels. They do not have to turn around in their tight tunnels. The gopher's tail is highly sensitive and acts as a "feeler" to guide the animal as it backs up through the tunnels. With its loose and stretchy skin, a gopher can go in reverse almost as fast as it goes forward. Gophers are antisocial creatures, living most of their days alone in their tunnel systems, many of which are hundreds of feet long. The mounds you can see on the surface are made up of the soil that was excavated from the tunnels.

65 Another Power Trail

The power trail that crosses I-70 just before mile 64 is linked to the one described earlier at 73W (p. 112). Other trails with different construction will cross the interstate just ahead as they converge to exchange power at the two generating plants in Colby, a coal-powered steam generator and an internal combustion plant. These modern power trails vividly contrast our modern lifestyles with those of past travelers on Kansas trails who never saw a power line and could not even imagine the wonders of electricity.

63 Mingo

Mingo, once a thriving railroad town, is named after a branch of the Sioux tribe. The Mingo Frontier Ag elevator on the left is another of the farmer cooperative grain storage and shipping facilities.

62 Dirt Poor

Early settlers and farmers had no understanding of how to care for this land. Grasslands were plowed up to plant crops, and without the thick grass roots tightly holding the soil in place, the land was left exposed and vulnerable to being blown or washed away by wind and water. Inch by inch, the topsoil eroded. Crops were planted in rows that ran up and down slopes instead of across them. When thunderstorms hit or the snow melted, water flowed down the furrows, washing away topsoil and leaving behind gullies. Farmers seldom realized they were losing the richest soil and potentially their livelihood.

In many areas today, the unproductive subsoils that had been covered for many centuries by fertile topsoil are now at the surface. The remaining nutrients in the soil are converted into crops. When crops are harvested, the nutrients leave the fields along with the crops by the truckload. Many farmers have had to turn to using large inputs of chemical fertilizers, which has caused pollution of groundwater that is used for drinking in some Kansas counties. Fortunately, farmers are developing better techniques that maintain soil fertility for future generations while still producing a bountiful crop today. One strategy is to leave the dead plant residue from the previous season on the field to help hold the soil and to partially reestablish the natural cycle of plant matter decomposition. Look for crop stubble left in the fields as you drive along.

People concerned about conserving soil fertility take the long-term view, as referenced in a popular conservation slogan: "We do

Plowing for soil conservation (US Department of Agriculture)

not inherit the land from our fathers, we borrow it from our children." All these efforts are made so that our children will not find themselves "dirt poor."

60 Hill's Cows

Four generations of the Hill family have worked the land around the 7X Cattle Company feedlot on the right. Those grain bins with the spiderweb tops store the corn and grain sorghum that is raised on this ranch. The cattle also eat corn silage, ground alfalfa, and rolled corn kernels. Feed is distributed to the cattle bunks that radiate out from the grain center. It's possible you could see 4,000 cattle here when the lots are filled. The livestock waste is useful fertilizer for nearby cropland.

Since this is a feeding operation, no cattle are raised from birth here. Instead, they come from nearby farmers who manage grasslands. Cattle are also purchased from the big Oakley livestock auction and from an auction in Burlington, Colorado. Sometimes, cattle from as far away as the grassy hills of Pennsylvania are brought here to be fattened on western Kansas grain.

58 Off to China

Wheat collected in the tall elevator at the right is destined for export. Rail grain cars filled here will unload in the Pacific Northwest to ships destined for China and other Pacific Rim markets. Other trains will head for Houston or Louisiana, where ships will take Kansas wheat to Europe, Africa, and the Mideast. Kansas wheat is one of the important export food products that the United States ships to hungry people all over the world.

The Frontier Ag complex here along the Union Pacific tracks was built to load 100-car trains with wheat and sometimes milo and transport them to cargo docks. The elevator, with its eight concrete bins and bright-yellow legs, receives grain from farmers within a 60-mile radius, an hour to an hour and a half away. The siding is designed to hold 100 empty hopper cars, which move under the filling chute to each receive 3,300 bushels, or about 100 tons, of grain. With the 10,000 tons loaded, the train takes off on the initial leg of the trip from Kansas to China.

57 Sunflower Snacks

The silver grain storage elevators you see ahead on the right are part of the Red River Commodities confection sunflower processing plant. This plant mostly produces seeds for humans to eat. Sunflower seeds are dehulled, producing kernels that have a unique taste. Their rich flavor and crunchy texture add a nutty dimension to recipes, whether they are used raw, roasted, whole, chopped, ground, or salted. The kernels are rich in protein and high in fiber, iron, and vitamin E.

Sunflower kernels are shipped from here to all parts of the United States and to Mexico and Canada. But the major market is confection food plants in California. Also, about 10 percent of the whole seeds are bagged and sold as bird feed. Often considered waste products, the hulls and damaged seeds are a valuable feed for cattle in nearby feedlots.

The sunflower is an American original. Unlike corn, which came from Central America, and wheat, which came to Kansas from the eastern United States and even as far away as Russia, sunflowers are native to the Great Plains. American Indians are believed to have cultivated and enjoyed the sunflower and used the nutty kernels for a quick energy food. Spanish explorers enjoyed them

Red River Commodities sunflower grain elevator

so much that they sent them back to Europe, and the plants have been cultivated in Europe and around the world ever since. You, too, can enjoy sunflower seeds as you travel because virtually every gas station and convenience store along I-70 sells bags of them for snacking.

56 The Prairie Museum of Art and History

Use Exit 54 ahead to visit the interesting collection of artifacts from people and places on the Plains. The Kuska Collection contains over 28,000 objects collected by Joseph and Nellie Kuska, residents of Colby for over forty years. The collection includes glass, ceramics, dolls, silver, clothing, textiles, and furniture. The museum also has a 1930 restored farmhouse, a sod house with furnishings from the late 1880s, and a one-room schoolhouse.

The most striking feature on the Prairie Museum of Art and History property is one of the biggest barns in Kansas! This structure was built by a family named Foster as a barn for showing cattle. As a hobby, the Fosters would take their show cattle to the American Royal Exposition in Kansas City and the National Western Stock Show in Denver. In 1992, the barn was moved 19 miles from the Foster farm to the museum to house exhibits depicting the history of agriculture in western Kansas.

55 Colby

You will know where the first exit to Colby is located when you spot the 10-foot-high Colby Municipal Utilities water standpipe. This glass-lined steel Aquastore structure is 14 feet in diameter and has a capacity of over 160,000 gallons. Colby is named after J. R. Colby, a Civil War hero who dreamed all his life of setting up his own town. On March 10, 1885, the Colby Townsite Company recorded the original plat for the town. Colby is located in the geographic center of Thomas County and is the county seat. Early settlers began to arrive in 1879. They remarked on how well the land was suited to raising cattle and hunting buffalo because large expanses of buffalo grass extended "as far as the eye can see." In the early 1880s, ranching, catching wild horses, and gathering buffalo bones to sell as fertilizer were the principal means of livelihood. In fact, after the buffalo herds were wiped out, people with no other source of income gathered buffalo bones from the thousands of carcasses that littered the Plains. They received from $6.25 to $8.00 per ton of

Big barn at the Prairie Museum in Colby.

bones, which were then ground up and sold as fertilizer. Carcasses were particularly common along railroad lines, where buffalo had been shot for sport from the railcars and left to rot.

52 Cranston Cattle Company Feedlot

Trees are planted for windbreaks at the feedlot ahead on the left. A line of trees will provide shelter for a distance of ten times their height. Protecting cattle from winter winds is one of the major challenges in feedlot operations. Studies have shown that with protection from winter winds, the rancher saves a lot of money in lowering the costs to feed the cattle. Windbreaks help in summer, too, as they reduce blowing dust that can create conditions that cause some animals to contract pneumonia. Read more about this feedlot and the cattle industry at 49E (p. 149).

50 Dust Bowl Days

For four long years beginning in 1933, farmers from Texas to the Dakotas battled hard against drought. Settlers had plowed up the native prairie grass and converted the land to row crops during periods of sufficient rainfall. This “sod busting” removed the protective blanket of grass that would normally hold the soil during dry years. With the grass removed, a conservation time bomb was set to go off in the next drought. When the next round of dry years hit, the crops withered, their roots shriveled, and the soil was left to blow away with the incessant Kansas wind. The years 1934 and 1935 were particularly bad. Brown dust clouds 2 miles high blew across the Plains. Dust storms halted autos and trains, leaving people stranded, often in total darkness. Some Kansas topsoil was carried a thousand miles east, where it settled on New York City. The irony did not go unnoticed when the US Department of Agriculture building was splattered with muddy raindrops. Even a steamship 200 miles offshore in the Atlantic reported falling dust!

On May 11, 1934, a storm lifted 300 million tons of topsoil into the atmosphere, roughly equivalent to the amount of earth moved to dig the Panama Canal. On April 10, 1935, a local newspaper reported, "After a brief cessation from yesterday's blow during the morning hours, a new storm swept in . . . and grew steadily worse until it was as dark as night before noon. Bright electric signs could hardly be seen across the street." It rained mud balls as the soil mixed with rain. Near Goodland, snow blew with the dust, making a dust blizzard and leaving drifts so high that they caused a train to derail. Housewives used rugs and towels to seal door and window openings, but nothing kept the dust from entering. The dust aggravated illnesses, and people both indoors and out covered their mouths with wet handkerchiefs. One farmer said that it seemed as if the entire state was being blown away.

Depending on the site, 2 to 12 inches of topsoil were lost. The heavier sand particles formed dunes, sometimes burying entire farm buildings and farm equipment. Farmers had trouble making payments on their land and equipment. As immortalized in folk songs by Woody Guthrie and in John Steinbeck's classic novel *The Grapes of Wrath,* many people headed for California. Others, virtually penniless, traveled back to cities in the East, looking for work or benevolent relatives. But Kansans were not easily driven off the land. As a western Kansas resident wrote in her journal:

> Dust whines against the windows unendingly. Food gets filled with it, clothes weigh heavy and smell chocking, and there is a grittiness about people's skin and hair and mouth that no amount of washing can get rid of. . . . But, like the original colonists, hope filters the atmosphere with a golden glamour

Dust clouds rolling across the plains. (National Archives)

> for a number. Some yet have a pure, unfounded faith in the benevolence of nature. They know the rains will fall and another boom will again bring new settlers to the county. A regular alternative of booms and droughts is inevitable. Those who stay know the conditions and expect to accumulate sufficient funds in boom times to carry them through dry years, and borrow money only as the next resort to suicide.

Those who stayed did so with a grin-and-bear-it attitude, joking about dust so thick that a prairie dog was seen digging a burrow 100 feet in the air or reporting they had seen birds flying backward so dust wouldn't get in their eyes. One survivor said that after a man was hit by a raindrop his friends had to throw a bucket of sand in his face to revive him. These tall tales illustrate how much resiliency and determination many people had to possess—and still do possess—to make Kansas their home.

The woman writing in her journal was partially correct, for there has always been a natural cycle of wet years and drought. But what she did not recognize—something many others still do not see—is that without topsoil, there cannot be boom times when the rain returns. Occasionally, blowing soil on the High Plains still reduces visibility and dangerously impedes traffic along this stretch of I-70.

46 Levant

Nobody knows how this town name came to be. Historians know that Stephen Waters, the founding father, requested the names of Waterville (after himself) and Fingal (after his hometown in Canada), but he was turned down on both counts. We do know that Waters applied for a post office in 1888 after the Rock Island line came through here. In those days, the post office often was named first, and the town took its name from that. It may be that Waters had planned and platted the town after a visit by a railroad representative in late 1886, but there's no evidence of a proposed town. No other town along I-70 has such a mysterious naming history.

45 Solitary Sentinel

Directly to the right of marker 45 is a lonely tree in a field. Oh, the stories these prairie trees could tell! These trees do not grow naturally here, and once they do get started, they grow slowly; they often mark the location of a homestead. Thomas Fuller wrote that "he who plants trees loves others besides himself." A tree may have been planted with the hopes that children would one day climb in it or swing from it or that hammocks would hang from it and lemonade would be sipped in its shade. The planter may have imagined birds singing in the tree and breezes blowing through its branches. Each of these lonely trees is a testament to a planter who cared about others out here on the Plains.

43 Another Historic Trail

That's the early highway US 24 that appears as merely a frontage road along the right side of the interstate. Most of I-70's path across Kansas follows the old US 40 corridor. But back near Oakley, 40 headed southwest toward Colorado Springs, as I-70 angled north toward Denver. However, I-70 follows the US 24 route from Colby into Colorado. US 24 connected cities in Colorado with Kansas City and Detroit. When these US highways were built, they attracted travelers who had been using railroads, thereby causing the reduction or even elimination of some railroad passenger service. Likewise, when more efficient interstates were built, they pulled traffic off these two-lane highways, and roadside businesses suffered. Today, the empty shells of abandoned gas stations, diners, and motels along US 24 are reminders of the road's important and prosperous past.

41 **Kansas Is Not Really Flat**

The dips and hills in the road ahead testify to the rolling landscape here on the High Plains of Kansas. Although Kansas is said to be flat, it's really just the open spaces and wide horizons that give that impression. Usually dry, the South Fork of Sappa Creek contributes to the topography here by forming a small valley during times when water flows in the creek. *Sappa* is a Native American word meaning "dark" or "black."

40 **How Did They Survive?**

This is a land of temperature extremes where it may be 100 degrees above zero or 10 below. There is little precipitation, and as a result, there are few trees. When settlers came west, there was not even enough wood to make campfires for cooking and certainly not enough to provide fires for warmth during the long, severe winters. There was no wood to build homes or make corrals.

The land offered grass and little else, so settlers learned to make sod homes for shelter from the heat and cold. They cut dense mats of prairie grass about 3 inches deep, 12 inches wide, and 2 feet long. Slowly, they would build walls out of this sod and then scavenge enough branches to support a sod roof. These dwellings were warm in the winter and cool in the summer. Some pioneers mixed the abundant native lime with water to plaster the walls of their "soddies."

Settlers gathered buffalo chips for heating and cooking. Dried chips burn quickly but provide ample heat for cooking. One account from a Kansas pioneer described using the chips—buffalo chips, unless they were dropped by Texas cattle—in this way:

> Chips make a tolerable fair fire, but of course burn out very rapidly; consequently, to keep up a good fire you must be continually poking chips in and taking the ashes out. Still we feel very thankful for even this fuel. It was comical to see how gingerly our wives handled these chips at first. They commenced by picking them up between two sticks, or with a poker. Soon they used a rag, and then a corner of their apron. Finally, growing hardened, a wash after handling them was sufficient. And now? Now it is out of the bread, into the chips and back again—and not even a dust of the hands!

Collecting buffalo chips (Kansas State Historical Society)

38 Brewster

The town of Brewster was founded in 1888 and was named after L. D. Brewster of Illinois. He was a director of the Rock Island Railroad, which passed just south of town. Without the railroad, the town would not have survived.

36 Mountain Time Zone

A sign on the county line road bridge here indicates it is time to turn back the clock. You have entered Sherman County (named in honor of General William T. Sherman, a prominent officer and Civil War hero) and left the central time zone. From this point west, you will be on mountain time, one hour earlier than before the bridge.

Like most everything else in western Kansas, the time zone idea is linked to the railroad. In 1883, there were about 100 different railroad times across the United States. Various localities had set their own time, declaring it was 12:00 noon when the sun was directly overhead. Yet when it was noon in New York City, it was only 11:55 in Philadelphia, 11:47 in Washington, DC, and 11:35 in Pittsburgh. The railroad officials tried to make their passenger schedules simpler and established their own railroad time for all towns along each route, but even this caused confusion. So the railroads agreed to establish four time zones across the United States, each centered on a meridian of longitude, 15 degrees apart. By 1884, a similar pattern of twenty-four time zones was established worldwide.

34 Jackrabbits

Watch for jackrabbits as you travel on through western Kansas. They are larger and have longer ears and hind legs than the familiar cottontail rabbits. Jackrabbits can quickly accelerate up to 40 miles per hour.

In the 1930s, jackrabbits were exported from this area to stock game preserves in Illinois. But they failed to survive there. Stocking of game animals was a common practice until the mid-twentieth century. Wildlife managers now know that releasing nonnative animals is costly and almost always fails. When it does succeed, it has devastating effects on the native wildlife. Even stocking native species is often costly and unnecessary. If good habitat is present, the animals will be there. If the habitat is poor, all the stocking in the world won't establish the animal, at least for the long term. Habitat is the key!

33 Tumbling Tumbleweeds

If you are traveling during autumn, you might notice another type of traveler—beachball-size plants rolling across the highway or piled up against the interstate fence. Maybe you even hit one with your car as it crossed the road in front of you. These are tumbleweeds, an icon of the dry, wide-open western plains seen in cowboy movies and sung about in cowboy songs. They seem to move across the land purposefully, like an animal on a mission. Fortunately, unlike animals, tumbleweed roadkills don't damage your car when you run over them. Kansas tumbleweeds are Russian thistle plants—another nonnative species—that, like many of the immigrants here, came to the Great Plains from Russia in the late 1800s. Tumbleweeds demonstrate an ingenious design for living in landscapes that are windy and open. After the first frost, the plant breaks off at ground level, and everything except the seeds dies. The plant is now a lightweight sphere that can easily be blown across the countryside, depositing up to 250,000 seeds along the way! Tumbleweeds continue on their seed-spreading cross-country trips until stopped by a fence or building. There, they pile up and remain until they decompose and go back into the soil.

31 Innovative Agriculture

When I-70 was constructed, fill dirt was frequently required. This was "borrowed" from adjacent fields, such as the one on the right here. In many places, a vertical bank was left in the farmer's field. Farmers have been innovative in returning these areas to production or developing new uses for them, such as serving as a feeding center. You will probably see bales of hay stored and trenches cut in the bank as a bunker silo. The openings can be lined with plastic and filled with chopped alfalfa or stalk corn, then covered to seal out the air. Silage develops in the oxygen-reduced bunkers, producing rich cattle feed.

30 Treating Soil Like Dirt!

As you have driven across Kansas, you have read about soil conservation. Agronomists study soil and take it very seriously. To them, what you see covering the fields is not dirt but soil. They say dirt is what's under your bed or fingernails. To them, dirt is misplaced soil.

Have you ever wondered what makes up soil? It is a mixture of very small particles worn from rocks; dead and decaying plants and animals (called organic matter); water; air; and billions of living organisms, most of which are microscopic creatures called decomposers. Decomposers participate in nature's cycle of life and death by converting dead organic matter into forms that can be taken up and used by living things. By making organic nutrients available, they improve the soil's fertility. Good soil is alive and keeps other things, including humans, alive as well.

Our soil is a national treasure. President Franklin D. Roosevelt correctly said, "The nation that destroys its soil, destroys itself." Our welfare is linked to the soil because nutrient-rich soil grows healthy plants, which in turn support healthy wildlife populations, healthy livestock, and healthy human populations. Put another way, good soil grows plants, animals, and people. Throughout history, civilizations have prospered because of their fertile soil. When they abused their soil and allowed it to wash or blow away, these civilizations crumbled. It's encouraging to note that along I-70, you have seen techniques such as terracing, grass waterways, and field windbreaks being used by farmers to save our soil and protect our nation's prosperity.

28 Ed & Son

Exit 27 marks Edson, population fifty. The town was named because Ed Harris and his son settled here in 1888.

A tragic event occurred just north of what is now Edson in 1867. Because of Indian uprisings, Lieutenant Colonel George Custer and 1,100 soldiers from Fort Hays (see 157E, p. 175) were camped along the Republican River north of this location. Lieutenant Lyman S. Kidder, along with a ten-man escort and an Indian guide, was sent with a message to Custer declaring, "Beware the hostiles." Unfortunately, Custer had become restless and had decided to travel northwest to Fort Sedgewick. Lieutenant Kidder found Custer's old camp and assumed he had headed south. On July 2, 1867, Sioux and/or Cheyenne Indians attacked Kidder and his party. None of the soldiers survived. Their bodies were found by Custer's men ten days later.

GOODLAND

26 Winning the County Seat

When counties were being formed, towns competed to be chosen as the county seat. These competitions were always bitter and sometimes even violent and destructive. You probably take your county seat for granted today, but in earlier times in this sparsely settled region, having the county government locate in your town was a big deal. Being the county seat "put the town on the map," so to speak, and held the promise of economic development, political clout, and enhanced civic status for the citizens.

Goodland, just ahead, captured the Sherman County seat, beating out several competing towns. According to *The WPA Guide to 1930s Kansas,* this is what happened. Prior to the founding of Goodland, a hard-fought and bitter election resulted in voters choosing the town of Eustis to be the county seat. At the vote count, people representing the different towns came heavily armed with clubs, bowie knives, and pistols, but amazingly, none of these weapons were used. When Goodland was formed, citizens in the towns that lost the election combined forces with the people in Goodland and held an election to snatch the designation from Eustis. Recalling the weapons brought to the last vote count, Goodland supporters ordered twelve repeating rifles from Pennsylvania to supplement their arms for this election.

Goodland won the 1887 contest without incident, but after the courthouse was built, leaders in Eustis refused to surrender the county records. The leaders of Goodland devised a plan to retrieve the records. They secretly hid 300 men in Goodland's empty courthouse and then sent their new sheriff to Eustis to arrest, individually, every man in that town! The entire male population was rounded up on false charges, including cattle stealing, wife beating, polygamy, murder, and even harboring a dog without a license. The men went willingly, anxious to clear their names before a judge. They were taken into a courtroom, where the judge began a mock trial.

Meanwhile, as soon as the trial started, Goodland's 300-man army headed for Eustis to seize the records. An old-time local resident, Colonel George Bradley, saw the men slipping away from the courthouse and figured out what was happening. He got in his buggy and rode to Eustis to confront the Goodland men. When they encountered Bradley, these men opened fire around his feet, then continued their raid on the Eustis courthouse. They successfully made off with all the records except for the official returns for the 1887 election, which were hidden in a trunk at the county clerk's home. Bradley, knowing this, stole the records from the clerk's home on his way back from Eustis. Later, a local banker who wanted to expedite Goodland's county seat designation then offered to hire—of all people—Colonel Bradley as a detective and pay him $1,500 if he could solve the crime and produce the stolen election records! But before Bradley could take advantage of this offer, the Kansas Supreme Court ruled that Goodland was indeed the county seat and the election records were no longer needed. Colonel Bradley then burned them.

Goodland residents experienced all this strife for the honor and, more important, the financial benefits of having their town as the county seat. Goodland is now a town of 5,700, whereas Eustis is not even on the map.

22 Rainmakers

Rainmakers first appeared in Goodland during the droughts of the 1890s. Frank Melbourne, billing himself as the "Australian Rainmaker," was offered $1,500 if he could make it rain 1 inch within a twenty-four-hour time limit. Announcements were posted in railroad stations throughout Kansas and Nebraska. It didn't rain in Goodland, but within twenty-four hours, flash floods occurred in Nebraska, causing such damage that officials of a number of towns began telegraphing Goodland, imploring the people there to shut off the rainmaker. Melbourne promised to tell the county his secret and donate a machine so the local people could make their own rain. But in July 1895, he admitted his scheme was a hoax, and the people ran him out of town.

Melbourne was just the first of many rainmakers here. For instance, a local chemist and a railroad agent had been conducting experiments similar to Melbourne's, and it happened to shower after one of them. So the two men formed a corporation and sold stock in it. Thereafter, Californians hired them to make rain in several valleys, and the Mexican government also sought their services, although Mexico's drought ended before they made Mexican rain.

Dr. L. Morse, a Goodland druggist, operated a rainmaking company for about twenty years. In the summer of 1892, the wheat was burning up in the fields. The postmaster paid Morse fifty dollars to buy chemicals to make it rain. Morse bought sulfuric acid and began his experiment at ten o'clock in the morning; by two o'clock, according to one report, the wooden sidewalks were afloat and children were using them for rafts. The railroad even got into the rainmaking business with its own rainmakers and three laboratory train cars, which toured the rails throughout Kansas.

Groundwater management districts here still try to modify weather by seeding clouds from aircraft. This modern rainmaking is done mostly to diffuse potential hailstorms that could destroy the crops.

20 First in (Helicopter) Flight

If you pass a car from North Carolina, you'll notice that its license plates feature the state motto, "First in Flight." But even though North Carolina has the Wright brothers and their aviation exploits, Goodland is home to America's first patented helicopter. Two Rock Island Railroad machinists, W. J. Purvis and Charles A. Wilson, designed, built, and patented their invention in 1909 and 1910. The machine used two counterrotating rotors to offset engine torque rather than the modern tail rotor. A full-size replica of the original machine can be seen in the High Plains Museum in Goodland.

19 The Big Easel

Yes, that is an easel with a painting on it way over there on the right. The easel is 80 feet tall and weighs 40,000 pounds. The "canvas" is composed of twenty-four sheets of standard plywood, providing a 24-by-32-foot surface on which artist Cameron Cross has reproduced one of Vincent van Gogh's sunflower paintings.

Cross put up his first big easel with a sunflower reproduction in his hometown of Altona, Manitoba. Since van Gogh created seven sunflower paintings, Cross decided to reproduce all of them and install them in different countries. His second is in Queensland, Australia; Goodland, here in the heart of sunflower country, was selected for the third site. The other paintings will go to areas with a connection to sunflower agriculture or van Gogh himself—places like the Netherlands, Japan, South Africa, and Argentina.

The sunflower painting was created with an industrial acrylic urethane enamel, the kind used on ships and on farm machinery that is exposed to heat, chemicals, and ultraviolet light. Ten layers of enamel were used to ensure that those big sunflowers would have a long life. Exit 17 will take you to the sunflower painting and to the High Plains Museum.

18 Good Land

The town was named Goodland not because the founders thought it was particularly "good land" but because a stockholder in the town company was from Goodland, Indiana. However, the name fits the Kansas city well, at least in regard to wheat farming.

Today, Goodland is a busy commercial center and one of the largest towns in northwest Kansas. It has adopted the clever motto "Goodland—On the Top Side of Kansas," referring to its position in the northwest corner and the fact that it has the highest elevation of any city in the state.

The bricks in Main Street were laid by Jim Brown in 1921 at the astounding rate of 150 bricks per minute, or more than 2 per second. And even at that great speed, Brown laid them so straight that no adjustments were necessary.

Sunflower painting

16 Living Snow Fences

The rows of pine trees on the right side of the interstate beyond the overpass serve as living and permanent snow fences. The trees will stop the wind, and snow will pile up behind the trees rather than on the roadway. You may recall seeing other living snow fences back at mile 229W (p. 63).

14 Caruso

The town at Exit 12 was indeed named after the famous Italian tenor Enrico Caruso. Sometimes called Caruso Station, it is another small railroad town. Apparently, the founders of this town appreciated opera or at least Caruso's talents, but the "opera houses" found in this and most of the small towns did not host opera companies. Rather, as noted back at Grainfield, they were venues for all sorts of entertainers that the railroads would bring to town, including stock companies and vaudeville acts. The opera houses served as a community gathering place, functioning much as a civic auditorium would today.

13 A Different Kind of Oil

Operators of the next elevator on the right specialize in buying sunflower seeds from fields within a radius of 60 miles or more. The ADM Company stores grain and ships sunflower oil as an ingredient for food industries. Tbe oil, similar to that which you purchase at a grocery, is extracted using high-pressure presses. About 28 percent of the seed is a light oil with a pleasant flavor. What remains is a protein-rich cake that is valued by local feedlot operators as a high-energy cattle feed supplement.

In the summer, you will see fields of bright-yellow sunflowers in the surrounding farms until they are harvested around the end of July. The sunflower is native to the fertile Great Plains. American Indians are believed to have cultivated and enjoyed the sunflower and used the nutty kernels for a quick energy food.

Spanish explorers enjoyed the Indian kernels so much that they sent them back to Europe. Ever since, sunflowers have been cultivated in Europe and around the world. Today in the United States, several varieties of sunflowers are grown commercially. There are two primary types of seed: one is used for oil, like the oils shipped to the storage elevators here, and the other, known as confection sunflowers, is the kind you buy to shell and eat the kernels. Confection sunflowers are handled in an entirely different manner, as described at Red River Commodities (57W, p. 117).

10 Ruleton and "the Rock"

At Exit 9 is the town of Ruleton, a small farming community that survived because of the Rock Island Railroad, also known as "the Rock." As mentioned previously, railroads gave life to many Kansas towns like Ruleton and caused the death of others—those they bypassed. Railroads served as an economic umbilical cord to the outside world. Even now, we see that as railroads themselves die off, many towns that were linked with them from birth struggle for survival on their own, many unsuccessfully.

The Frontier Ag elevator along the railroad tracks to the right stores and ships grain from area farmers. This elevator receives the major grains—wheat, corn, and milo. It also specializes in collecting and shipping pinto beans, an increasingly important crop for western Kansas farmers.

9 Controversial Critters

The area from here to the state line is prairie dog terrain, the kind of area where these animals build their towns. Prairie dogs are fascinating social creatures that get their name from their doglike "bark." They like areas with short grass, where they can stand on their hind legs and look out over the vegetation to detect danger.

Prairie dog burrows provide homes for many other forms of wildlife, including burrowing owls, snakes, and the endangered black-footed ferret. Before the land was converted to ranches and farms, dog towns stretched for many miles and contained millions of prairie dogs. The population of prairie dogs on the Great Plains today totals only about 1 percent of the presettlement population. Ranchers sometimes poison prairie dogs because they compete with the cattle for grass. So, although they may have been nearly eradicated, you might still see their mounds. Depending on your perspective, prairie dogs are destructive pests, cute and cuddly creatures, or a key part of the prairie ecosystem. You're more likely to see prairie dogs as you travel west into Colorado.

7 Rest Area

Before you leave Kansas, the terrain at this rest area provides one more vista of rolling hills to assure you the state is not truly flat. A historical sign here explains that this Dwight D. Eisenhower Highway was designated in August 1973 by the US Congress as "a legacy of safety and mobility that has brought all Americans closer together."

6 The Wayward Wind

If you have been traveling across Kansas, you already know that the wind seems to blow continuously here. You've already seen two wind farms, and a third can be spotted ahead just across the state line. The incessant wind aggravates and agitates some people to the point that they cannot take it anymore. Over the years, many residents have left the state to seek calm days in tree-filled terrains back east or farther west. But others have stayed and put the wind to work with windmills that pump water to the surface and wind turbines that produce electricity. Rather than detesting the wind, resilient residents have learned to have fun with it, and some are even inspired by it. The Goodland Chamber of Commerce has sponsored wind wagon races each fall. Contestants hoist sails on homemade wagons and race down a stretch of Highway 24.

The wind inspired Fred Atchison to write the following poem:

The Prairie Wind
I'm thinking of you, prairie wind
running free across Kansas plains
and see the evidence of our presence
billowing seas of golden grain

You etch your mark on sandstone cliffs
sculptures carved by a timeless hand
and move soft brushes of prairie grass
drawing circles across the sand

It is humbling when I realize
these soft breezes reaching me now
whispered lullabies to the Indian child
before the prairie was put to the plow

Late nineteenth-century wind wagon (Kansas State Historical Society)

4 The High Point

At this spot, you are at the highest point on I-70 in Kansas. At mile 3.7, the elevation of the roadway is 3,910 feet above sea level. Back where the interstate crossed into Kansas from Missouri, the elevation was only 760 feet. It is our hope that you have had many high points in your journey across our state.

3 Mountains, Real and Imagined

About 20 miles off to the left, in a pasture on private ranchland, is the highest spot in Kansas, called Mount Sunflower. The US Geological Survey officially plotted the elevation of Mount Sunflower at 4,039 feet above sea level—not exactly an ear-popping height! However, Mount Sunflower is not considered a true mountain because there isn't a 2,000-foot altitude change within a 10-to-20-mile radius of the peak. Even so, many folks like to "conquer" Mount Sunflower, just because it's there.

Many first-time travelers to Colorado expect to see real mountains soon after crossing the state line. It is normal for eager families to look hard at the horizon with anticipation of seeing the first snow-capped peaks. Indeed, travelers have been doing this since the days of the wagon trains. But the landscape and scenery in Colorado will not be much different from that in Kansas for quite a while, since you are still about 150 miles from the front range of the Rockies. That means many more miles of High Plains grasslands and crops lie ahead.

2 Beaver Creek and the Border Town

The name of Beaver Creek reminds us that although it is dry today, this creek once had enough water to support beavers. Today, water is becoming scarcer in this region as groundwater is pumped for irrigation.

There is one more exit in Kansas: Exit 1 marks the town of Kanorado. This town with the hybridized name taken from the two bordering states was declared a city in September 1903 and currently has about 200 residents.

Happy Trails!

You are now entering Colorado. We are pleased that you chose I-70 for your travels and that you have used this book to add to your adventure. We trust that this guide has been an enjoyable companion, providing you with a greater appreciation for and understanding of the many significant sights along I-70 in Kansas. We hope that as you traveled across our state, you were pleasantly surprised by our topography, history, natural beauty, prosperity, and productivity. Most of all, we hope you will return soon to travel more Kansas trails.

Eastbound

Most of you who are entering Kansas from Colorado will have recently experienced the majestic Rocky Mountains. It has been said the Rockies will take your breath away, but the pleasant, peaceful landscapes of Kansas will give it back to you again. We hope that you will catch your breath as you drive across Kansas.

1 **The High Point**

Exit 1 marks the town of Kanorado. South of Kanorado is the highest point in Kansas—Mount Sunflower, with an elevation of 4,039 feet above sea level. These next few miles will be the high point of your trip along I-70, at least in terms of elevation. From a peak of 3,910 feet at mile 3.7, travel east is all downhill; you will drop more than 3,000 feet by the time you get to Kansas City.

2 **The High Plains**

Kansas consists of eleven distinct regions, each differing in elevation, vegetation, precipitation, topography, wildlife, and history. You will pass through four of these regions if you travel I-70 across the entire state. To the surprise of most people—and in spite of what you may have heard—none of these four regions is flat.

You have entered Kansas in the High Plains region, which covers the western third of the state. This is the largest, highest, and driest region in Kansas. It receives only between 16 and 20 inches of precipitation per year, and the elevation ranges from about 4,000 feet above sea level along the Colorado-Kansas border to 2,000 feet at the eastern edge of the region. The High Plains have a reputation for being windy and for having extreme temperatures (both cold and hot) that can fluctuate wildly, sometimes changing by 60 degrees in twenty-four hours.

3 **Sunny Sherman County**

Known as the Mountain Climate Capital of Kansas, Sherman County has an average humidity of only about 27 percent, with 300 days of sunshine per year. This abundant sunshine provides the solar energy that is converted by crops into food energy and stored in the grain that grows in the bountiful fields you will drive past. When you eat a piece of bread or corn, you are eating a bit of sunshine, getting your energy from solar energy that traveled 93 million miles to a place like Sherman County, Kansas, and then to your table.

Sherman County receives only about 16 inches of precipitation annually, so the streams here are usually nothing more than dry gullies, or washes. As you crossed the Middle Fork of Beaver Creek, you probably noticed that it is dry. But the gullies on both sides of I-70 offer proof that the rivers occasionally run; these gullies were created by water washing away the soil when the area has a "gully washer" of a thunderstorm. The name Beaver Creek indicates that at one time, there was a steady supply of water here to support beavers.

Sherman County was established in 1869 and named in honor of General William T. Sherman, a Civil War hero and prominent officer in the US Army. In the late 1800s, Kansas was called the Great Soldier State because so many Civil War veterans settled here. In fact, there were more Grand Army of the Republic members per capita in Kansas than in any other state. No wonder that forty-six Kansas counties are named for Civil War soldiers, most of whom died in battle.

5 Goodland

Just ahead is Goodland, the seat of Sherman County. Early on, towns would compete to become the county seat. Read the story of how Goodland won that competition at 26W (p. 127).

6 Official Kansas Welcome!

At the Travel Information Center ahead, you can receive not only tourism information but also a free cup of coffee and a warm welcome. The Kansas flag will be waving in the wind (we can almost guarantee the wind), and you can get a close-up view of the state seal, both of which are described in the introduction (p. ix).

7 Ruleton: "The Rock and a Coop"

The tall structures along the railroad to your left comprise a Frontier Ag elevator that stores grain from area farms. You will see many grain elevators in the miles ahead. For clarity, we refer to the entire cluster of structures as the "elevator." A single tall, round storage structure is a "bin." Sometimes bins are called silos. We will use silo to describe the similar on-farm, cylinder-shaped structure. An elevator, the cluster of bins (and frequently other structures), has a single mechanism to take grain to the top; its name comes from the fact that the grain is "elevated" to the top of the tall storage bins. In one type of elevator, buckets attached to a moving belt scoop the grain and carry it upward. At the top, the grain is discharged to one of the chutes, where it flows by gravity down into one of many storage bins.

You will see numerous Frontier Ag facilities across northwest Kansas. The major grain crops stored and shipped from them include wheat, corn, soybeans and milo (which is also called grain sorghum). The elevator at Ruleton stores the major grain crops and for food processors, pinto beans that are becoming a significant new crop for this region.

Frontier Ag is a full-service, member-owned agribusiness cooperative (called a co-op for short and generally spelled coop) offering grain, feed, agronomy, fuel, and transportation products and services to its members and other customers. A cooperative consists of members who unite to buy supplies and market their products more profitably. A basic code specifies democratic con-

Frontier Ag grain elevator

trol, with each member having one vote and a share in the profits in proportion to the amount of his or her patronage. The elevator staff acts on behalf of the members to market their products just like any company that manufactures a tool or machine. For details about "The Rock," see 10W (p. 132).

10 A Different Kind of Oil (13W, p. 132)

The elevator that you see on the left is one of ADM Company's grain operations. ADM is among the world's largest agricultural processors and ingredient providers. It concentrates on sunflower seeds at this location. Seeds are trucked here from fields within a 60-mile radius, sometimes farther. The seeds are crushed at the elevator to extract the sunflower oil that is sold to food processors.

11 Caruso (14W, p. 131)

Most towns along I-70 are named for settlers, soldiers, or places back east, but this next town was named for the Italian tenor Enrico Caruso.

12 Super Sprinklers

The large metal structures in the fields are center-pivot irrigation systems. The long arms move slowly over the crops like the hand of a clock while spraying water pumped from a well. These are not your typical lawn sprinklers! Deep well pumps deliver water from wells, sometimes up to a mile away, to feed the arm. The machine slowly sweeps around the field, pivoting from the center, where the water enters. Water flows out through the long arm with sprinkler heads hanging from it. Electric motors drive the wheels slowly so the arm makes one revolution in twenty-four hours or longer, sprinkling the crop within the circle. Most irrigation arms are a quarter mile long and cover 130 acres, but some extend for a half mile, thereby watering 568 acres out of the 640 acres in a square-mile field as they sweep above the crops. From the air, these circles make western Kansas looks like a pond with giant green lily pads.

In this area and in the miles ahead, you will see many more center-pivot irrigation rigs in the fields. Precipitation is scarce in the High Plains; therefore, farming benefits from irrigation water found in the Ogallala Aquifer, an enormous underground water source the size of Lake Huron. The aquifer extends at varying depths from north Texas into South Dakota. It allows farmers to raise crops, especially corn, that otherwise would be impossible to grow in this dry region. These crops are sold to grain markets and to feedlots to grow cattle that in turn also consume water. Packing plants have moved here to be close to these feedlots, and they, too, depend on the grain and consume large amounts of water.

Irrigation alone accounts for 85 percent of all water used in Kansas, and 92 percent of all groundwater used is devoted to irrigation. In some areas, the aquifer is being depleted fourteen times faster than it is being recharged from rains. This "mining" of groundwater has caused some wells to go dry, which means that wells must be dug deeper at great expense or irrigation must be turned off. Because the region's economy is based on irrigated crops, many fear that when it becomes infeasible to continue mining this groundwater, the economic consequences could be disastrous.

15 Living Snow Fences

The rows of pines on the left side of the interstate were planted to serve as living snow fences. You will see several of these fences over the next few miles. Other examples of trees being used to block the wind will be seen at miles 49 and 58 and throughout your trip across the High Plains.

16 Goodland (18W, p. 130)

This town is surrounded by good land for growing wheat, which you might assume was how this community got its name. But in fact, it was named for Goodland, Indiana, so the name was not meant to make a statement about the quality of the local land.

17 The Big Easel (19W, p. 130)

Exit 19 will take you to the enormous Vincent van Gogh painting that can be seen off to the left. To honor the role of sunflowers as a cash crop in this region, one of van Gogh's sunflower paintings is reproduced here on an 80-foot-tall easel.

18 First in (Helicopter) Flight (20W, p. 129)

Just north of the van Gogh is the High Plains Museum, which has the world's first patented helicopter. Take Exit 19 for both the giant easel and the museum.

19 "A Dry and Thirsty Land"

You are traveling through irrigated croplands. Great civilizations such as those of the Babylonians, Assyrians, Sumerians, and others throughout history failed because their food was produced in dry regions requiring irrigation and their irrigation systems eventually became inefficient. These collapses in agricultural production led to scarce commodities, poverty, and even wars between nations. Here in Kansas, the wars are fought at the state level, with legal battles between Colorado, Nebraska, and Kansas. Water is the lifeblood of the Great Plains.

People here have been so desperate for rain that they sometimes have turned to rainmakers. Read the story about the "Australian Rainmaker" at 22W (p. 128).

20 Pump Protection

Small shelters like the one at the right along the fence row or out in the field protect motors and pump controls at irrigation wells. Each center-pivot irrigation machine has its own well, equipped with a deep well turbine pump to lift water from the Ogallala Aquifer. In some places, the water is more than 300 feet below the surface. Pumps are powered by electricity or by diesel or gas engines. The pump at mile 21 uses a 413-horsepower Chrysler gas engine to deliver 650 gallons of water per minute through a 2.5-inch pipe, at a pressure of 30 pounds per square inch. During the seven days it takes the machine to complete a full circle, the pump will have delivered more than 65 million gallons of water to the cornfield.

Legally, groundwater belongs to the state of Kansas. Farmers can apply for a "water right" permit by demonstrating that they can use groundwater productively. This is called "perfecting" a water right.

22 Spiderweb Bins and Blue Silos

The spiderweb-like towers and chutes radiating from the top of the bins on the horizon to the right signal on-farm grain processing. At this farm, as many as 2,000 head of cattle may be fed. When trucks arrive, grain is elevated in the tall center shaft by a conveyor of buckets. It is then directed through one of the tubes connected to the round grain bins. You'll get a closer look at them at miles 48 and 49 ahead.

Irrigation pump protector

A half mile down the road, additional grain is stored in the tall, blue Harvestore silos. You can see one of these standing alone to the left of the grain bins. Many of these glass-lined, steel silos can be spotted across Kansas. The unique design allows storage of hay or grain that is too wet for conventional storage, such as grain that is not completely ripe. It can also store fodder, the whole plant—stalks and seeds. Wet crops are "ensiled" to turn them into a rich feed in the oxygen-controlled Harvestore environment. There is more at 33E (p. 144) about ensiling in a silo to slightly ferment the plant material, enhancing its value as feed.

24 "A Newer Garden of Creation"

That's what Walt Whitman called this region in a poem called "The Prairie States." While traveling across these High Plains, he also wrote the selection presented at 95W (p. 104).

26 Ed & Son (28W, p. 127)

The Kidder Massacre site is 13 miles north of Edson on North Edson Road 27.

The Frontier Ag elevator at Edson now mostly collects sunflower seeds. Until recently, however—indicating how markets and crops

Bins and silos

change—about 1.5 million bushels of wheat (more than 400 railcars full) were shipped annually to a flour mill in Utah. Farmers from as far away as Colorado and Nebraska sign annual contracts to bring grain here daily during the harvest season.

28 The Wayward Wind (6W, p. 133)
It seems like the wind blows ceaselessly here in the region Ian Frazier called "the airshaft of the continent," but some locals use the wind and even have fun with it.

31 Don't Treat Soil Like Dirt! (30W, p. 126)
People concerned about conserving soil take the long-term view, as suggested in a popular conservation slogan, "We do not inherit the land from our fathers, we borrow it from our children" (see also 62W, p. 114).

33 Silos
The tall, cylindrical objects seen near barns are silos. Silos, such as those on the right, are used to make silage, a succulent feed for livestock, especially on dairy farms. Damp grain, hay, or alfalfa is placed in the sealed cavity of the silo, where it ferments, making a

nutritious feed for cattle. The fermentation breaks down the plant material, making it easier to digest. From the early 1900s until the 1950s, silos were made of concrete or wood. Then, as mentioned at mile 22, another option became available—the dark-blue, glass-lined steel Harvestore silo, which makes a richer feed. Some farmers dig trenches and put chopped crops in them to ferment. You will see several of these trench silos along I-70. One recent innovation is a large, tube-shaped plastic bag that is filled with plant material and sealed. It essentially functions as a silo lying on its side. Before long, an old-fashioned upright silo may be a thing of the past.

34 Thomas County (74W, p. 111)

Ahead is Thomas County, established in 1873 and named in honor of Civil War hero Brigadier General George H. Thomas.

Exit 36 goes to Brewster, visible on the left. Brewster was named after L. D. Brewster of Illinois, a director of the Rock Island Railroad when the town was founded in 1888. Like most western Kansas towns, it would not have survived without the railroad.

36 Tumbling Tumbleweeds

You might have noticed another type of traveler as you drive—beachball-size plants rolling across the highway or piled up against

Harvestore silo

the interstate fence. Maybe you even hit one with your car as it crossed the road in front of you. These are tumbleweeds, an icon of the dry, wide-open western plains seen in cowboy movies and sung about in cowboy songs. They move across the land almost purposefully, like an animal on a mission. Fortunately, unlike animals, tumbleweed roadkills don't damage your car when you hit them. Kansas tumbleweeds are Russian thistle plants—another nonnative species—that, like many of the immigrants here, came to the Great Plains from Russia in the late 1800s. Tumbleweeds are ingeniously designed for living in landscapes that are windy and open. After the first frost, the plant breaks off at ground level, and everything except the seeds dies. The plant is now a lightweight sphere that easily can be blown across the countryside, depositing its seeds along the way. Tumbleweeds continue on their seed-spreading cross-country trips until stopped by a fence or building. There, they pile up and remain until they decompose and go back into the soil.

38 Time Zones (36W, p. 124)

Don't speed up, but it's later than you think! At the Thomas County line marker, you left the mountain time zone and lost an hour. Turn your watch and car clock ahead one hour for central time. Four Kansas counties bordering Colorado use mountain time; the rest of Kansas is on central time.

39 Kansas Is Not Really Flat

Notice the rolling landscape in this area. Western Kansas is thought of as flat, but it is really just the open spaces and wide horizons that give this impression. Later in the trip across Kansas, you will drive through the Smoky Hills and the Flint Hills—regions that are not at all flat.

40 Homes on the Range

Cattle ranches are common throughout the High Plains, and most are large compared with those farther east. It takes more acres to support each head of cattle out here where grass is short and sparse. A herd that could live on a few acres in Missouri, for instance, would need hundreds of acres to survive on the High Plains. Here on the short-grass prairie, the only plants that survive are those that tolerate very dry conditions. Plants like cactus or yucca and grasses such as buffalo grass and blue grama can last through the long, hot periods between rains. These grasses are important for holding the soil and are good for grazing livestock.

Ranches here grow more than beef. Grama grass is a good source of food for jackrabbits and prairie dogs, which in turn are good food for hawks and coyotes. Finches, longspurs, and other birds eat the grama seeds, and North America's only kind of antelope, the pronghorn, grazes these grasslands.

41 Bison

Imagine this entire landscape covered by a lawn of short, green grass. That is the way it looked at one time. Then imagine buffalo, more accurately called bison, by the millions roaming and grazing on this green carpet. That is the way it was before settlers arrived. Between 12 and 20 million bison roamed the Plains, with some herds large enough to cover an area 5 miles wide and 50 miles long. Herds were so densely packed that one observer in 1860 described a passing herd as a "monstrous moving brown blanket" that would take days to pass by a campsite.

The arrival of the railroad quickly eliminated bison from Kansas. At first, the white people killed the bison only for their meat and hides, but soon after the railroads arrived, bison were killed from trains by sport hunters and often left to rot. By 1875, there were so few bison left that Kansas passed laws to protect the remaining few. But it was too late. This slaughter of the bison not only eliminated a source of fuel and food for settlers but also helped to seal the fate of the Plains Indians, who depended on bison herds for their own survival. In fact, this dependency provided additional motivation for some "buffalo" hunters who wanted to remove this food source from the Indians so that they would leave the region.

Today, bison can be seen on ranches where they are raised commercially like cattle—for example, near Fort Hays (mile 157), between miles 234 and 235, and on the Plumlee Buffalo Ranch (mile 326). Although the meat is still mostly a novelty, many Kansas restaurants serve buffalo steaks and buffalo burgers as an alternative to beef. Watch for small herds of these impressive mammals as you drive along I-70, and try to imagine what it must have been like when millions of bison roamed this land.

Bison skulls to be ground up to make fertilizer

43 How Did People Survive?

Depending on the season, outside the comfort of your car as you travel along I-70 the temperature may be 100 degrees above zero or 10 below. Besides being a land of temperature extremes, western Kansas is an environment with little precipitation and, as a result, few trees. When settlers came west, they could not find wood to build homes or make corrals. There was not even enough wood to make campfires for cooking and certainly not enough to provide fires for warmth during the long, severe winters. To survive, settlers had to make use of the few resources the land offered—sod and buffalo chips (40W, p. 123).

45 Levant (46W, p. 122)

Several theories exist, but nobody knows with certainty just how this town got its name. No other Kansas town along I-70 has such a mysterious designation.

46 Dust Bowl Days (50W, p. 119)

In the 1930s, western Kansas became part of the dust bowl. Skies were blackened and roads and buildings were blanketed with soil

Sod house (New York Public Library)

that had blown wildly across the landscape. Read about these storms at 50W and 143W (p. 119 and 89).

49 Feedlots

The Cranston Cattle Company feedlot on the hill ahead to the right is one of several hundred small feedlots that you'll see across western Kansas. Don Cranston says they limit their operation to 999 cattle because environmental regulations require operators with 1,000 or more cattle in a feedlot to implement far more extensive and costly waste-handling procedures. Cranston primarily has a cow/calf operation with 400 cows that give birth to calves each year. The additional cattle are purchased from area farmers or at auctions. The animals are fed locally grown grain, corn, barley, milo, and protein-rich by-products, such as sunflower hulls from the Red River Commodities plant in Colby and distillers grain from Western Plains Energy in Oakley.

At about ten months of age, a calf will weigh around 700 pounds and be ready to go to a finishing feedlot. That's correct, calves can add about 2 pounds every day! One of the biggest challenges in operating a feedlot is marketing at a price that will pay for all the feed and labor that is required and also cover the investment in facilities. Severe cold and snow pose a significant challenge to the cattle farmer, too. Feed must be gotten out to bunks that may be filled with snow or ice, and water tanks may be frozen.

Cattle feeding is one of Kansas's major industries. Cash receipts from cattle sales have generated almost $8 billion annually, and over 18,500 people have jobs in the Kansas beef industry. In addition, feedlots provide a significant market for crops from local farms. Kansas ranks third in the nation in number of cattle, with 5.8 million. That means there are twice as many cattle as there are people in Kansas!

51 The Prairie Museum of Art and History (56W, p. 118)

At the next exit, a restored farmhouse from 1930, a sod house with furnishings from the late 1880s, and a one-room schoolhouse can be seen at the Prairie Museum of Art and History. The museum houses an interesting collection of artifacts from people and places on the Plains. From the interstate, you can see to the left a most striking feature—one of the biggest barns in Kansas.

52 Colby

This town was named after the Civil War hero J. R. Colby. Read about its history at 55W (p. 118). As you pass by the town, there is a 140-foot-tall tower on the left at Exit 54. It stores over 160,000 gallons of city water. The coated-steel tank, called an aquastore, is 14 feet in diameter.

54 Sunflower Snacks (57W, p. 117)

On the left at Exit 54, you see silver grain storage elevators at the Red River Commodities confection sunflower processing plant. In contrast to the sunflower seeds that will be pressed for oil (like those in the elevator back at mile 10), the products of this plant are mostly intended for human consumption. Sunflower seeds are a popular snack in Kansas and are sold in virtually every convenience store. The sunflower seeds you munch on may have come from nearby fields or from this very processing plant.

55 Wheat for the World (58W, p. 116)

Wheat collected in the tall yellow elevator at the left is destined for export. Rail grain cars filled here will head for cities along the Gulf of Mexico, where ships will take Kansas wheat to Europe, Africa,

Grain for the world

and the Mideast. Other trains will unload this wheat in the Pacific Northwest to ships destined for China and other Pacific Rim markets.

56 Kansas Skies (141W, p. 90)

Although Montana calls itself the Big Sky Country, Kansas, too, has impressive skies. There are about 300 sunny days each year, and when skies are not clear, they often are embellished with beautiful and powerfully majestic clouds. We hope you enjoy the spectacular Kansas sky.

But Kansas skies are not always a pleasant diversion. As you travel across the state, you need to keep an eye on what's going on in the sky. Although tornadoes have occurred in all fifty states, only Texas and Oklahoma have more than Kansas. Moreover, Kansas has the distinction of having more F5 tornadoes than any other state. To see a tornado from afar is awe inspiring. To witness one up-close is terrifying. If you see a tornado along the highway, do not try to outrun it. Experts suggest leaving your vehicle and lying flat in a roadside ditch.

Regardless of the season, if skies look threatening listen for weather reports. You can also hear weather reports at each rest area. Nature can express its majesty and power not only in ways that can destroy crops but also in ways that can take a deadly toll on travelers. At 141W (p. 90), read what poets and playwrights have written about these skies.

57 Semi Story

As you drive I-70, you will pass many semis and maybe even consider it a nuisance to have to share the road with them. But these trucks play a key role in all of our lives. Sixty-eight percent of all goods in the United States (about 60,000 pounds per American every year) is delivered by semitrucks.

Each year, a semi will average 45,000 miles, but long-distance trucks average close to 100,000 miles annually. In total, semitrucks drive about 140 *billion* miles a year in the United States.

The term *semitruck* comes from the trailer, which only has wheels on the rear. Since the trailer has no front wheels, it can be used only when it is being pulled by a truck. The combination of a truck or tractor pulling such a trailer is known as a semitruck, a semi-tractor-trailer, or merely a semi for short. Because many of the trucks have a total of ten wheels and the trailers often have eight wheels, they are sometimes called 18-wheelers.

These trucks get between 4 and 8 miles per gallon, with an average of 6.5 miles per gallon. Going up one of the Flint Hills or Smoky Hills here in Kansas, they might only get 2.9 miles per gallon, but going down those same hills, their mileage may shoot up to more than 20 miles per gallon. As you pass semis, notice whether they have metal "skirts" hanging below the trailers. These relatively new features reduce the aerodynamic drag of swirling air under the trailers and increase fuel efficiency by about 5 percent. Notice, too, whether a trailer has an Underrun Protection Guard to prevent a car from sliding under the trailer in the event of a rear-end crash. This issue was first brought to light when actress Jayne Mansfield died after her sports car slid under a trailer, causing severe head injuries. Read about popular truck brands and trucking companies at 243W (p. 58).

59 Rails to Riches

Here, you cross over more railroad tracks. Read about the lasting impact of the railroads at 337W (p. 29).

Mark Twain wrote, "A railroad is like a lie—you have to keep building it to make it stand." This notion certainly was played out in Kansas as railroads kept being built across the Plains. As towns sprang up along the railroads, wagon roads and then state and federal highways were built alongside the rail routes to connect the towns. For most of its route, I-70 follows one of the Union Pacific lines across Kansas to Kansas City.

Today, railroads transport large quantities of grain from small farm communities to larger markets where the grain is sold and processed. The white grain elevators, regularly spaced about 8 to 10 miles apart, mark the location of the railroad tracks and serve as a constant reminder that railroads are still vital to the economic survival of western Kansas.

62 Mingo

On the right, you can see the town of Mingo and the Frontier Ag elevator, a farmer cooperative. Mingo is named after a branch of the Sioux tribe.

63 Energy Trails

Electricity is routed along overhead transmission line "trails"; it is another avenue of commerce across the state. The line paralleling I-70 is a major corridor for carrying electricity. One measure of the amount of power is voltage, or the pressure that moves current through the lines. To move electricity through your home takes 115 or 230 volts. To move power through lines along city streets or out to farms, about 6,900 volts are used. For the long lines that connect eastern and western Kansas, much bigger lines are required. The line here operates at 115,000 volts.

You will see structures that support double that voltage and more. The construction will include more rugged steel-frame towers with longer and thus heavier insulators used to separate the cables from the support beams, such as those seen at mile 280 ahead. This line connects the power-generating plants in Colby with plants in Great Bend to the southeast. From Colby, transmission lines carry electricity east and west along the same trail you are following. Watch as other lines operating at different voltages cross I-70.

65 Pocket Gophers (66W, p. 114)

You may have noticed the mounds of sandy soil along the roadway. They are made of soil excavated from the tunnels of plains pocket gophers.

66 Kansas Sharks (79W, p. 109)

At one time, this area was a warm and shallow tropical sea. Shark teeth, coral, and other remnants of this ancient ocean are found in this area and can be seen up-close at the Fick Fossil Museum (Exit 76).

68 Monument Rocks

The Monument Rocks Natural National Landmark is located on private property 26 miles south of Oakley (Exit 70). These rocks are impressive chalk bluffs and pyramids poking high out of the prairie. Native Americans used them as a lookout perch, and they were a landmark for travelers along the Butterfield Overland Despatch (BOD) stagecoach line on their way between Atchison (near Kansas City) and Denver. I-70 closely parallels the route of this passenger and express stagecoach from here to Kansas City. It was the shortest but most dangerous route across the Plains. The stage ran three times a week, taking eight to twelve days to make the one-way trip. The BOD began on August 1, 1865; however, it ended operation less than eighteen months later because of a lack of protection from Indians and decreased gold mining in Colorado. Just think, you can make this same trip in about eight *hours* rather than eight *days* and with nothing to fear except other drivers.

70 Eliza, not Annie

Take Exit 70 south and drive 4 miles to visit the Buffalo Bill Cultural Center. There, you will learn about Buffalo Bill and see an enormous, larger-than-life bronze statue of him on his favorite horse, Brigham. The center also is a gateway to the scenic and geologically rich Western Vistas Historic Byway. While there, you can visit the gift shop and enjoy a free cup of coffee.

People assume that the town of Oakley, founded in 1885, was named for the famous female sharpshooter Annie Oakley. But in fact, it was named for Eliza Oakley Gardner-Hoag, mother of David Hoag, who founded the town. This does not make for quite as good a story, but who can argue with a son honoring his mother? Annie never made it to Oakley, although some of the West's most famous riders did pass through this area. In 1868, William "Buffalo Bill" Cody and William Comstock, both scouts with the US Cavalry and Union Pacific Railroad, competed in a buffalo-shooting contest 3 miles west of town. It was after he won this contest that Cody began to be called Buffalo Bill.

72 Jackrabbits (34W, p. 125)

Another interesting mammal found in the High Plains is the black-tailed jackrabbit, which is larger and has longer ears and hind legs than the familiar cottontail. It can quickly accelerate up to 40 miles per hour. Watch for jackrabbits as you travel through western Kansas.

73 Yucca (75W, p. 110)

Yucca, or soapweed, grows on both sides of the interstate along banks and out in the fields to the right just ahead at mile 74. It looks like a shrub, with spikes pointing out in all directions, and has large white flowers during spring and early summer. The sharp, spiny leaves stay green even in winter. Read about the many uses of this interesting plant at 75W (p. 110).

Yucca

74 Logan County

You will just clip the corner of Logan County, named after General John Alexander Logan, a Civil War veteran and US senator from Illinois during the years 1871 to 1877 and 1879 to 1886. The story of this county's name illustrates the rancor and divisiveness of early politics on the Plains. The county was originally named for John P. St. John, a Kansas governor. But St. John lost to a Democrat in the race for governor in 1882 after receiving an unprecedented third-term nomination. When he ran for president as a Prohibition Party candidate, some Republicans blamed him for taking enough votes from the Republican candidate to cost them the election. St. John's role in these losses to Democrats infuriated Republican legislators, so they changed the name of the county to Logan. Governor St. John was not totally wiped off the map, though. The town of St. John in south-central Kansas still bears his name.

75 Gove County

You now enter Gove County, created in 1868 and named in honor of Captain Grenville L. Gove, who had died four years earlier in the Civil War. The soldiers of Company G under Captain Gove's command had been so famous for being the best drilled unit that when they marched, people came just to watch. For the first few years, the only residents of Gove County were a few railroad workers and buffalo hunters. The first settlers arrived in 1871, many from Pennsylvania.

Before Gove County existed, many people traveled through the area and kept right on going. The discovery of gold near Pikes Peak in 1858 caused many folks to head west along the Smoky Hill Trail, which crossed the county just south of I-70. You'll read more about this trail and the Butterfield Overland Despatch that used it in the pages ahead.

76 Renewable Fuel from Crops

The interconnected cluster of bins and tanks a mile north at Exit 79 is the Western Plains Energy (WPE) plant. WPE began operations in 2004 to provide a new market for grain from local farms. At that time, grain prices were down due to surplus, and farmers were looking for alternative uses for their grain crops. Local farmers Brian Baalman and Jeff Torluemke organized a group to build the ethanol plant here. The simple idea to improve the value of local grain has led to a tremendous value-added industry for the region, producing about 50 million gallons of ethanol annually.

WPE purchases both corn and milo (grain sorghum) from area farms within a 150-mile radius of the plant. The grain is ground into a "meal" and slurried with water and enzymes, added to convert the starch into sugar. This "mash" is cooked, then transferred to fermenters. The resulting "beer" is separated from the "stillage" and distilled to fuel-grade ethanol. Ethanol production uses only the starch in the grain. One-third of every bushel returns to farms as a high-protein cattle feed. The stillage is sent through a centrifuge to separate the solids, which are dried to become distiller's grain, an animal feed supplement comparable to soybean meal. Other products include distiller's oil, corn gluten feed, and bio-oil. WPE has grown from just a grain outlet for farms to a leader in renewable fuel production, with multiple products and benefits to the regional economy.

79 Frozen Cattle Pools (84W, p. 108)

In 1886, a blizzard killed thousands of cattle near this spot. Winter weather still can be dangerous to livestock as well as travelers on I-70. Listen for weather reports before crossing western Kansas and read about the blizzard of 1886 at 84W (p. 108).

81 Hellendale Ranch (82W, p. 108)

To the left, notice the trench bunkers lying right along the highway where haylage (fermented hay used for feed) is produced. You may see as many as 1,200 Holstein dairy cattle, with their familiar black-on-white patches, in the pens at the Hellendale Ranch headquarters. New heifer calves are added every six to eight weeks. As they grow, they move from small pens to the larger lots. Farm manager Cheryl Madison grows most of the feed for the cattle on the ranch, which was founded in the 1930s and extends for about 3 miles along I-70.

83 Dryland Farming

Fields without irrigation rigs may indicate that this area is devoted to dryland farming. When the prairies were first cultivated, irrigation water was not available, so farmers developed techniques for dryland farming. This type of farming conserves precious groundwater. To allow moisture to build up in the soil, dryland farmers often leave some fields unplanted for a year. They plow these fallow fields to kill weeds and keep the soil loose enough to soak up what little rain they receive. By the second year, the land has accumulated enough moisture for wheat or sorghum to grow successfully. Sometimes, farmers can get two crops before having to leave the ground fallow once again. Improved varieties of crops developed specifically for dry areas are resulting in dryland yields unheard of just a few years ago. You may notice these cultivated but unplanted fields as you drive through western Kansas.

84 Grinnell: Home of Early Jerky

German farmers founded Grinnell in 1870. They shipped wheat and cattle out by railroad. In 1872, Grinnell had two large sod buildings for drying buffalo meat. In this arid climate, meat could be stripped off in layers and hung to dry. People called this meat "jerked" because of the way it was torn from the buffalo's carcass. You can buy similar jerked meat in the form of beef jerky at convenience stores along I-70.

86 "Going to the Dogs"

Quickly glance right at the mile marker just beyond the overpass, and you will see pens that had been used for greyhound dogs. Raising and racing greyhounds is both a serious vocation and a popular pastime in Kansas. The greyhound pedigree goes back 4,000 years. The dogs, which are designed for speed, have been clocked at speeds of 45 miles per hour! The Greyhound Hall of Fame is ahead at Abilene (Exit 275).

87 The Dinosaur War (90W, p. 105)

The chalk beds of Gove County were a gold mine of prehistoric bones. Read details about the work of paleontologists Edward Drinker Cope and Othniel Marsh here in the late 1860s and early 1870s at 90W (p. 105).

90 A Gambrel Roof

That barn at the farmstead ahead on the right has a gambrel roof. On a gambrel roof, there are two added ridges parallel to the center peak ridge extending the length of the roof, giving it a flatter slope at the top with steeper sections at the sides. The design is created with a truss-type bracing inside that strengthens the roof. The primary advantage of this type of construction is that it provides a high, open loft where a large volume of loose hay can be stacked. That is why the gambrel-roofed barn became popular on farms in this hay and cattle country. Of course, with the availability of big, round bales and tractors to move them, you no longer find people putting loose hay in a hay loft.

You will see other types of roofs at farmsteads, including simple one-slope lean-tos, simple gable roofs, and two-slope roofs. There will be roofs that slope up from all four sides; if there is a single slope, it's called a hip roof, whereas if there is a double slope similar to a gambrel on four sides, it's a mansard roof.

91 Skyscrapers

Fred Atchison, a forester and poet, wrote this poem about the High Plains landscape.

Security
The vastness of the prairie would be
overwhelming
Were it not for a canopy of blue sky
pinned neatly along the horizon
by grain elevators.

As you drive along, note these rural white skyscrapers pinning the sky to the horizon—some visible from as far as 20 miles away. Plains people call them prairie cathedrals.

Gambrel-roofed barn

92 Grainfield

The next town on the left is Grainfield. In an area of many grainfields, this name was appropriate back in 1879 when a little girl riding down the trail in a wagon commented to a Union Pacific Railroad official, "Oh, what a pretty green field!" The man, who had been sent by the railroad to lay out the town site, recalled the girl's comment and decided to name the new town Grainfield. Today, wheat grows right up to the edges of town, making Grainfield one of the most obvious and appropriate town names along I-70.

An ornate opera house built in 1887 is listed on the National Register of Historic Places. In the early days, stock companies would arrive by rail and put on plays or concerts for three to five nights and then move on to another town. Since local schools did not have auditoriums, the opera house was also used for dances, holiday celebrations, and graduations.

At one time, the Grainfield Grain Elevator Company purchased grain at harvest and then sold it back to farms within a 20-mile radius as winter feed. Today, all of the 1.6 million bushels of grain delivered here annually from area farms are shipped to other locations. Eighty percent of the wheat is transported by rail to markets in the United States, but some of the remainder is sent to ports on the Gulf of Mexico for shipment to China.

Corn production has increased in recent years due to the development of drought-resistant varieties and because of increased demand to supply cattle feedlots. Nearly all of the corn brought here is shipped by truck to huge feedlots around Garden City and Scott City, Kansas.

This elevator at this location specializes in shipping grain of a specific quality. A state inspector certifies the grade and quality of the grain being loaded before the railcar or truck leaves the property.

95 The Wheat State

One of Kansas's nicknames is "the Wheat State." Nearly one-fifth of all wheat grown in the United States is grown here. In most years, Kansas produces more wheat than any other state, typically 400 million bushels. There are 61,000 farms in Kansas, and about 31,000 of them grow wheat. If all the wheat produced was loaded onto railcars, the train would stretch from western Kansas to the

Atlantic Ocean. Half of the crop is exported to other countries every year. About 10 percent is used for animal feed, and another 4 percent is required as seed for the next year's crop.

Kansas grows winter wheat, which is planted and sprouts in the fall; it goes dormant during the winter months, grows again in the spring, and is harvested in early summer. Wheat is a grass whose seed belongs to the cereal group. It contains gluten, the basic structure needed to form the dough for breads, rolls, and other baked goods.

Kansas is number one in flour milling in the United States. The state is also the top producer of wheat gluten, the natural protein derived from wheat. Gluten, when dried, is a tan, free-flowing powder with a high protein content. High-protein flour from hard red winter wheat is best for making bread. Medium-protein flours can be used for making biscuits, all-purpose flour, quick breads, mixes, and other baked goods.

One 60-pound bushel of wheat seeds provides about 42 pounds of white flour, enough for about seventy 1-pound loaves of white bread. Recent statistics show the average American consumes about 144 pounds of wheat flour per year. Whole wheat flour includes the insoluble bran that makes up the outer coat of the kernels and yields about 14 percent more loaves.

The gluten (protein) and starch that make wheat suitable as a food product are increasingly being used in nonfood and industrial applications. Gluten, which is elastic and can form films, is useful for preparing adhesives, coatings, polymers, and resins. Wheat starch is used as an adhesive on postage stamps and holds the bottom of paper grocery sacks together. One acre of wheat stubble produces approximately two bales of wheat straw. This becomes the main component of straw particle board, used for furniture, flooring, and cabinets.

One bushel of wheat weighs 60 pounds. A gondola railcar will hold 200,000 pounds, or 100 tons—about 3,333 bushels. A highway truck typically carries 40 tons (1,350 bushels), which equals the production from about 25 acres. As you drive for a mile past a wheat field along I-70 and look a mile beyond the highway fence, imagine enough grain being harvested from this field to fill eight to ten railroad cars or twenty-five to thirty trucks.

In 1820, army explorer Stephen Long reported that this land was "almost wholly unfit for cultivation, and of course uninhabitable." If he could only see it now and realize how wrong he was about these productive lands!

99 Park

The tall, white prairie cathedrals and the steeple of the beautiful Sacred Heart Church, built in 1898, mark the town of Park. Originally called Buffalo Park, this is another of the stations on the Union Pacific Railroad. The town was named for the great herds of bison that roamed the area. Gove County was a popular place to hunt buffalo, and one early resident of Park was allowed to join an Omaha Indian buffalo hunt. The man's journal described how the specific posture of a scout on his horse would indicate buffalo were in the area. He noted the way the Indians' arrows were grooved to indicate which tepee the hunter came from. These grooves also allowed blood to flow out of the wound the arrow created. The Indians used all parts of the buffalo: skins for shelter and warmth, meat for food, and sinews for sewing and bowstrings. Most of the meat was cut into 1-inch-wide strips and dried in the sun.

101 Farms in the Forest

Notice how the farms here are hidden among a dense stand of trees. As we've discussed, weather conditions are harsh on the High Plains. Consequently, farmers plant rows of trees, called farmstead windbreaks or shelterbelts, on the north and west sides of their farmsteads. Settlers planted trees because the treeless plains seemed empty and they missed the forests of their eastern homes. Today, farmers and ranchers plant and maintain these shelterbelts for protection from the brutal winter winds and for shade during the hot summers. Read more about the importance of shelterbelts at 123W (p. 95).

103 Cottonwoods

Notice the cottonwood trees on both sides of the interstate, growing in low spots where water can collect. The cottonwood, the state tree of Kansas, gets its name from the soft, white, cotton-like hairs attached to its small seeds, which allow them to drift gently on the breeze. Cottonwood trees grow quickly, but they produce light, brittle wood. Native Americans made a tea from cottonwood bark and also fed the bark to their horses. Ian Frazier, in *Great Plains,* noted how cottonwoods "lean at odd angles, like flowers in a vase." He also remarked on how the bison loved to rub against the cottonwood's bark, which is ribbed like a tractor tire. In fact, in areas with cottonwoods, according to Frazier, "in the shedding season, the river bottoms would be ankle deep in buffalo hair."

106 Quinter

This town was founded in 1886 by a group of Dunkards, also known as Baptist Brethren. It is named after the Reverend James Quinter, a Pennsylvania immigrant and church elder.

Castle Rock Road got its named from a delicate chalk formation with a tall spire that towers above the prairie; it is on private land about 20 miles south of Quinter. The formation, a remnant of the ancient seabed, is known as Castle Rock. Fossils of more than 200 organisms have been found around Castle Rock.

107 Corn Bunkers

Look to the right to see long, flat bunkers that provide supplemental on-ground storage for Frontier Ag, a cooperative that also owns the tall storage bins in Quinter. The supposedly temporary storage was created in 1998, a particularly good year for corn production, and it has been used in succeeding years ever since. Each bunker holds a million bushels of corn!

Although the railroad was important for grain shipping, all the grain both arrives and leaves by truck today. Some corn is fed to cattle in nearby feedlots. Most, however, is trucked to grain millers for processing into corn products such as starch, corn sweeteners, and ethanol fuels. Frontier Ag affiliates have storage elevators in eleven surrounding towns. They cooperate with each other by specializing in the storage and marketing of different grains.

108 Corn (132W, p. 92)

You have been driving past many cornfields. Corn leads the nation in terms of acres planted, bushels harvested, and dollar value of the harvest, making it America's number one crop. Kansas is a leader in corn production. The many uses of this native grain are described at 132W (p. 92).

110 Strong Sorghum, Mighty Milo

Compared with corn, grain sorghum is typically a shorter, stronger, and bushier plant. The plant may reach 3 or 4 feet tall and will have a large seed head on top. Since both sorghum and corn are grass crops, the plants look somewhat alike, especially early in the growing season. But unlike corn, sorghum can be grown in dry, windy regions because it can tolerate longer periods with no rain.

Its roots go deep into the soil to get moisture, and the seed heads are produced late in the year, generally after the hottest weather. The low, stocky plants resist being toppled over by the strong winds of western Kansas. Anyone who has seen a cornfield after a severe thunderstorm will understand why many farmers choose to raise sorghum.

Kansas leads the United States in production of grain sorghum, growing more than 40 percent of the nation's crop. Over 80 percent of the rounded, starchy seeds are used as livestock feed. The plant also is a useful source of clean-burning ethanol fuel for automobiles. The by-product of ethanol production is distiller's grain, another valued, high-nutrient livestock feed.

Sorghum is one of the world's oldest crops, believed to have grown among the wild plants of Africa. The first seeds may have been brought into the United States on slave ships during the late 1700s. Besides grain sorghum (often called milo), three other sorghum groups are grown in Kansas: grass sorghum for animal feed; sweet sorghum for making syrup; and "broom corn," whose fibers are used to make brooms.

113 Trego County

This county was established in 1867 and named in honor of Captain Edward P. Trego, who died during the Civil War at the Battle of Chickamauga. This county was hit hard by the dust storms of the 1930s, as explained at 143W (p. 89).

114 Collyer

This town is named for the Reverend Robert Collyer, a poet, author, and Unitarian minister. Collyer was the president and financial supporter of an organization in Chicago that in 1878 formed a Soldiers and Sailors Colony here for veterans of the Civil War and their families. Collyer never came to his colony; in fact, he left Chicago in the 1890s to be pastor of the Church of the Messiah in New York City. However, he sent one or two books each week to Collyer, creating a circulating library for the settlers.

Many soldiers did not know how to farm, and others were physically unable to do farmwork. Few of the veterans came with any money, so when crops failed, most of them either headed for cities to look for work or returned to homes in the East. Those who remained were eventually joined by a colony of Irish settlers and a Czech colony as well.

115 The Lipp Farm

The red barn on the right was the center of the Lipp farm operations for nearly a century. Phillip Lipp arrived from Russia in 1907 and established a typical farmstead of the time. At this location, he built a house of sod and started farming the surrounding 160 acres. In 1917, the red barn was built, with a two-story farm home being added later.

The barn was the farmer's factory and storehouse. The workhorses were housed here, along with fifteen milk cows. Since animal feed was required all year long, bins were used to store crops produced on the farm, and there was a high center loft for hay forage. In this system, the grain and hay fed to the animals were converted into milk and cream, eggs, and meat.

Many barns of this type still exist across Kansas. However, few have animals, and little grain or hay can be found in them. They may house a car, a tractor, or field machinery, but they no longer serve as a center of production. Tractors have replaced horses, freeing up land that once was used to produce feed for them. Dairies that specialize in milk production can afford refrigerated storage and sanitized operations that are not economical for small herds. Planting, cultivating, and harvesting machines are designed to greatly reduce the drudgery of farming and improve safety while making it economical to greatly expand farm operations. Large barns are no longer needed.

A great-grandson now operates the Lipp farm, but he does not occupy the farmstead. The operation has expanded to 1,500 acres, and winter wheat and milo are the primary crops. Some Sudan grass is raised as well. This tall grass, in the sorghum family, is cultivated for livestock feed. It was introduced from Khartoum, Sudan, in 1909 by the US Department of Agriculture. It is one of the best drought-resistant plants, so it is well adapted to the drylands of western Kansas. Moreover, Sudan hay has a higher nutritive value than most other grasses, and the livestock, especially pigs, like it.

The grain produced on the Lipp farm is not fed here. It is trucked from the fields to elevators like those you see along the railroads. From the elevator, it might go to area feedlots or dairies, but more likely, the elevator is just the first stop on the way to a distant market.

117 Capturing an Iron Horse

The line of telephone poles on the left marks the railroad track that parallels I-70. Along these tracks in 1868, Indians tried to capture a locomotive "alive" by taking telegraph wire, doubling it back and forth several times, and stretching it across the track, with an Indian or two holding each end. Needless to say, the "iron horse," running at full steam, tore through the snare like a rampaging buffalo crashing through a spiderweb.

118 Windmills

Windmills have been used by Kansas farmers and ranchers since the late 1800s to harness an ever-present, inexhaustible Kansas resource—the wind. Windmills attached to pumps lift water from wells for livestock, crop irrigation, and occasionally household needs. Here on the right, you see a windmill pumping water into a tank from which cattle can drink. Wind continues to be a welcome power source for pumping water, and for some farms, it is a

Lipp farm barn

method to generate electricity. Ahead, you will see a new generation of wind turbines designed to more effectively convert the wind force to electric power. These turbines will dwarf the windmills you see along the interstate, with their blades sweeping a circle the equivalent of half a football field from the top of a 200-foot-tall steel tower.

119 Volga Germans (119W, p. 97)

Like the Lipp family back at mile 115, most of the original settlers in this area were Volga Germans. The Volga Germans descended from German families who migrated to the Volga River region of Russia in the 1700s. Although they lived in Russia, they maintained their German language and customs.

The German immigrants found the landscape and climate in western Kansas to be similar to that of Russia. They adapted well to this region, having been hardened by conditions in the Ukraine. They used what nature provided, perhaps better than any other immigrant group. Many other European pioneers moved on as the frontier moved westward, but the Volga Germans stayed to raise their families and crops.

121 Rocks on Their Way to the Sea

Because soil is made up of particles that have been weathered and worn from rocks and because erosion by wind and water is a universal natural phenomenon, it has been said that soil is rocks on their way to the sea. Although the movement of soil into the sea is inevitable, farmers try to slow down the trip.

Modern farmers are employing more environmentally friendly techniques that conserve topsoil, moisture, and nutrients. They use minimum tillage and leave residue plant material from previous planting seasons on the surface to hold moisture and slow the wind. They practice contour plowing (planting crop rows that curve across the slope) and create raised terraces that catch the rainwater, allowing it to soak into the soil rather than run off, carrying soil with it. Ahead on the right, you can see the curved terraces and concrete outlets of terraces that direct excess water runoff into the roadside ditch. All these strategies help hold soil particles in place and prevent them from moving toward the sea. Watch for these farming practices as you drive through Kansas.

123 Big Creek Valley

Off to the south for the next 30 miles or so, you can see the Big Creek valley. Lines of trees hugging the edge of the creek mark the location of this stream. You are in the Big Creek watershed, meaning water from all the surrounding fields runs downhill into this creek (another indication that the land is not flat). King Solomon wrote in the Old Testament Bible that "all streams flow to the sea." Big Creek eventually flows into the Smoky Hill River, which becomes the Kansas River ahead (mile 298). The Kansas River flows into the Missouri River at Kansas City, which in turn flows into the Mississippi near St. Louis. The Mississippi then empties into the Gulf of Mexico beyond New Orleans. Indeed, even the waters of Big Creek here in the middle of the continent eventually flow to the sea.

125 WaKeeney

You are welcomed to WaKeeney, on the left, by an A-14 Tomcat navy fighter jet in Eisenhower Park along I-70 at the first exit; a World War II Iwo Jima memorial at the second exit; and flags at the Kansas Veterans Cemetery just at the north edge of town. A local travel and tourism council member explained, "It's a patriotism thing with us."

"Beautiful location and surrounded for scores of miles by the most fertile agricultural land in the world"—this is how some settlers saw WaKeeney, Kansas, as farming drew them to settle here. WaKeeney has been a town since 1878. That same year, people from all over Trego County fled to WaKeeney for protection from a group of Cheyenne Indians. The next year, they chose it as the county seat.

WaKeeney was named by combining the names of Albert Warren and James Keeney, owners of the Chicago real estate company that surveyed and plotted the town site in 1878. These men chose this spot along the route of the Union Pacific Railroad exactly halfway, or 322 miles, from Kansas City and from Denver. They had big plans for their "Queen City of the Great Plains," including 18-foot-wide brick streets.

In 1974, the Trego County Courthouse was used to film several scenes for the movie *Paper Moon*.

126 Merry Christmas

Since 1950, WaKeeney has been known as the Christmas City of the High Plains. It claims to have the largest Christmas tree and lighting display between Kansas City and Denver. Each year, prior to Thanksgiving, the residents build a 35-foot Christmas tree made up of 2,300 pounds of fresh evergreen branches, 1,100 yards of hand-tied greenery garlands, and over 6,800 lightbulbs. If you are traveling through during the holidays, you might want to stop and get in the Christmas spirit.

128 Ring-Necked Pheasants (71W, p. 112)

Watch for pheasants along the roadside and in the fields. Kansas is consistently one of the top three states for pheasant hunting. Hunters from all over North America come to the state during the opening week of pheasant season in November. As a result, pheasant hunting contributes well more than $75 million to Kansas's economy annually.

Pheasants are not a native bird, having been introduced to the United States from China. In 1760, Ben Franklin's son-in-law tried unsuccessfully to introduce the birds to his farm. But by the late 1800s, pheasants had been established in several parts of the country. They were first introduced in Kansas with the release of 3,000 birds in eighty-four counties in the spring of 1906.

130 The Lifeline

As I-70 parallels the Union Pacific tracks on the left, consider how the railroad affected every facet of life on the Plains for more than fifty years until paved highways were built in the 1920s. Besides all sorts of people, vast amounts of food, furniture, fuel, and other freight also arrived by train—a lifeline from the East. In return, buffalo skins, grain, cattle, and stories of romance and rowdiness on the range traveled the tracks eastward. As railroads die off, many towns that were linked from birth with this economic lifeline struggle for survival, and many don't succeed.

131 Kansas Pines

At the next rest stop and at locations all along I-70 (particularly at interchanges and rest areas), you will see pine trees. Most of these are Austrian pine, a species native to Europe. Kansas has the distinction of being the only state other than Hawaii that has no native species of pine. In other words, until settlers and others planted them, no pines grew in Kansas. All the pines you see here today are native to other lands.

132 Field Windbreaks (144W, p. 88)

We have seen how people plant rows of trees as shelterbelts or windbreaks around their farmsteads to provide shade and protect themselves from the winter winds. But on the right horizon, you also see rows of trees that have been planted along a field. These field windbreaks have many benefits for people and wildlife alike. They prevent the wind from blowing the soil from fields; they help crops conserve moisture by reducing evaporation; they protect livestock and wildlife from winter winds; and they are used as snow fences to prevent snow from drifting across roads.

134 Cargill Elevator (135W, p. 92)

The four-bin storage complex on the left is operated in conjunction with the Cargill terminal in WaKeeney, ahead. Sitting along the Union Pacific Railroad tracks, this is one of the company's significant shipping centers. Trains of 100 cars are loaded every week, many destined for ports in Texas and the export market. In the busy harvest season, three or four trainloads are shipped weekly.

135 Ogallah (136W, p. 91)

The name Ogallah, originally spelled Oglala, was taken from a tribe called the Oglala Sioux, a division of the Teton Sioux who lived in South Dakota. Experts disagree over the exact meaning of the word *Ogallah.* Some say it means "to scatter one's own," whereas others claim it means "she poured out her own."

At the elevator on the right are four of Cargill grain storage bins, each with a capacity of 110,000 bushels. Wheat and milo begin their integration into the company's global operations. Sitting along the Union Pacific tracks, this becomes a busy shipping center at harvest time. Trucks bring grain from as far as 50 miles west, 40 miles east, 40 miles south, and 60 miles north. Trains of 100 cars are loaded three or four times per week during the harvest. You often see railcars on the siding lined up, ready to move under the filling chute. Cargill officials have explained that they have developed expertise for preserving the identity of products such as those shipped from this spot. The differentiated products sustain their distinctiveness in overseas markets.

Read at 136W (p. 91) about the Smoky Valley Scenic Byway, a historic canyon, and the many recreation opportunities around Cedar Bluff Reservoir.

137 Buffalo Bill

Here, as you cross over the Union Pacific Railroad tracks, imagine Buffalo Bill Cody galloping along this route. In fact, he did exactly that. The stretch of railroad you just crossed was completed in 1868 as part of the Union Pacific Railroad that connected Kansas City to Denver. Buffalo Bill came here to supply the railroad construction workers with buffalo meat during those years. He claimed to have killed 4,280 buffalo near this location in only eighteen months!

138 Growing Precious Trees

Many more trees grow in western Kansas now than during settlement days. When settlers first arrived, a single tree was a precious commodity—almost an oddity. Shade was scarce, but so was wood for building or burning, and as a result, settlers cut and used most of the few trees they encountered.

Ogallah was the location of the first state tree nursery in Kansas. The Kansas State Forestry Station was established in 1887 along the Union Pacific tracks. It seems strange to locate a tree nursery so far west in such an inhospitable climate for trees, but this location demonstrates the early recognition by state officials that trees were a valuable resource on the High Plains for fuelwood and construction. In 1865, just four years after being granted statehood, the Kansas legislature passed a law that said anyone who planted 5 or more acres of trees for wind protection or timber would be paid fifty cents per acre for twenty-five years. Subsequent amendments increased the payments to two dollars per acre and later required plantings of at least 160 acres. In 1873, the US government passed the Timber Culture Act, which gave settlers 160 acres of land for free if they planted 40 acres to trees. The trees had to be planted no more than 12 feet apart. Planting a 40-acre "timber claim" required about 12,000 seedlings. In 1878, the act was amended to require only 10 acres of trees to receive the 160 acres of land.

All in all, over 2 million acres of trees were planted under this act. The Ogallah Tree Nursery raised the seedlings to supply to settlers participating in these programs; in 1887, it grew 1,960,200 trees. Most trees did not survive long, and in that sense, the program was a failure. But those that did survive provided the settlers with welcome summer shade and protection from the winter winds, if nothing else. The Timber Culture Act was repealed in 1891 due to widespread fraud, and the forestry station nursery closed in 1913.

140 Riga Road

The trees with a grain elevator rising above them mark the location of Riga, a small town situated along the Union Pacific Railroad. The town was named by the Volga Germans; the name means "ridge of sand."

142 Plows

The original tilling of the tough Kansas sod was done by plows pulled by oxen, which, unlike horses, did not need supplemental feed but could maintain their energy by eating range grass. Now, farmers pull plows with powerful tractors complete with air-conditioned cabs and guidance from computers, lasers, and even satellite positioning data to ensure straight rows.

144 Ellis County (175W, p. 78)

Ellis County is named for George Ellis, a Pennsylvania man who came to Kansas and enlisted in the Twelfth Kansas Infantry. Ever since, this has been one of the best oil-producing counties in the state. On the right, you can see two of the many oil wells in Ellis County.

Where does the crude go after it is lifted from the ground? A network of pipes connects the wells with those storage tanks. It is then picked up by tanker trucks and transported to refineries. In some cases, it is piped directly to refineries near Wichita or as far away as Texas.

145 Ellis: Three Museums

The town of Ellis has three small museums. The Ellis Railroad Museum focuses on Union Pacific Railroad history and offers a 2.5-mile, one-third-scale train ride.

The Bukovina Society of the Americas Museum honors the immigrants and culture from the province that was once part of the Austrian Empire and now is divided between Ukraine and Romania. There is a small collection of books and artifacts from Bukovina emigrants. As you can imagine from its location on the eastern slopes of Eastern Europe's Carpathian Mountains, Bukovina and its people were deeply affected by both world wars in the last century. As a multiethnic province, Bukovina has several spellings,

Kansas State Forestry Station (Kansas Forestry Service)

but all mean "Land of the Beech Trees." The Bukovina Society of the Americas welcomes everyone with interest in the history and culture of this land.

The Walter P. Chrysler Boyhood Home and Museum tells the story of inventor and automobile manufacturer Walter Chrysler, who grew up in Ellis during the 1880s and gained experience as a mechanic. Walter learned about engines while working on the railroad. His first job as an apprentice paid five cents an hour. Before long, he was forging steel to make his own tools. Because of the quickness and quality of his work, he was soon a master mechanic.

Chrysler's boyhood home contains his personal memorabilia. The museum also displays a Chrysler car from 1924, the first year Chryslers were made. Maybe you are driving a car that bears Walter's name. Every day, Chryslers pass his hometown as they travel I-70.

Other notables who spent time in Ellis include Wyatt Earp and Buffalo Bill Cody. Walt Disney's grandfather and father both lived here as well.

147 Wind Farm

The wind turbines seen to the left are part of the Buckeye Wind Energy Center's 200-megawatt project, which covers more than 28,000 acres in Ellis County. The 112 turbines have the capacity to produce enough energy to power 104,000 homes. Invenergy, based out of Chicago, developed this site along with 67 other wind farm projects in the United States, Canada, and Europe.

Ahead, you will see an even larger wind farm up-close and learn more about how these facilities work.

148 White Roads

The crushed limestone used to pave the county roads is particularly white in this area. After you pass mile 149, you will see a road cut that clearly reveals the limestone layers, similar to those that provide the road-surfacing rock. These layers were formed at the bottom of a warm, ancient sea that covered this region.

151 Yocemento (156W, p. 85)

Across the valley on the right, the grain elevator marks Yocemento, its name derived from a combination of the words *Yost* and *cement*. In 1906, I. M. Yost and Professor Erasmus Haworth met in Hays and decided to build a cement plant on a ridge called the hogback. Behind the elevator, you can still see this ridge, now much reduced by quarrying operations.

154 "When in Rome . . . "

Looking up the Big Creek valley to the right, you will see another area where Buffalo Bill Cody left his mark. At the young age of twenty-one, he cofounded Rome, the first settlement in Ellis County, located near Big Creek. Fully confident that he was going to get rich selling lots in the new town, Cody sent for his wife and child back in St. Louis, and they joined him in Rome to start this new life. The town boomed, and within just a few months, it had a population of over 2,000 people, mostly railroad workers. Five saloons thrived on Main Street alone! But when Cody unknowingly offended a railroad official, the man decided to have the railroad depot built in newly formed Hays City instead. This marked the end of Rome, as the citizens and businesses, including the Cody family, moved to Hays City. Rather than making money in real estate, Cody lived up to his nickname by shooting buffalo for the railroad. It paid him $500 a month, plus expenses, to provide buffalo meat for railroad workers.

156 Stone House

The Roth house near the highway on the right was built of native limestone blocks in 1866. The Roths, along with their six sons and two daughters, migrated to Hays by way of Brazil after leaving Germany and living for a time in Russia. They were wheat farmers and probably lived on the land for many years before claiming ownership. The first records at the Register of Deeds office show that Joseph Roth filed a homestead claim for the farm in 1897. He purchased an adjacent 320 acres in 1904, and this land was farmed until it was sold for the adjacent warehouse/factory. The house was restored in 1975, and a buffalo grass prairie was reestablished around it to preserve a reminder of how early settlers lived. Notice the post rock fence along the property; you'll see many more in the miles ahead, with a story at 200E (p. 184).

Big batteries are made at the EnerSys plant next to the stone house. Read about them at 158W (p. 84).

157 Fort Hays (166W, p. 82)

Use Exit 157 or 159 to reach the Fort Hays State Historic Site. There, you will find a visitor center and three original buildings from the fort. Across from the fort, you can see bison close-up in the city's Frontier Park.

Forts such as Fort Hays provided peace of mind for settlers. As railroads moved west through Kansas, so did the settlers, And this encroachment into "Indian" territory sparked conflicts between settlers and Native Americans. To protect the settlers traveling along the rails and trails, the I-70s of the 1800s, the federal government built military posts along the way. One of the forts on the Smoky Hill Trail was Fort Fletcher, built along the Smoky Hill River in 1865. After a flash flood in 1867 that almost killed General George Custer's wife, that fort was relocated and renamed Fort Hays to honor General Alexander Hays, a hero at Gettysburg who had been killed in 1864 at the Battle of the Wilderness.

159 Sternberg Museum of Natural History

The white dome beneath the water tower ahead on the right is Fort Hays State University's Sternberg Museum of Natural History. If you or your children get excited about fossils and dinosaurs, then this is a great place to stretch your legs. Here, you can see the famous "fish-within-a-fish" fossil and walk among spectacular, life-size automated models of dinosaurs in their natural environment. Children get hands-on experiences with specimens in the Discovery Room. The museum, with a collection that includes 3.7

million specimens, is named to honor two generations of the Sternberg family, who collected spectacular fossils. George F. Sternberg joined the university in 1927. He established the fossil collection and played a major role in the study of North American fossil vertebrates and the science of paleontology. The museum's paleontology collection has the third-best collection of flying reptiles in the world, mostly from Kansas. If you have already passed Exit 159, you can still visit this fine museum by exiting at Commerce Parkway (Exit 161) and turning left to Twenty-Seventh Street. Canterbury Drive leads directly into the museum parking lot.

162 Boot Hill (160W, p. 84)

In Hays, Boot Hill was the final resting place of many an overzealous cowboy or unwary pioneer. A statue known as *The Homesteader* marks the location. Hays is believed to be the home of the original Boot Hill Cemetery, where men were buried with their boots on.

164 Iron Crosses of the Prairie

At Exit 168 ahead, you can visit the St. Fidelis cemetery just south of I-70 and north of the town of Victoria. It contains the fascinating and ornate iron cross grave markers that were the subject of a PBS documentary titled *Prairie Crosses, Prairie Voices: Iron Crosses of the Great Plains.* From 1870 to 1930, iron crosses were popular grave

Sternberg Museum

markers on the Great Plains from Canada to here in Kansas, particularly in Catholic cemeteries. The wrought iron was tough enough to withstand the winds, fires, blizzards, and prairie thunderstorms, and in this strength, they represented the strength and resilience of the settlers themselves. Crosses were made by local blacksmiths, many of whom learned the blacksmithing trade back in "the old country" of the Volga and Black Sea regions of Russia. Blacksmiths would vary their intricate designs to tell the story of the deceased without the use of words. The size, shape, color, and design of the wrought-iron crosses have personal and cultural significance. As blacksmithing became a lost art in the mid- to late twentieth century, marble, granite, and cement markers became more popular than iron crosses. Check out these historic pieces of folk art, and see if you can read the stories they tell of the people they honor.

166 Cathedral of the Plains

Exit 168 also leads to the Romanesque-style Basilica of St. Fidelis with its forty-eight historic stained-glass windows and its twin

Iron crosses of the prairie

spires rising 141 feet toward the heavens. You can see this church ahead on the horizon to the right.

Devout Catholic Volga German settlers built three churches prior to the construction of the Cathedral of the Plains, with its twin steeples. The present church's construction was begun in 1908 and completed in 1911, using native fence post limestone, quarried south of Victoria. According to the church history, each church member aged twelve or older was asked to give forty-five dollars a year and six wagonloads of stone to help construct the building. More than 125,000 cubic feet of stone were cut by hand, loaded on wagons, and hauled to the building site. Masons dressed the stone and placed it by hand. Each stone weighed between 50 and 100 pounds.

Read more about this beautiful church, including how an English duke contributed to the church fund, at 171W (p. 80).

167 A British Colony

The town of Victoria was founded by Sir George Grant, who wanted to form an aristocratic British colony in the United States. In 1871, he bought land from the Union Pacific Railroad and named his settlement after Queen Victoria. Two years later, he arrived with a group of wealthy young men who would be supported from home while the colony was being established. According to *The WPA Guide to 1930s Kansas,* they brought along fine horses, Southdown sheep, and the first Aberdeen Angus cattle to America. However, the young men, being far away from home, took no interest in farming. Instead, they spent their nights partying in saloons and dance halls and their days riding across the prairie chasing coyotes and jackrabbits for entertainment. Homesick for England's lakes, they dammed Big Creek to make it navigable for 8 or 9 miles. Then, they used their parents' wealth to buy a steamboat and have it floated west on rivers and pulled across the Plains on a large ox cart until it reached Big Creek. *The WPA Guide* quoted a historian as saying, "Kansas has witnessed many incongruous spectacles . . . but never before or since was there such a mirage-like sight as a steamboat chugging along in the midst of the prairie filled with a cargo of young British merrymakers."

Volga Germans also formed a colony adjacent to Victoria. Having come from the harsh steppes of Russia, they were well trained for conditions on the Plains, and unlike the young British men, they were skilled in agriculture. They prospered and eventually absorbed Victoria when the British abandoned it during the inevitable hard times.

As with most towns in Kansas, Victoria's survival was tied to the construction of the railroad. A memorial on the south side of town marks the graves of six track workers killed near here by Cheyenne Indians in 1867 while working on the new Kansas Pacific Railroad line.

169 Abandoned Air Base (172W, p. 79)

On the left behind the trees, you can see structures of the abandoned Walker Army Airfield, where until 1946 thousands of airmen trained for flying the Boeing B-29 Superfortress bomber.

171 An Avenue Exit

This is one of only two exits for an "avenue" along I-70 in Kansas. The other one is for First Avenue in Topeka, about 200 miles east. Having only two exits for avenues in more than 400 miles across the state illustrates the rural character of Kansas.

172 St. Ann's Church

St. Ann's Church in Walker, with its towering steeple, is a prominent landmark. It was constructed in 1904 using local limestone. Although close to the Cathedral of the Plains, it reflects a simpler construction. The smaller parish benefits by having a priest come from the big cathedral at Victoria to conduct services.

174 Water-Loving Willows

Ahead, notice the willows growing along the stream. Willows and water go together. Old Testament prophets, Shakespeare, and a multitude of writers and artists for centuries have linked willows and water. Read more about willows' characteristics and how the trees have been used at 177W (p. 77).

176 Russell County

You are now in Russell County. This county, which was established on February 26, 1867, and the city of Russell ahead were named after Avra P. Russell, a captain in Company K, Second Kansas Cavalry, who fought in the Civil War. He died of battle wounds in 1862.

177 Buffalo "Wallows"

Watch closely on the right in the low, wet area for a circular patch of grass that looks different from the rest of the terrain. This is a small buffalo wallow. During the spring calving season in the past when the weather got warm, the bison would wallow on the ground to try to rid themselves of their heavy winter hair. This would compact the soil and make a depression. If water was present, they would wallow in it and later carry the mud away, creating a bigger depression. As a result, buffalo wallows would form, some 2 to 3 feet deep and spreading across several acres. These wallows became dust baths or water holes for the bison. Even now, more than 140 years later, you can see different plants growing on that spot because of soil changes caused by the wallowing buffalo. Wallows are common throughout the region; in fact, golfers on the Ellsworth Golf Course (mile 217E ahead) play through a buffalo wallow on the number 6 fairway.

178 Sinkhole (180W, p. 77)

The pond on the right at mile marker 179 is the result of a sinkhole. Note the dip in the road here. Over the next couple of miles, you will notice several dips that have been caused by sinkholes beneath the roadway.

180 The Coyote and the Doodlebug

As you can see by the many oil rigs, Russell County's economy is largely supported by oil. The oil boom in the county has been credited, oddly enough, to a coyote and a "doodlebug," as described in the account at 186W (p. 76).

182 Wonderful Wetlands

Wetlands such as the marsh you will see ahead on the right are extremely valuable areas, for they serve as a natural sponge to soak up floodwaters and as nature's filter, removing pollutants. Wetlands also allow rains to replenish the groundwater rather than run off, a vital function out here on the Plains where people rely on the groundwater for irrigation and nearly all their water needs.

The largest inland marsh in the United States and one of the world's most ecologically important wetlands, about 30 miles south of Exit 225, is Cheyenne Bottoms, the 20,000-acre "Jewel of the Prairie." More than 25 kinds of ducks and geese have been seen at the Bottoms, and at times, they have numbered in excess of 600,000 birds. Besides the large numbers of waterbirds, Cheyenne Bottoms is an important rest stop for the endangered whooping crane. In all, at least 330 species of birds have been identified at the Bottoms. It is a wonderful wetland and a wonder-filled place to visit even in its tenuous condition. A detailed description is available at 228W (p. 63).

184 Oil Patch Russell

The oil-drilling rig on the left at the Oil Patch Museum is evidence that oil continues to play a central role in Russell. In the outdoor collection are rotary drilling rigs, pulling units, pump jacks, and the early steam engine power units. You can walk through an actual oil storage tank and see exhibits telling the story of the oil industry around Russell.

Derricks, like the one at the museum, once dotted the landscape. But in the 1950s, they were all removed for the scrap metal by teams of men from Texas. Witnesses said it was quite a sight to watch as the men, by hand, "flipped" each derrick up into the air so it would come down on its top rather than just tipping it over. This prevented joints and beams from being bent on impact with the ground. Then, like a NASCAR pit crew, the men would feverishly dismantle the derrick and load it for shipment back to Texas.

185 Sober Senators

Russell was once known as Fossil Station because of the rich fossil beds nearby. Fossil Lake, along the right side of the interstate, still reflects that original name. A group of seventy settlers from Ripon, Wisconsin, came here in the winter of 1871. Early accounts state that they were "good, sober, industrious people" who prohibited gambling and saloons. When *The WPA Guide to 1930s Kansas* was written in the 1930s, the authors noted that the German Russian population was still made up of "good, sober, industrious people." Russell is now most famous for being the hometown of longtime senator and presidential candidate Bob Dole. It is also the birthplace of another prominent US senator, Pennsylvania's Arlen Specter.

187 Parking Area

You have seen trees planted for windbreaks at farmsteads. Here, though, trees have been planted to protect the perimeter of the rest area, and fiberglass windscreens protect the individual picnic tables, a reminder of how the wind affects many aspects of life here on the Plains. A historical marker makes you aware that you are driving on the Eisenhower Interstate System, which has been designated by Congress for its "legacy of safety and mobility that has brought all Americans together." As you approach Topeka (346E), you will read about the very first section of the interstate system.

Notice the short stone fence posts at the parking area. You will learn more about them ahead at mile 200.

190 Big, Round Bales (213W, p. 68)

Here or on other farms ahead, you may spot big, round 1-ton hay bales that look like giant biscuits of shredded wheat. These bales, which will be used to feed livestock, are created with machines invented by an engineer from Kansas. Dr. Wesley Buchele grew up on a farm having to load and store hay by hand. This was heavy,

Round bales of hay

backbreaking labor. Read about his big, round bale invention at 213W (p. 68).

191 Water Associations (192W, p. 73)

That slim tower off to the right is 110 feet tall but only 10 feet in diameter. It holds 60,000 gallons of water and provides water pressure for the Post Rock Rural Water District. Throughout history, the quality and quantity of water resources have been a determining factor in where communities are located and the type of commerce that develops. In Kansas, over twenty governmental agencies address water-related issues.

192 Bunker Hill

The next town is Bunker Hill, which was named after a town in Ohio by settlers who arrived in 1871.

Beyond the water tower just north of town is the Bunker Hill Cemetery. At the east end of the cemetery is the grave of a young Pawnee chief named Spotted Horse, who died of typhoid fever in 1874. His father, also a Pawnee chief, had converted to Christianity and requested a Christian burial in the whites' cemetery for his son. The grave of Spotted Horse lies near those of Civil War veterans and early settlers.

194 Hawks (305W, p. 41)

As you drive along, watch for large hawks sitting along the highway on fences or trees. Most will be red-tailed hawks, which are common year-round wherever there are trees. They, along with the trees, will become more common as you travel eastward across the state. Between April and September, you may also see Swainson's hawks, although they become rarer as you drive east. These hawks have a dark upper breast, like a bib, and a distinct dark-and-light pattern under the wings when soaring. In the winter, while the Swainson's hawks are in South America, rough-legged hawks come down to visit us from the Arctic. They have varying degrees of black and white feathering, with some of them being almost all black.

197 Dorrance: The NBA Comes to Kansas!

Ahead on the right, you can see the town of Dorrance. Like many towns in Kansas, it is named after a railroad man, in this case, O. B. Dorrance. He was the Union Pacific Railroad superintendent at the time of the town's founding. But today, Dorrance is best known as the home of a company that has an influential presence in the National Basketball Association and in gyms and stadiums across the country.

Until recently, all NBA basketball rims and backboards were made in Dorrance. Now, Pro-Bound Sports manufactures the Pro-Bounder ball returner, which is used by the Chicago Bulls and other NBA teams during practices. Pro-Bound also makes many of the basketball goals and backboard supports used in gymnasiums and arenas around the United States.

This Dorrance firm has played a significant role in shaping the modern NBA basket and backboard. The company is credited with inventing the snap-back rim used by NBA and college teams. This was an essential development after NBA star Darrell Dawkins began breaking backboards with his powerful dunks. In addition, the size of NBA backboards was changed from 4 feet by 6 feet to 3.5 feet by 6 feet as a result of a suggestion from this Dorrance company. Pro-Bound convinced NBA administrators to cut the bottom 6 inches off the backboard to reduce injuries, since that part of the backboard was irrelevant to the shot anyway. Next time you watch an NBA game, think of little Dorrance, Kansas, and its link to the NBA.

199 Wilson Lake

Wilson Lake, about 5 miles north of the interstate at Exit 199, is considered by many to be the prettiest lake in Kansas. The US Army Corps of Engineers created the lake by damming the Saline River as a flood control measure in 1964. The grasslands upstream along the Saline keep it one of the clearest lakes in the state. The grass holds the soil in place when it rains, unlike areas with extensive cultivated fields where more soil washes into the water from the cropland. Wilson Lake has over 9,000 acres of water and over 100 miles of shoreline. Good numbers of walleye, striped bass, and smallmouth bass make fishing popular. Waterskiing, windsurfing, picnicking, camping, and hiking nature trails are also popular activities here. The drive along the south shore is one of the prettiest in Kansas. Exit 206 also leads north to the lake.

200 Post Rock

At the last parking area and over the past 20 miles, you may have noticed stone fence posts such as you see here on the left side of the highway. You are entering the heart of "Post Rock Country," which means post rocks will be visible along I-70 until you leave Lincoln County, about 40 miles ahead. Stone fence posts created from limestone have been used so extensively in this area that they are an identifying feature of the landscape. The Post Rock Country is from 10 to 40 miles wide and stretches about 200 miles from the Nebraska border south to Dodge City.

This area's development is strongly tied to the limestone. As the saying goes, "Necessity is the mother of invention." With so few trees around, the settlers, some skilled in masonry and stone-cutting, used the area's limestone in place of wood. Limestone is unique in that while the stone is covered with earth and protected from the elements, it remains relatively soft. Upon exposure to the air, however, chemical changes take place that turn the stone hard. Here, the limestone is in thin layers and near the surface, which makes for convenient excavation. Limestone post rocks and block-houses were a natural outcome. At 190W (p. 74), read the whole story about the 40,000 miles of post rock fences that remain.

Post rock fence post

202 Abandoned Homes (204W, p. 71)

You might have noticed an interesting-looking, yellowish limestone farmhouse on the left back at mile 201. It was built sometime before 1910 and abandoned in the late 1950s when the last residents moved to Wichita. Many abandoned homesites over the next 20 miles (such as the one just before mile 205 on the left) were built in the early 1900s when homesteading was at a peak. Today, each abandoned homesite marks the end of somebody's dream of making a living from this land. There is a move to combine adjacent farms into larger acreages.

204 Scenic Byway to the Garden of Eden

At Exit 206, you can connect with the Post Rock Scenic Byway and go north to the Garden of Eden, which contains dozens of concrete sculptures, a glass coffin with the corpse of the sculptor who made them, and a limestone and concrete cabin that is listed on the National Register of Historic Places (see 209W, p. 69).

205 Czech Capital

To the right, you can see the town of Wilson. The Midland Hotel here was used in the movie *Paper Moon*.

A Czechoslovakian named Francis Swehla promoted settlement in Wilson, and today, it is the Czech capital of Kansas. Ethnic foods and traditional handicrafts are available, and during festivals, original Czech costumes are worn and traditional meals are prepared.

At Exit 206, the products of 250 Kansas artists, authors, craftspeople, and food producers are sold at the Kansas Originals Market. This cooperative association has been featured in the magazine *Midwest Living,* and since opening in 1991 it has sold Kansas products to people in all fifty states and more than a hundred countries on six continents, bringing in more than $2 million to the artists and artisans since opening in 1991.

Wilson claims a unique relationship with Alaska, for that state's first governor, Walter Eli Clark, married Neva McKittrick, a Wilson resident.

206 Wind Turbines

For the next 25 miles, you will be driving through a wind farm owned by Enel Green Power North America, Inc., the world's largest producer of renewable energy. Each tower stands 80 meters

(265 feet) high and is topped by an electricity-generating turbine that is capable of producing 1.5 megawatts. At typical efficiencies, this is enough energy to supply the needs of 332 homes. This "farm" has 155 towers, meaning that, collectively, it could serve the needs of more than 50,000 households. (As you pass, some blades may not be turning because the winds are not sufficient or because maintenance is underway.)

The wind turbines seen here are three-bladed, upwind, horizontal-axis turbines with a rotational diameter of 72 meters (240 feet). Each blade is 35 meters (115 feet) long with yaw control to keep the rotor pointed into the wind. The turbines are designed with an active blade pitch control to regulate the turbine motor speed as wind force changes. The horizontal shaft is geared to produce a high-speed drive for an electromagnetic generator. A wind speed of 6 miles per hour will start the turbine turning, and the unit will shut down if the wind speed exceeds 50 miles per hour.

Enel Green Power leases land from the farms where the towers are located. The contract allows for access roads to be built during construction as well as easements for maintenance. Contracts vary, but in general, the farmland continues to be used as it has been previously, for crops or grazing. The towers are connected via underground electric cables that run on to the Midwest Energy Post Rock 230-kilovolt substation. From the substation, electricity is fed into the grid for distribution to factories, farms, and homes.

209 The Smoky Hills

Back about 50 miles, near Hays, you left the High Plains region and entered the Smoky Hills region. The changes are not abrupt between the regions. Instead, gradual changes occur in the land and vegetation. The Smoky Hills were so named because in the summer, they are obscured by a smoky-looking heat haze.

The elevation of this region is about 2,500 feet at its western edge and drops to 1,400 feet at its eastern border. Although the overall elevation change is only 1,100 feet, considerable ruggedness is evident over short distances. I-70 generally is located along the upland surface; along the Saline River, just north of the interstate, the river has cut canyons 300 feet below the upland in places. There is a little more rainfall here than on the High Plains, an average of 24 inches annually.

The Smoky Hills are rich with natural resources, and they provide much of Kansas's prosperity. Oil, natural gas, and salt are taken from underground. On the surface, the rich soils produce sorghum, wheat, soybeans, hay, and new varieties of drought-tolerant corn.

Throughout the region, you can expect to see sunflowers and other wildflowers such as plains indigo and prairie primrose. Upland vegetation called midgrass prairie consists mostly of buffalo and grama grass interspersed with taller grasses such as bluestems. Increasingly, you will see patches of forest along streams.

Buffalo, elk, grizzly bears, and wolves once roamed the Smoky Hills. Today, you might see coyotes, wild turkey, and/or deer in the fields along I-70.

211 Black Wolf

This small hamlet, 5 miles south, is named after a well-liked Indian chief. For many years, this spot was famous for the following sign, posted south of town:

Black Wolf, Kansas
Population 41
Speed Limit, 101 Miles Per Hour
Fords, Do Your Damnedest

212 The Lighted Cross Church

Dwarfed by the wind turbines, the quaint white Excelsior Lutheran Church on the left is known as the Lighted Cross Church. The cornerstone for this church was laid in 1908, and the adjacent cemetery has markers for people with birth dates in the early to mid-1800s, pioneers who came to farm these hills and now rest in them.

The church's cross is 65 feet tall. It is lined with forty-eight lights that are lit from dusk to dawn, making it conspicuous from the interstate in an otherwise dark stretch of road. The cross arm is a circle of lights 16 feet in diameter, arranged so that the arm appears in perfect proportion from any direction. A fund has been established so the lights will continue to glow even if the continually diminishing congregation no longer exists. The landmark is so prominent that donations from travelers have been delivered when only a "Wilson, Kansas 67490" address is used.

213 Deer Crossing (200W, p. 13)

You may see two different kinds of deer in central Kansas, white-tailed deer and mule deer. White-tailed deer are found throughout Kansas, whereas mule deer are found only in the western two-thirds of the state. Deer were essentially eliminated from Kansas in the 1930s, but their numbers have increased dramatically since then as they adapted to agriculture and even city life. Deer annoy farmers and gardeners by eating crops. But more serious problems are caused when deer try to cross highways and tragic accidents result. About 10,000 deer-car accidents occur each year in Kansas. Be alert, especially in the fall during rutting season.

214 Don't Fence Me In

The fences at the side of the I-70 right-of-way have been installed to deter animals from wandering onto the roadway. Read more about the use of fences and the development of barbed wire at 92W (p. 105).

217 Ellsworth (224W, p. 65)

You are traveling through Ellsworth County, which was established on February 26, 1867, and named after 2nd Lieutenant Allen Ellsworth of Company H, Seventh Iowa Cavalry. He established a small fort here in June 1864, on the banks of the Smoky Hill River. In 1866, this fort was renamed Fort Harker and moved to a new site a mile or so away (see 221E, p. 190). During its short history, Fort Ellsworth was attacked twice by Indians; on one occasion, a raiding party drove off fifty horses and five mules from the fort. No deaths were reported from either attack.

Exit 219 leads south to the town of Ellsworth, which was constructed near the fort site in 1867. A branch of the Chisholm Trail ran here from Oklahoma. The other branch ran to Abilene, Kansas. Ellsworth prospered from the cattle trade, as explained at 224W (p. 65).

218 The Twenty-First-Century Farmstead (220W, p. 66)

At the top of the Exit 219 ramp, in back of the service station, there is a cluster of buildings. This is the center of the Helvey Farms operations, a 6,000-acre spread. The self-contained farmstead of old—with its home and garden, livestock barn, barnyard, and silos—has given way to this machinery repair and parking center with fuel and chemical supply tanks.

221 Fort Harker

Established as Fort Ellsworth in 1864, the fort was renamed Fort Harker two years later to honor Captain Charles Harker, who died of wounds received at the Battle of Kennesaw Mountain during the Civil War. This fort provided protection to the stagecoaches and military wagon trains traveling the Fort Riley Road and Smoky Hill Trail. The fort could hold about 700 soldiers and 1,400 civilians. It is reported that a young Bill Cody took his first scouting job at the fort in 1866. It was while hunting buffalo for the railroads the next year that he became known as Buffalo Bill. Distinguished generals who visited the fort included Grant, Sheridan, Sherman, and the infamous Custer.

For three weeks in 1867, cholera swept through the fort. That experience led the post surgeon, Dr. George M. Sternberg, to become a leading authority on communicable diseases.

Fort Harker provided protection for the Butterfield Overland Despatch when it began operation in 1865 along the Smoky Hill route to Denver. A lack of protection to the west of this area contributed to the BOD's demise after eighteen months of operation. The Fort Harker Museum in Kanopolis contains artifacts and war memorabilia, displayed in one of the fort's original buildings.

After Fort Harker was closed in 1872, many families headed out along the river, where they dug homes out of the earth and lived underground like the common prairie dogs. One man, Charles Grifee, became a modern caveman. The son of a miner from Colorado, he chiseled his way into the Dakota sandstone with a pickax to create caves that served as his permanent home in the rock. Carvings and petroglyphs created by Native Americans and early settlers can be seen on the walls of caves in this area.

223 "Metropolis, Kansas"

Ahead, south of Exit 225, is the town of Kanopolis. It got its name from the vision of a new town to be called "the Capital Metropolis" or "Kansas Metropolis." *The WPA Guide* called it "one of the most extensive 'paper' towns ever conceived" and reported that "the promoters kept the presses busy day and night printing advertisements of what they dreamed would be a big city by 1900." The town was designed for 150,000 people! Four city blocks were set aside in the plans for the state capitol building. However, despite the best efforts of the Populist Party in 1893, the statehouse remained in Topeka. These ambitious plans never came to pass, but the town has survived. One mile east of Kanopolis is the Independent Salt Company, the oldest continually operating salt mine in the United States. In 1887, rock salt was discovered at the site 850 feet below the surface by people drilling for gas and oil.

224 Mushroom Rock Rest Area

There is a history plaque about the Smoky Hills region at this rest area. Here, you can photograph and climb on a mushroom rock outcropping. This formation is typical of the ones found on eroded bluffs in the Smoky Hills. The wind- and water-eroded limestone layers create a menagerie of forms and imaginary figures.

225 Elkhorn Creek Valley

Ahead, as you cross the Elkhorn Creek valley, you are in the heart of the Smoky Hills. Just past Exit 225, you will cross the creek and experience more of the rugged terrain of this area—another indication that, at least along I-70, Kansas isn't flat. The name Elkhorn reminds us that before the settlers arrived, elk were common residents here on the Kansas grasslands.

Mushroom rock at the parking area.

228 Land of Lincoln

Lincoln County was established on February 26, 1867, and named after Abraham Lincoln, who had been killed two years earlier. Because Kansas was antislavery and remained part of the Union, President Lincoln was a hero here. After George Washington's name, Lincoln's is the most popular choice among political place-names in the country. In fact, this Lincoln County is one of twenty-two counties in the United States.

Note the rows of redcedar trees planted as another living snow fence along the left side of the interstate.

229 Spite Fence

On the right, just down the slope, there are two stone post fences running parallel to each other and a few feet apart. These parallel fences, with woody vegetation between them, are sometimes called spite fences. Such fences were built where there were disputes or at least confusion between landowners about the exact location of property lines; they also were put up when there were disagreements about fair and equal maintenance of fences that were directly on property lines. The space between the fences is sometimes called the devil's lane. You will see more of these devil's lanes, which are filling in with shrubs where cattle cannot graze.

230 Pioneer Problems

Kansas farmers still face hardships, but they pale in comparison to the difficulties faced by the original pioneers. Early settlers cut fence posts from rock, lived in houses of sod, burned buffalo dung for fuel, and inhabited a lonely land. Until they planted trees, they had no shade to protect them from the harsh summer sun and no shelter from the cold winter winds.

The Plains Indians resented the invasion of settlers who were taking their land and killing their buffalo. Kiowa and Cheyenne war parties responded by attacking the settlers. Lincoln County was the site of many deadly Indian raids during the 1860s and 1870s. The worst year for Indian attacks was 1874, when Cheyennes raided settlements along the Smoky Hill and Saline Rivers, killing soldiers and settlers and destroying or stealing their property.

Early farmers faced other hazards as well, among them drought, economic depression, blizzards, and grasshoppers. National economic depressions affected Kansas in 1887 and 1893. Blizzards in the mid-1880s killed hundreds of thousands of livestock animals and many people. But lots of pioneers withstood economic difficulties and bad weather and stuck it out.

The one thing pioneers could not be prepared for was the grasshopper invasion of 1874. According to *Kansas: A Land of Contrasts,* the grasshoppers appeared suddenly in late July and August in such numbers that they blotted out the sun. In some places, they covered the ground 4 to 6 inches deep. People watched in amazement and consternation as food and grain disappeared almost instantly. Clothing was eaten off people's backs, and even the soft wood of tool handles was devoured.

The victims fought back using kerosene as an insecticide and beating grasshoppers with sticks and boards. They raked grasshoppers into piles, like leaves, and set them on fire. But their efforts to fight the insect enemy were in vain.

In *Kansas: A Land of Contrasts,* one local resident gave a vivid account of the incident:

> We were at the table; the usual midday meal was being served; one of the youngsters who had gone to the well to fill the water pitcher came hurrying in, round eyed with excitement. "They're here! The sky is full of 'em. The whole yard is crawling with the nasty things." Food halfway to the mouth fell back upon the plate. Without speaking the whole family passed outside. Sharp spats in the face, insects alighted on the shoulders, in the hair, scratchy rustling on the roofs, disgusted brushing of men's beards, the frightened whimper of a child, "Are they going to eat us up?" Turkeys gobbling the living manna as fast as their snaky heads could dart from side to side; overhead the sun dimmed like the beginning of an eclipse, glinted on silver wings as far as eyes could pierce; leaves of shade trees, blades of grass and weed stems bending with the weight of clinging inch-long horrors; a faint, sickening stench of their excrement; the afternoon breeze clogged with the drift of descending creatures.
>
> Not much was said, children huddling against their mother, whose hand touched lightly the father's arm. . . . The garden truck had disappeared, even the dry onions were gone, leaving smooth molds in the ground empty as uncorked bottles. Fruit hung on the leafless branches, the upper surface gnawed to the

Buffalo hunters' dugout (Kansas State Historical Society)

core. The woods looked thin, as in late autumn. Water troughs and loosely covered wells were foul with the drowned hoppers.

234 Buffalo Ranch

If you look to the right at the ranch with the tall flagpole, you might see a herd of bison. As mentioned previously, buffalo ranching provides the buffalo burgers and buffalo steaks that are served in many Kansas restaurants. And just like the early settlers, modern people make coats and blankets out of the animals' pelts. During spring and fall, flocks of gulls often are seen feeding around the bison.

235 Dog Soldiers (215W, p. 67)

During the late 1800s, ruthless bands of renegade Indians called Dog Soldiers roamed these hills. They attacked settlers, ignoring peace treaties and the orders of their own chiefs.

236 Saline County: Saltwater in Kansas

In 1806, Lieutenant Zebulon M. Pike, traveling to what is now Pikes Peak, camped near this location. During his stay, he sampled the stream water and found it tasted salty, or "saline." In his report to the government, Pike wrote that the region was "The Saline River Country," hence the name of both the river and the county. Saline County was organized in 1859.

Bison, Kansas state animal and US National Mammal (US Fish and Wildlife Service)

Pike was not the first European to visit this county. That distinction was earned by the Spanish explorer Coronado, who came this far east on his 1541 expedition from Mexico City in search of the Seven Cities of Gold. Can you imagine his disillusionment at coming upon a salty stream with no sign of gold and no cities?

237 Nature's Sanitation Crew (216W, p. 8)

From mid-March until October, turkey vultures will be seen along I-70 performing their cleanup duties. You can distinguish these scavengers by their red, unfeathered heads and by their distinctive soaring, tipsy manner of flight on black wings held upward above the horizontal.

239 Brookville

About 5 miles south of the interstate lies the town of Brookville. Once a cattle-shipping site and division point on the Union Pacific Railroad, the town bustled in the 1870s with 2,000 residents, several general merchandise stores, two lumber yards, flour and feed stores, and two hotels. Because the town was a division point for the railroad, train crews lived here and took the trains a specified distance in either direction, where they would turn them over to the next crews. They would then work on other trains for the return trip to Brookville.

Turkey vulture (Lowell Johnson)

One business that remained in town after the Union Pacific moved its division farther west was the Brookville Hotel. Originally known as the Cowtown Café and then the Central Hotel, the Brookville has had many notable guests, including Buffalo Bill Cody; J. C. Penney; and Henry Chrysler, father of Walter Chrysler, founder of the Chrysler Corporation. The hotel became famous for its fried chicken dinners. During World War II, military personnel at the nearby Smoky Hill Air Force Base patronized the hotel by the hundreds.

The owners have now moved their business to Abilene. At this new location, at Exit 275, a replica of the Brookville still serves family-style chicken dinners to travelers, just as the original hotel did in the 1800s.

241 Sunflowers

This is wild sunflower country. Throughout the summer months, watch for many varieties of this yellow flower, which was chosen as the state flower in 1903.

Again, as in western Kansas, you are entering an area where farmers grow commercial varieties of sunflower. You may have al-

Union Pacific steam locomotive and crew (Kansas State Historical Society)

ready noticed large sunflower fields along I-70. The sunflower is an American original. Unlike corn, which came from Central America, and wheat, which came to Kansas from the eastern United States and even as far away as Russia, sunflowers are native to the Great Plains. American Indians cultivated them and used their nutty kernels for a quick energy food. They also produced a yellow dye from the petals. Spanish explorers enjoyed sunflowers so much that they sent them back to Europe, where they were widely used as an ornamental plant. Sunflowers were never really viewed as a food plant until they reached Russia. There, sunflower oil was commercially manufactured, and the Russian Orthodox Church left it off the list of foods prohibited from being consumed during Lent.

When sunflowers are blooming, you can see how their heads all follow the sun across the sky in unison. In fact, that is how they got their name, from the fact that they always face the sun. Sunflowers are a prominent crop here, and Kansas is regularly one of the top three states in terms of sunflower production. As seen in western Kansas, companies process sunflowers to make oils and birdseed and, of course, to produce the seeds you buy at convenience stores to munch on as you travel down I-70.

243 A World of Wildlife

South of Exit 244, a section of Kansas prairie has been transformed into a beautifully landscaped zoological park. The Rolling Hills Zoo, a 95-acre prairie oasis, is dedicated to conserving and propagating rare and endangered wildlife. You can see a rare white camel, an Indian rhino, and more than 100 kinds of animals, ranging from aardvarks to orangutans. A 64,000-square-foot museum has wildlife dioramas representing habitats in Africa, Asia, the Arctic, and four other regions. Some of these exhibits have robotic human figures that speak to visitors, allowing them to experience the wide world of wildlife.

245 Hedgerows

Throughout this region, you will see fields bordered by hedgerows—single rows of rather short, rounded trees. The trees are Osage orange, often called hedge or hedge apple. Before the days of barbed wire fences, hedgerows were planted to serve as natural fences. Osage orange is a dense, bushy tree with thorns on the branches; when planted close together, they make a nearly impenetrable fence that is touted as being "horse-high, bull-strong, and pig-tight." Although native only to Texas, hedgerows were a common sight as far away as New England even before the Civil War.

The wood of the Osage orange is hard and strong. It is used to make fence posts, crossties, and archery bows. In earlier times, it was used to make wagon wheels. The hedge apple or hedgeball is a softball-size, lumpy, yellow-green fruit that is not edible. Hedgeballs are sold at farmer's markets to people who believe they repel insects and spiders from homes.

246 Bombs Away!

You can see a long way here in the Smoky Hills. Back across the valley to the right, the small, flat-topped hill forming the highest point along the southern horizon is called Soldier Cap. That particular hill is 11 miles away. From this distance, the landscape seems pastoral and peaceful, but looks are deceiving. Soldier Cap is located on the Smoky Hill National Guard Range, where jets from McConnell Air Force Base in Wichita and other bases conduct target practice with their air-to-ground delivery of precision-guided weapons.

During World War II, the Smoky Hill Army Air Base was the

B-29 Superfortress bomber (National Archives)

training center for the first B-29 Superfortress units. B-29s built in Kansas played prominent roles in the success of European and Pacific operations.

248 Breadbasket of the World

The first railroad car full of wheat was shipped from Saline County to New York City in 1870. By 1880, the town of Salina had three flour mills and six grain elevators. More than 120 years later, wheat still plays a major role in Salina's economy, as evidenced by the enormous Cargill-Salina grain elevator seen to the right, with its 140 bins that are 150 feet tall.

Sixty percent of the storage capacity at this elevator is used for hard red winter wheat that comes by truck from farms within a 30-mile radius. About 85 percent of the wheat is destined for export to hungry people in the rest of the world. It is shipped out in 100-car trains to be loaded on ships at Texas and Louisiana seaports. Cargill also purchases and stores sorghum, corn, and soybeans here.

249 Salina (257W, p. 54)

William A. Phillips, a lawyer and newspaper writer, and several other men founded the town of Salina in 1858, at the confluence of the Saline and Smoky Hill Rivers.

251 Blue Beacon

The sign for the original Blue Beacon truck wash can be seen ahead at the next exit, on the left. The concept of a fast multibay truck wash was started here in 1973. There were other truck washes at that time, but drivers commonly had to wait in long lines, and the wash could take forty-five minutes. Blue Beacon introduced high-pressure sprays that made it possible to wash a truck in ten minutes, and it also emphasized attentive customer care. The company now has a nationwide network of about 100 locations, many with three bays to maintain its short-line, fast-wash reputation.

253 Aviators

Several important people related to aviation have come from Salina. These include Glen Martin, who in 1908 flew the first aircraft that took off under its own power; he also invented the first parachute and the first bomber and founded Martin Aircraft in California. Another Salina aviator, Tom Braniff, was the founder of the now-defunct Braniff Airlines. And then there is Steve Hawley, a NASA astronaut who flew on the maiden voyage of the space shuttle *Discovery.*

In 2005, seventy years after Kansan Amelia Earhart attempted to fly solo around the world, adventurer Steve Fossett—the first person to circumnavigate the globe solo in a balloon—took off on the

140-bin Cargill grain elevators

first solo, nonstop flight around the world from Salina's airport. In just over sixty-seven hours and without refueling, he landed back here in Salina. This location was chosen because its airport, the former Shilling Air Force Base, has a runway that is more than 2 miles long. The 25,000-mile flight was financed by Virgin Atlantic Airlines chief Richard Branson. The British billionaire declared, "Virgin Atlantic is delighted to be launching this historic record attempt from Salina, Kansas, and I hope that we can add Salina to the roll call of sites like Kitty Hawk which have been the setting for milestones in aviation history."

254 Bottomlands and Uplands

As you cross the Saline River, notice how the flat bottomlands are planted in wheat, soybeans, and other crops, whereas the hilly uplands are covered with grass. Besides the obvious difference in terrain that limits the operation of farming equipment, the bottomlands have deep, rich, productive soil from the silt that is deposited when the river floods. The hills have relatively poor, shallow soil that needs to be protected from erosion with grass cover.

256 Iron Mound

For the next 5 miles as you look back across the Saline River valley, you can see Iron Mound on the southern horizon. This apparent mountain has an elevation of 1,497 feet and is capped with Dakota sandstone. The mound was formed because the sandstone is less prone to erosion and remains in place while the surrounding soil erodes.

257 Eastern Redcedar

Redcedars are the small evergreen trees you will see growing in the grasslands and along the roadside. The redcedar is not really a cedar but instead is a member of the juniper family. Redcedars grow in open and sunny places, often encroaching into grasslands unless they are burned. Although ranchers do not like them because they compete with the grass, redcedars have many positive attributes. If you have been traveling from western Kansas, you've seen redcedars planted in windbreaks and living snow fences.

Because of its color, fragrance, and presumed ability to repel moths, redcedar wood is used in chests, wardrobes, and closet linings. Cedarwood oil is used for making many other fragrances.

Woodenware and many of the wooden novelties sold at tourist attractions are made from redcedar. At one time, most wooden pencils also were made from redcedar (and the tree was known as pencil cedar), but now, only about 10 percent of pencils come from this tree. Redcedars are in the top five trees used for Christmas trees.

Redcedars benefit wildlife by providing year-round shelter from enemies and the elements. Birds use them for nest sites, and the trees' berries are eaten by many kinds of birds, as well as raccoons, skunks, foxes, rabbits, and other mammals. Although most redcedars in Kansas eventually fall victim to fire or cutting, one tree on an undisturbed rocky bluff in Missouri is well over a thousand years old!

260 New Cambria

Exit 260 south leads to New Cambria, which was named in 1872 by the town's founder, S. P. Donmyer. This settler was born in Cambria Township, Pennsylvania, so the name honors both his Pennsylvania birthplace and his Welsh heritage.

261 Alfalfa

Alfalfa was introduced to Kansas here in Saline County. In 1874, according to *The WPA Guide,* Dr. E. R. Switzer planted alfalfa seed he had bought in California for fifty cents a pound. Later that year, a grasshopper plague and drought seemed to destroy the new crop, but when rains came in September, the alfalfa sprang back to life. Switzer thought any crop that could withstand drought and grasshoppers would be just the thing for a place like Kansas.

Alfalfa can be identified by its small, round leaves and bluish or purple blossoms. It is not planted in rows, and so it appears to cover the whole field. When the plants are 12 to 20 inches tall, the alfalfa is cut, dried, and baled. The crop then grows back and can be cut again. Some farmers chop the green plants to make silage, as explained at 33E (p. 144). Depending on the amount of rain that falls, farmers take three or four cuttings of alfalfa from a single field each year.

Alfalfa is a major crop for Kansas, with over 3 million tons being harvested annually according to the USDA Census of Agriculture. As mentioned previously, those big, round bales of alfalfa weigh about 1 ton each, so if all of the alfalfa in Kansas were hauled to market, 75,000 trucks would be required. Of course, much of the hay stays on the farms to be eaten by livestock. Alfalfa is a nutritious feed, rich in proteins, minerals, and vitamins. Cows fed alfalfa produce sweet-tasting milk.

Alfalfa knows how to get a drink. Its roots penetrate deep into the soil in search of water. In fact, in some varieties, the long, stringy roots go down 25 feet. The crop also enriches the soil with nitrogen. Bacteria on the roots take nitrogen from the air and change it into plant food. Look for this beneficial plant as you drive east. It will become increasingly common as you proceed.

263 Motherly Love (258W, p. 53)

Mary Ann "Mother" Bickerdyke, the famous Civil War field nurse, lived in Saline County and was responsible for bringing more than 300 families into the county after the war. She cared for veterans and their families during the era when Kansas was known as "The Soldier State."

264 Solomon River

Contrary to what you might assume, this river was not named for the Old Testament king. Instead, its name derived from the word French fur trappers used for a leader of the Louisiana Territory—*Salmon*. Explorer Zebulon Pike passed across this river in 1806, and in his journals, he interpreted it to be Solomon's Fork. Explorers reported witnessing this river being drunk dry by an enormous herd of buffalo.

265 Historic Abilene Ahead

At this rest stop, you will be introduced to historic Abilene, a city that played a pivotal role in the development of Kansas and the United States as a whole. Abilene was one of the first cattle boomtowns, as a terminal of the Chisholm Trail. James Butler "Wild Bill" Hickok briefly served as the town marshal in the early days of Abilene.

Some independent, or non-Bell, telephone companies originated in Abilene, including the company that became Sprint. The town was also the birthplace of winter wheat planting in Kansas. In addition, Abilene was the home and the final resting place of President Dwight D. Eisenhower. The Eisenhower campus here includes the Presidential Library, a visitor center, the Presidential Museum,

Ike's boyhood home, and President Eisenhower's grave in the Place of Meditation chapel. Ike's wife and son are buried next to him.

Don't forget that the historic Brookville Hotel, described back at mile 238, is now located in Abilene. Those famous chicken dinners are served in the re-created hotel just to the left at Exit 275. Read much more about Abilene's contributions at 275E (p. 206) and 279W (p. 48).

266 Dickinson County

This county was created by an act of the Kansas territorial legislature and signed into law by Governor John W. Geary on February 20, 1857. It perpetuates the name of Daniel S. Dickinson, a US senator from New York who introduced legislation that helped create the Kansas Territory.

Just across the county line (Exit 266) is the town of Solomon. It is located at the junction of the Smoky Hill and Solomon Rivers and was named in 1865 after the latter. Early on, it was expected that the seat of Dickinson County would be located near here, but ultimately, Abilene gained that distinction. Solomon's economy was built on salt. By the 1870s, salt producers were shipping about 10,000 barrels a year from salt mines in the area.

268 Abilene's Museums

The Museum of Independent Telephony collection in Abilene includes a silver-dollar pay phone, candlestick phones, a Wonderphone, a potbelly phone, and a little pink "Princess" model. You are invited to operate the switchboard and touch many pieces of telecommunications gear to feel how they operate. C. W. Parker, who became known as "the Amusement King," built his first carousels in Abilene in the 1890s. One of his early carousels, operated by its original steam engine, is now at the Dickinson County Historical Society Museum.

Abilene is known as the "Greyhound Capital of the World," and the Greyhound Hall of Fame located here presents facts and stories about greyhound dogs and racing. The grandest museum in Abilene is the Eisenhower, which has exhibits and significant artifacts from General Eisenhower's military career, World War II, and Ike's days in the White House.

270 Sand Dunes

Notice, particularly on the right, that the sculptured landscape is different from the hills you have been seeing thus far. Under a blanket of grass dotted with cedars are sand dunes. These dunes formed over many thousands of years as sand blew up from the Smoky Hill River valley on the right. The coarse sand particles piled up, leaving these uneven surfaces on which grass took root and developed a thin, stabilizing topsoil layer. Read about sand and loess (wind-blown) soils at 270W (p. 50).

271 Abilene Ahead

The blue watertower ahead signals that you are fast approaching the edge of the historic town of Abilene, which was founded by Timothy F. Hersey in 1858. Mrs. Hersey chose the name of the town by allowing her Bible to fall open and picking a name from that page. The Bible opened to the third chapter of the book of Luke, where the name Abilene appears in the first verse. Appropriately enough, the name means "city of the plains."

272 Chocolate Factory (274W, p. 49)

At Exit 272, you can visit the Russell Stover plant and buy a wide assortment of sweet treats at bargain prices. At this plant, employees make and package 90,000 pounds of candy each day! The layout of this 401,500-square-foot plant is highly efficient. Raw materials are stored in separate silos for bulk sugar, corn syrup, milk, and cream. In-process storerooms hold nuts, chocolate, bag sugar, cocoa, fruit centers, and other ingredients. Separate production areas are designated for candy forming, chocolate melting, nut processing, caramel and fudge cooling, and hand dipping. Finished candy is stored in a 44,000-square-foot freezer maintained at subzero temperatures. This facility has its own box-making plant, a laboratory for in-process testing, and its own wastewater plant. Read about the history of Russell Stover at 274W (p. 49).

273 Bulgur Wheat

Each of the seventy-two grain elevator bins sporadically seen over the next 2 miles on the south horizon is 143 feet tall. The bins store wheat and barley for another important market. Every day, 25,000 bushels of wheat are cooked at this mill in Abilene to produce bulgur, which is one of the most important products that the

US Agency for International Development (USAID) supplies when there is a famine or other international disaster. Quantities of barley come from farms in Montana and North Dakota to be processed and warehoused here, just as the local wheat is, for USAID.

Bulgar is grain kernels that have been steamed, dried, slightly scoured, cracked, and sifted for sizing. The result is a parboiled, cracked wheat or barley. Arab, Israeli, Egyptian, and Roman civilizations consumed dried cooked grain as early as 1,000 BC. Bulgar is sometimes sold in supermarkets as pilaf or tabouli mix. Stored in airtight containers, it will keep well for six months. It more than doubles in volume when it is cooked in water or broth. From this plant in Abilene, 110-pound red, white, and blue bags of bulgur wheat are shipped by rail to ports in Louisiana and Texas, to be transported to famine and disaster sites. When it is not being used as disaster relief, bulgur is used in meatloaf, soups, stews, and casseroles or stirred into waffles, pancakes, muffins, salads, and baked goods to add a nutty flavor without adding fat.

275 Abilene: End of the Chisholm Trail

At the end of the Civil War, Texas cattle ranchers faced a big problem: they had more than 5 million longhorns on their rangelands but no way to send them to cities in the North or East. Joseph McCoy, an Illinois livestock dealer, knew he would be a wealthy man if he could move the longhorns to eastern markets, and he learned the railroads could haul the cattle if he could get them to a pickup point. In 1867, he selected Abilene.

McCoy immediately bought land for his stockyards and built a hotel. He sent messengers south to spread the word to drive cattle toward Abilene. On September 5, 1867, the first rail shipment of cars filled with cattle left Abilene for Chicago.

The route followed by cattle drives to Abilene was an extension of the Chisholm Trail. The trail, which had been employed by Indians, traders, and the army before cattlemen began using it, ran from the Canadian River in present-day Oklahoma north to a trading post at Wichita and then on to Abilene. After four years of cattle drives, the trail was 200 to 400 yards wide, bare of vegetation, and lower than the surrounding terrain. The trail was marked only by the occasional bleached skull of a longhorn or the grave of an unlucky cowboy.

Abilene marked the end of the trail for many a cowboy, and so it also marked payday and the comforts of "civilization." Abilene became a wild and open frontier town. Nightclubs, saloons, and gambling establishments contributed to Abilene's reputation as the wildest town in the West. In 1869, soft-spoken Tom "Bear River "Smith took the job of sheriff and held it for over a year. One of Smith's first official acts was to issue an order that no one was allowed to carry a firearm within the city limits. His ability and courage were respected, and even the most troublesome cowboys obeyed this law or paid the consequences. Unfortunately, in 1870, Smith was shot while trying to arrest a man in a nearby town.

James Butler Hickok, better known as Wild Bill Hickok, replaced Marshal Smith. Wild Bill's manner of dress and his deadly aim with a gun were legendary. According to *The WPA Guide,* his wardrobe ranged from the well-known fringed buckskin to a Prince Albert coat, checkered trousers, embroidered waistcoat, and silk-lined cape. Wearing a fancy two-gun rig (either silver, pearl-handled pistols when formally attired or a pair of army revolvers when in casual dress), he set up office in the Alamo Saloon. As for his shooting, it was said that he could hit a coin tossed in the air or keep a can dancing in the dirt. The exact number of men he killed is unknown (only two killings have been documented in Abilene, and one of those was a case of mistaken identity), but Hickok was not at all shy about shooting at more than cans and coins. He is quoted in *The WPA Guide* as saying, "Killing a bad man shouldn't trouble one any more than killing a rat, or a mad dog." Wild Bill bore out the saying "Live by the sword, die by the sword"; he was killed by a gunshot to the back of the head while playing cards in Deadwood, South Dakota.

Soon after Wild Bill left Abilene, the railroads connected with towns farther west, thereby diverting the cowboys and crime to those western towns. Almost 3 million head of cattle had been shipped from Abilene to eastern markets.

279 Enterprise (283W, p. 47)

Across the valley to the right is Enterprise. It was founded in 1873 and quickly became a milling center for wheat.

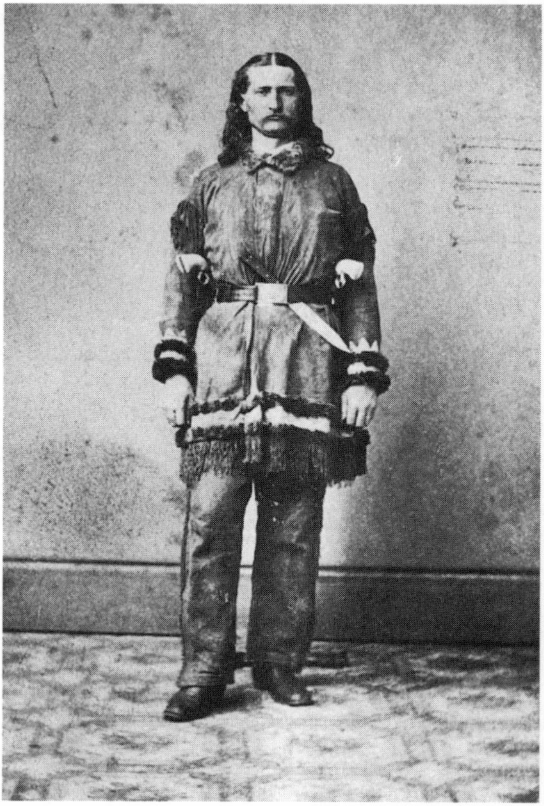

Wild Bill Hickok (Kansas State Historical Society)

282 Another Power Trail

Along I-70, you've crossed trails used by Native Americans and settlers, railroads carrying farm products to market, and roads for trucks and cars. Other "trails" transport electricity.

Power lines that will cross and then parallel the interstate are constructed to carry different amounts of electricity. One determination of the amount of power is voltage, or the pressure that moves current through the lines. To move electricity through your home, it takes 120 or 240 volts. About 6,900 volts are used to move power through lines along city streets or out to farms. To connect eastern and western Kansas, the electric line here is designed for 345,000 volts. It carries electricity from the Jeffrey Energy Center (see 320E, p. 219) to Salina and south to Hutchinson.

The three widely separated lines on these poles indicate a three-phase transmission. A single-wire neutral line at the top of the poles is a grounding neutral. You can tell the line carries high voltage by the wide spacing between cables and the long insulator hangers used to attach the cables to the tower frames. In your home wiring, a single layer of insulating tape can keep electricity from sparking off. As the voltage increases, greater separation is required. So when you see an electric line, note how the cables are separated; the greater the distance, the higher the voltage. Together with longer, heavier insulators, it takes bigger cables to carry more power.

These modern power trails vividly contrast our lifestyles against those of past travelers across Kansas who never saw a power line and could scarcely imagine the wonders of electricity.

285 Chapman (287W, p. 46)

This town was once known as Little Ireland because it was settled by Irish immigrants. It is home to the first county high school in the United States and to Joe Engle, one of our nation's premier pilots and astronauts. Read more about Engle at 287W (p. 46).

286 Why Are Barns Red?

That barn ahead at the pretty farm on the left is typical of the red barns across the countryside. Red was the color of choice for painting barns for many years, probably because the ingredients for red paint were inexpensive and easy to mix. You can learn more about traditional red barns (and other colors used more recently) at 196W (p. 72).

288 Wings over the Prairies

More than 475 different kinds of birds have been seen in Kansas. In about fifteen minutes, you will be entering an area of expansive tallgrass prairie. Read descriptions of prairie birds such as upland sandpipers, nighthawks, and meadowlarks at 328W (p. 33). The most distinctive prairie bird is the prairie chicken, which is discussed further at 308W (p. 40). Watch for these prairie birds as you drive through the miles and miles of rolling prairie ahead.

289 Geary County

This county was originally named Davis County after Jefferson Davis, secretary of war from 1853 to 1857. During the Civil War, Davis became president of the Confederate states. Thereafter, legislators

Western meadowlark, the Kansas state bird (Lowell Johnson)

tried to change the name of the county, but locals objected to having a new name. The efforts failed. In 1889, long after the war was over, the legislature finally changed the county's name to honor Kansas's third territorial governor, John W. Geary. Geary went on to be mayor of San Francisco, where the famous Geary Street is named for him.

290 Kansas's Largest Lake (297W, p. 44)

Exits 290 and 295 will take you to Milford Lake, the largest lake in Kansas. It was created by damming the Republican River. Below the dam are a nature center and a modern fish hatchery operated by the Kansas Department of Wildlife and Parks. These facilities are open to the public and offer nature trails, exhibits, and educational tours.

292 Head of the Kaw

Just a few miles ahead at mile 298, I-70 will cross the Smoky Hill River near its junction with the Republican River. Two miles from the bridge, these rivers form the Kansas River, commonly called the Kaw. Several attempts were made to found a town where the rivers join, but they all failed until one appropriately named Junction

City was finally established in 1858. At one time, settlers wanting to build a town there tried to reach the spot by steamboat traveling up the Kansas River, but they got stuck on a sandbar before they made it and decided to settle at that location instead (see 300W, p. 44).

Explorer Captain John C. Frémont, heading west in 1843, camped near this spot. "The Pathfinder," as Frémont was called, reported great numbers of elk, antelope, and friendly Indians here. Today, an elk herd has been reestablished on Fort Riley, and the animals once again roam the region.

294 Sausage Factory

The large white manufacturing facility on the left produces all types of smoked sausage and packaged pork products. It is a plant of Smithfield Foods, the world's largest pork processor and hog producer, and it operates as Armour-Eckrich, a part of the John Morrell Food Group.

You have probably purchased an Eckrich or Armour package of sausage that was produced here. This location was selected for the plant in 1995 after an extensive search and evaluation of locations in more than 1,300 counties across the Midwest. Key factors in selecting Junction City included the local population's strong work ethic and the availability of capable workers. Read about the history of these meatpacking companies and the meat industry at 296W (p. 45).

295 Fort Riley

Built in 1853, Fort Riley was originally named Camp Center because of its location near the geographic center of the United States. The name was changed to Fort Riley to honor Major General Bennett C. Riley, from Buffalo, New York, who led the first military escort along the Santa Fe Trail in 1827. A cholera epidemic broke out during the fort's construction, and more than 100 people died. Most soldiers were spared because they were away on an Indian campaign. Fort Riley provided protection for travelers on the Santa Fe and Oregon Trails and later for the builders and passengers on the railroad. Before the Civil War, cavalry units stationed at Fort Riley "policed" the recently opened territory in response to bloodshed between pro- and antislavery factions.

General George Custer was second in command at the fort, and he rode to the Little Big Horn from here. After the Plains Indians were removed from the area, many forts closed. However, Fort Riley remained open at the request of Lieutenant General Philip Sheridan who wanted it to serve as the army's cavalry headquarters.

Fort Riley's cavalry school became the only one in the United States and the largest in the world. Horse soldiers were trained until 1950, when all the units became mechanized. Because of the emphasis on horses, the fort produced the US equestrian team for all Olympic Games between 1894 and 1947. Many of our best-known military leaders trained and served here, including Jeb Stuart, Robert E. Lee, and George Patton, who passed though Fort Riley several times. When duty called for World War I, World War II, Korea, Vietnam, and the Persian Gulf, tens of thousands of soldiers went to war directly from Fort Riley. During World War II alone, 150,000 men were inducted and trained here. The base is home to the First Infantry Division, known as the Big Red One. This unit was made famous by the movie of the same name, which starred Lee Marvin.

The base covers 157 square miles, making it the largest nontraining military base in the nation. The US Cavalry Museum (Exit 301) features dioramas that depict life in the cavalry and show the progression of the equipment and uniforms from the Revolutionary War to World War II. In addition, there are original artworks by Frederick Remington and memorabilia from George Patton and other famous military heroes. The house that Custer lived in at the fort has been preserved and is open to the public.

298 First Capitol

Exit 301 leads to the first territorial capital of Kansas. Andrew Reeder, the territory's first governor, had real estate investments here, obviously influencing his decision on where to locate the capital. Reeder told the Pawnee Town Company, in December 1854, that he intended to meet with the legislature at the town of Pawnee on July 2, 1855, provided a suitable building could be made available. As soon as it became known that Pawnee might be the capital, settlers began to arrive in droves and camped on the prairie beside the Kansas River.

Work began on the capitol building in the spring of 1855 and continued through Sunday, July 1. Although there was a hole in the west side of the upper story and several floorboards were not

Fort Riley parade ground, 1897 (Joseph J. Pennell Collection, Kenneth Spencer Research Library, University of Kansas)

nailed down, the legislature convened in the unfinished building on July 2 as planned.

However, the legislators were not happy with Pawnee as the capital because it was too far from their homes. So just two days later, they passed a bill transferring the seat of government from Pawnee to Shawnee Mission, near Kansas City. Governor Reeder vetoed the bill, but his veto was overridden. The legislators hastily gathered their belongings and headed for Shawnee Mission, leaving the unfinished stone capitol behind. Pawnee's days as the territorial capital of Kansas were over.

Governor Reeder was opposed by members of the proslavery faction because they saw him as too favorable to Free-Staters. On July 28, 1855, he was removed from office and charged with purchasing Indian lands, speculating in town property, and endeavoring to influence the value of town lots in Pawnee. Fearing for his life, Reeder left Kansas disguised as a woodcutter.

300 Atomic Cannon

Straight ahead on top of the ridge, you can see an atomic cannon, one of only three in the world! This cannon was designed during the Cold War to shoot a nuclear warhead and hit targets more than 20 miles away.

Atomic cannon

301 Marshall Field

Fort Riley's Marshall Airfield is on the left. Vehicles and helicopters stored here were used in Iraq. The vehicles were painted tan, rather than the normal army green, to blend in with the desert sands. Hap Arnold, the first commander of the US Air Force, got his start in aviation by flying biplanes from this field in 1912. Today, the field is used primarily by helicopters based at Fort Riley.

302 The Flint Hills

The Flint Hills region actually began a while back, just east of Salina, but the hills will be more pronounced over the next 45 miles. These hills may be the most picturesque region along I-70 and, indeed, one of the most pleasant landscapes in the United States. They form a band running north and south from Nebraska to Oklahoma across the entire width of Kansas. The area is named for the chert, or flint rock, that covers the slopes. As you will see by looking at the flat-topped hills, they could more accurately be called the Flint Valleys because erosion has cut into the otherwise flat terrain to create these "hills." The eastern edge of the Flint Hills forms Kansas's most rugged landscape, with slopes rising more than 300 feet.

Besides the picturesque scenery, the Flint Hills provide unexcelled pastureland. Eighty-eight kinds of grass grow here. The region averages about 28 inches of precipitation per year. Flint Hill streams are usually clear, with rocky limestone bottoms and banks, because their watersheds are mostly grass and grass holds the soil in place even after a rain.

At one time, 142 million acres of prairie existed in the United States. Today, less than 5 percent of that prairie remains, most of it right here in the Flint Hills. Tallgrass prairie persisted in the Flint Hills because the soil was too shallow and rocky to be plowed up and converted to cropland, as was done in Illinois and other prairie states. On both sides of I-70 over the next 30 miles, you can see that the construction of the interstate involved cutting into the hills to level out some of the ups and downs of the terrain. The limestone is a sedimentary rock, made by sediments accumulating one layer at a time. Materials such as the remains of mollusks and corals settled to the bottom of the ancient sea that once covered this area, as mentioned previously.

The rainbow of layers in the road cuts results from a colorful type of shale that is interlaced among the limestone layers. Shale is formed when clay or silt is compressed and hardened into rock, in this case after the articles settled to the sea bottom. Notice the very shallow surface soil layer. It is no wonder that these Flint Hill prairies have never been converted to cropland.

306 Konza Prairie

McDowell Creek Road (Exit 307) leads to the entrance of Konza Prairie. This 8,616-acre prairie, which continues along the left side of the interstate between here and Exit 313, is a world-famous ecological research site. The prairie ecosystem involves complicated interactions between plants, animals, soil, climate, and fire. If any of these elements change, the entire prairie system changes. Kansas State University scientists study the plants and animals that live here, as well as the ways in which cattle and bison grazing and prairie fires affect the prairie ecosystem. Even the National Aeronautics and Space Administration (NASA) has been involved in research here.

The Konza Prairie is part of the tallgrass prairie that once extended from Texas to Canada and from the Dakotas through Iowa to Illinois and Indiana. Enormous herds of grazing animals such as bison, elk, and pronghorn antelope were a vital part of the vast tallgrass ecosystem before European settlement. Today, cattle have replaced these native grazers.

Nearly 600 different species of plants have been found on Konza Prairie, including 86 kinds of grasses. Typical grasses are big bluestem, switchgrass, Indian grass, and prairie cordgrass. Several types reach more than 6 feet tall, and two species, prairie cordgrass and Indian grass, have been known to grow 8 feet tall. More than 200 kinds of birds have been seen on the Konza. A herd of about 250 bison live alongside almost 40 other kinds of mammals and 34 kinds of amphibians and reptiles, including 15 species of snakes!

The name Konza comes from one of the more than 100 variants of the name given to the Kansa Indian tribe. This is also the source of the name Kansas.

309 Rest Area

The sunflower sculpture, about 20 feet tall, on display at this rest area was carved from limestone in conjunction with a stone symposium held in October 1986. Artist Robert Rose was joined by a nineteen-member carving team for the project, in partnership with the Kansas Department of Transportation and the Kansas Sculpture Association. Stone for the sculpture was donated by the Bayer Stone Company. A historical marker at the rest stop interprets the Flint Hills area.

310 The Little Apple

Exit 313 north leads to the city of Manhattan, which calls itself the Little Apple to avoid confusion with the *other* Manhattan. The city is home to the Flint Hills Prairie Discovery Center, a state-of-the-art interactive museum that interprets the Flint Hills to children and adults alike. Kansas State University is also located here. Because of its internationally recognized agriculture and veterinary programs, the university is now the site of the Department of Homeland Security's National Bio and Agro-defense Facility. Read more about the founding of Manhattan and KSU at 316W (p. 38).

312 Council Grove

About 30 miles south at Exit 313 is the historic town of Council Grove, located along the Santa Fe Trail. Beyond Council Grove on K-177 are the Flint Hills Scenic Byway and the Tallgrass Prairie National Preserve. Part of the National Park System, both offer inspiring views of the expansive Flint Hills landscape.

Sunflower sculpture

The Santa Fe Trail, which started in Missouri, had been used by Native Americans for centuries and then by fur traders and explorers to reach Santa Fe, the Spanish capital of the Nuevo Mexico province. The United States negotiated with the Osage Indians for passage across their lands along the route of the trail. It was from this council with the Osage that the town took its name.

On September 1, 1821, William Becknell and several other men left Missouri, and by mid-November, they were in Santa Fe. Becknell was so encouraged by the success of his first journey that he decided to try another the following year. His second trip was not as easy as the first, as run-ins with Osage Indians and near dehydration almost ended the men's lives.

The following story tells of one of the hardships the men of the second party faced after they left Council Grove on their journey in western Kansas:

> The men proceeded along their forward course without being able to procure any water, except for what was in their canteens. As these sources were exhausted the men were reduced to the cruel necessity of killing their dogs and cutting off the ears of their mules, in the hopes of quenching their thirst with blood. This only served to aggravate the already parched members of the second party.
>
> The men searched many days for water and were frequently led astray by mirages and false ponds. Not realizing they had almost reached the banks of the Cimarron River, their last hopes fading quickly, the men believed they were about to die.
>
> Suddenly, a buffalo fresh from the river's side, and with a stomach full of water, was discovered by a couple of men in the party. The hapless intruder was immediately dispatched and an invigorating draught procured from its stomach. One of the men mentioned afterward that nothing ever passed his lips which gave him such exquisite delight as his first draught of that filthy beverage.

When the Santa Fe Trail was the main highway between Missouri and Santa Fe, Council Grove was the most important point along the route because it was on the Neosho River and surrounded by forests and lush grasslands. Trail animals such as horses, cattle, and oxen were fattened on tall prairie grass and allowed to rest and drink before heading out on the long journey to Santa Fe. Timber was critical for repairing wagons and their axles. Since large trees were scarce west of Council Grove, timber suitable for replacement axles was gathered here and slung under wagons headed west.

Seth M. Hays established a trading post just west of the Neosho River in 1847. Hays's business grew to include a restaurant along the trail—the Hays House Restaurant, which opened in 1857 and is still in operation today. It is said to be the oldest restaurant west of the Mississippi River. Famous guests visited the Hays House, among them General George Custer and Jesse James. Seth Hays himself was close to fame himself, with Daniel Boone being his great-grandfather and Kit Carson his cousin. The Hays House Restaurant is still a popular spot with travelers along modern-day trails.

318 St. George (319W, p. 37)

Not one but three men named George founded the town of St. George, just north of this location. The westbound story (p. 37). explains why they did it and why one of the men was considered a saint.

320 Jeffrey Energy Center

From hilltops over the next 25 miles, you will see three smokestacks on the horizon to the left. They mark the Jeffrey Energy Center, the largest power plant in Kansas. This plant, more than 20 miles north of I-70, can produce 2,250 megawatts of electricity. It burns relatively clean coal brought in by rail from eastern Wyoming. Thousands of acres of land and lakes around the power plant have been designated as a wildlife refuge and the Oregon Trail Nature Park. Those high-voltage electric power lines that have crossed I-70 are interconnected with the Jeffrey plant to carry electricity across Kansas.

321 OK Corrals

The fencing and structures on both sides of the interstate make up corrals. Corrals are needed to treat sick cattle and to herd them together for loading on trucks headed for market, feedlots, or other pastures. They were made famous in cowboy movies and are still an essential part of ranching.

The newest corrals have curving alleys and solid panels that help calm the cattle. They are designed to effectively direct the livestock into different pens and sort them safely and efficiently. Attention is given to providing smooth surfaces and control gates that protect animals from injury. The corrals include features that make it practical for one cowboy to manage a herd alone when necessary.

322 Wabaunsee County (346W, p. 26)

You will be entering one of the few Kansas counties whose name was taken from a Native American tribe or chief. Wabaunsee, a warrior chief of the Potawatomi tribe, never lived in Kansas but was born in Indiana in 1760 and died there in 1845. The first settlers in the county were a band of outlaws known as the McDaniel Gang, who preyed on wagon trains traveling on the Santa Fe Trail.

323 Skeet Tower

In a pasture at the right just before Exit 324 is a wooden tower from which targets are launched for shooting skeet. Skeet is a sport in which shooters use shotguns to fire at saucer-shaped targets. As in trapshooting, the target is thrown into the air from a metal-sprung trap. Some targets are thrown in pairs at different levels, and the shooter is challenged to bring down both of them. Although sometimes called clay pigeons because they were originally made of clay, today's targets actually are made from a mixture of silt and pitch.

The word *skeet* is a Scandinavian term for "shooting." The sport was invented in 1920 in Massachusetts and gained nationwide popularity in the 1930s. Today, it is a popular competitive-shooting sport, and it also provides bird hunters with opportunities to develop their shooting skills during the off-season.

Exit 324 takes you to Grandma Hoerner's factory and store, where you can see the Hoerner family's famous applesauce being cooked and canned. You can also purchase many of their natural

Skeet tower

and organic sauces and preserves products, which are shipped to more than 5,000 stores nationwide. Read more about this family business at 326W (p. 35).

324 Beecher Bible and Rifle Church

About 6 miles north of this exit is the Beecher Bible and Rifle Church. In May 1854, the Kansas-Nebraska Bill passed in Congress, giving each of those two territories the right to vote to be either a slave state or a Free State. Consequently, people living in free or slave states relocated to Kansas in hopes of influencing the vote. Charles Lines of New Haven, Connecticut, favored a Free State and raised money to send colonists to the Kansas settlement of Wabaunsee.

In the spring of 1856, sixty people met at the North Church in New Haven and prepared to leave their jobs and move to Kansas to cast their votes. Henry Ward Beecher opened the meeting with an eloquent antislavery address. He also promised the congregation that he would donate twenty-five rifles and some Bibles for the Connecticut Company going to Kansas if the audience would provide twenty-five additional rifles. When the group left Connecticut, the rifles were packed in boxes labeled "Bibles" in an effort to smuggle them into Kansas.

In April 1856, the group arrived at Wabaunsee and set up camp. Some New Englanders found pioneer life too difficult and returned home. The ones who stuck it out formed the Prairie Guard, which fought in many skirmishes with proslavery groups, including traveling to Lawrence to defend it against proslavery border ruffians from Missouri. The New Englanders completed the Beecher Bible and Rifle Church in 1862. Kansas became a Free State as a result of efforts of antislavery groups such as this one.

326 Wamego and Alma

Exit 328 leads to Wamego (9 miles north) and Alma (3 miles south). Just before this exit, on the right, you might see some of the seventy-five bison at the 400-acre Plumlee Buffalo Ranch. Tours are available and are especially fun during late spring when you can see the cute 40-pound calves with their mothers. The Plumlees raise "buffalos" for breeding stock and for meat that is sold to area grocery stores. They say that "buffalo are smarter than cows and less ornery than horses!" Alma is a quiet and quaint town featuring a main street lined with original limestone buildings. The Alma Creamery makes and sells a variety of cheeses and milk from local dairy farms. You can visit the store and schedule a tour of the creamery.

Wamego is the birthplace of Walter Chrysler of automotive fame. You may recall that his boyhood home was back in Ellis (see 145E, p. 172). Wamego residents also are proud of their Columbian Theater. A local banker built it in 1895 to house artifacts purchased at the 1893 Columbian Exposition in Chicago, which celebrated the four-hundredth anniversary of Columbus's discovery of the New World. Windows in the theater came from the Brazil Building at the exposition and were among the first metal-framed windows ever built. The most valuable artifacts are six large murals (each 9 by 13 feet) depicting American prosperity, painted by Francis David Millet. Millet had been the art director for the exposition and was famous for his larger-than-life murals. This painter was also a larger-than-life hero in death: he died on the *Titanic* after saving many women and children by helping them into lifeboats. The Columbian Theater was one of the top playhouses west of Chicago well into the twentieth century. It has been restored and is an active venue for plays and concerts.

Just down the block is the Oz Museum, displaying one of the world's largest private collections of *Wizard of Oz* memorabilia, and in the city park, a Dutch windmill built in 1879 still grinds grain. See 329W (p. 33) for details about the Oz Museum and the windmill.

328 Sleeping Buffalo Mound

The hill on the distant horizon ahead is often referred to as Sleeping Buffalo Mound. It is 11 miles away! You will see it up-close and cross over it at mile 339 ahead.

329 Weigh Station (330W, p. 33)

You may have noticed an odd-looking pole hanging over the road here. It signals a weigh station (or chicken coop, as some truckers call them) that lies ahead. Such poles send signals to boxes in trucks that let the drivers know if they must stop or if they can continue down the highway.

Freight has always been carried on Kansas trails. Today, the Kansas Corporation Commission determines what can be hauled and which routes commercial traffic can travel through the state.

Sleeping Buffalo Mound

At weigh stations, trucks are weighed and checked for safety, and state workers determine whether all appropriate road and fuel taxes have been paid. Weight and size limits are described at 330W (p. 33), and you can read more about semis at 243W (p. 58).

330 Mill Creek

For the next 3 miles, you will pass through flat and fertile bottomlands surrounded by hills. This is the floodplain for Mill Creek, which once provided waterpower to a grist mill. It is one of fourteen Mill Creeks in Kansas!

This bottomland is planted to crops of corn and soybeans, unlike the grassy hills that are grazed by cattle. The deep, rich soil was deposited over thousands of years by the flooding of Mill Creek.

331 Wine Country (334W, p. 31)

At Exit 333, you will see the Wildwood Cellars Winery outlet on the left. This is the largest licensed winery in Kansas. It is one of more than two dozen wineries in the state with tasting rooms. Wildwood Cellars' signature product is elderberry wine. The elderberry plant, with dark-purple berries, is considered a noxious weed, and it grew wild on the Brewer family farm. In 1988, however, in an effort to make the farm more profitable the brother and sister team of Dr. John Brewer and Merry Bauman began producing and commercializing elderberry wine, jelly, and a concentrate that can be added to drinks and other products.

Wildwood Cellars continues a long tradition of wine making in Kansas. The Kansa Indians were growing grapes in the area at least as early as 1794. In 1865, the community of Doniphan started vineyards along the Missouri River and made wines to offset the loss of trade with riverboats, which were being replaced by the railroads.

332 Paxico: Antique Town

Paxico, between Exits 333 and 335, is regionally known for its antique stores. Anyone interested in antiques should take a few minutes to explore this charming town. Pottery made here has been featured in national magazines.

Paxico got its name from a Potawatomi medicine man named Pashqua. The land here was part of the Potawatomi Reservation, but in 1868, the government sold some of it to the Atchison, Topeka and Santa Fe Railroad. The railroad ultimately decided to build its tracks farther south, and so, in turn, it sold the land to the Rock Island line. Two towns, Paxico and Newbury, were vying for the railroad to come to their site. The Rock Island decided to build along the banks of Mill Creek, so both groups compromised and jointly chose a new site along the railroad. On December 30, 1886, six blocks with 100 lots were laid out. By July of the next year, the new Paxico had a three-story hotel, two dry goods and grocery stores, two blacksmith and wagon shops, a billiard hall, a barber shop, a restaurant, a shoe shop, a drugstore, two lumber yards, and several other buildings under construction. The population peaked in the early 1900s, with about 400 people living there. The population is about 200 today.

335 Guard of the Plains

Try to spot the sculpture ahead, among the trees on top of the hill. Many local people believe that this work, titled *Guard of the Plains,* represents a howling coyote. From any angle—and to a viewer who has a bit of imagination—it does resemble a coyote with its head thrown back, howling skyward. However, the sculptor, James Kirby Johnson, created the piece to symbolize a windmill and honor the vital role windmills played in harnessing the wind for the good of humans on the Plains. You can hike the trail at the rest stop ahead to get an up-close look at the sculpture.

336 Rest Stop

The next rest stop features modern picnic shelters, a historical marker telling about the settlement and development of this region, and a memorial to highway workers killed on the job. It also offers native wildflower plantings and a woodland trail that leads to the top of the hill and provides panoramic views of the Flint Hills.

337 Real Coyotes

You may have already spotted coyotes in the fields along the interstate. Sometimes, you'll see them crossing the interstate, and often, if you notice roadkills along the shoulder, you'll see coyotes that did not make it. Coyotes are most active at night, but you may see one during the day, especially in the morning and evening. They eat almost anything—plant or animal—and this versatility is one reason why their numbers are increasing in Kansas and throughout the United States. Now, they even can be found in cities, howling at a streetlight rather than the full moon!

338 Sleeping Buffalo Mound (341W, p. 28)

You first saw Sleeping Buffalo Mound 10 miles back. Notice as you drive over the mound and head down the back side that on the right, the vegetation is almost entirely grass. The rancher on the right side burns the prairie annually to promote lush, nutritious grass for grazing. Burning controls weeds in the prairie, as well as the invasion of woody plants. Read more about prairie fires at 341W (p. 28).

340 St. Marys (342W, p. 28)

St. Marys, located about 12 miles north of I-70 on what once was the Oregon Trail, originally was a Jesuit mission to the Potawatomi Indians. The mission later served as a training school for the Indians, then a school for Catholic children and a Jesuit seminary; it finally closed in the 1960s.

341 Hudson Ranch

For the next 3 miles, you will be driving by the Hudson Ranch. This property is more than 10,000 acres and is just one of the large ranches owned by the Hudson family in Kansas. Parts of this ranch extend for miles along the interstate.

The Hudson Ranch is a "cow-calf" operation. At any given time, 1,200 mother cows may be on the range. Some calves are sold, others are sent to Oklahoma or Texas to graze, and still others are sent to feedlots to gain weight. Some calves are raised all the way to market weight and then sold. Every year is different on the ranch as ranchers respond to weather, forage conditions, and market prices.

The ranch is mostly native grass, but a few thousand acres are pastures of nonnative "cool season grasses," which allows for year-round grazing. Providing water for the cattle is just as important as providing nutritious grass for them to eat. Farm ponds are visible on the right. The ranch has about fifty ponds, with at least two in each square mile of ranchland. The Hudson's home is perched high on a hill to the right at mile 343.

343 Gullies

You may notice some depressions and gullies in the pastures on the right, especially near the ponds. Erosion is increased when cattle use the same trails every day to drink from the ponds. Grass near the trails is eaten and trampled, and it no longer holds the soil in place. Water washes down these paths and causes depressions and then gullies. Banks form along the gullies. As cattle walk on the banks, the soil collapses and crumbles. The next rain washes away this soil, thereby making the gullies deeper and wider. This process will continue until the banks are stabilized with new grass or shrubs.

344 Tall Tower (350W, p. 24)

For the next few miles, you can see the 1,440-foot-tall KTKA-TV transmission tower on the right. Read about the impact of structures like this on bird life at 350W (p. 24).

345 Willard and Rossville

About 3 miles north of the next exit is the town of Willard. It was once the site of Uniontown, which was established as a trading post for the Potawatomi Indians in 1848. Uniontown suffered two outbreaks of cholera and was burned and abandoned in 1859.

Just north of Willard across the Kansas River is the town of Rossville. Rossville was named for William Ross, who came from Wisconsin in 1855 and later served as a Potawatomi Indian agent. William's brother, Edmund Ross, became a US senator in the 1860s and cast the deciding vote against the conviction of President Andrew Johnson after his impeachment by the House of Representatives.

346 Shawnee County: Home to a Historic Highway

Pioneers first settled in Shawnee County along Mission Creek, which you will cross ahead near mile 351. The county, established in 1855, was named for the Shawnee Indians.

You are traveling on a historic piece of highway. The 8-mile stretch of I-70 from the Shawnee County line to the Topeka city limits was the first section of the US interstate system to be completed. It was opened on November 14, 1956, less than four months after President Eisenhower signed the Interstate Highway Act of 1956. This, then, is the birthplace of the nation's interstate system, the largest public works project in US history.

Ike had traveled across the United States from Washington, DC, to San Francisco on what is known as the Great Motor Truck Convoy of 1919. This convoy of army vehicles was meant to test both our nation's roads and the vehicles that had been used in World War I. The results were not good. Most roads were dirt, bridges collapsed along the way, vehicles constantly broke down, and the convoy averaged only a few miles per hour. Ike personally wrote the dismal trip report for the tank corps, concluding that our nation's road system needed great improvement, as did our military vehicles. An early piece of legislation leading up to the Interstate Highway Act was, in fact, called the National Defense Highway Act.

Eisenhower gained additional experience with roadways in Europe during World War II. Hitler's autobahn moved military and civilian vehicles efficiently. This impressed upon Ike the importance of having good highways to move military personnel and equipment; he also understood the importance of being able to evacuate cities quickly in the event of attack. In fact, one of the goals of the highway act was to link all cities having a population greater than 50,000 people. So, to a significant degree, interstate highways are an artifact of war and especially the Cold War with the Soviet Union. They were born out of the need for evacuations, not vacations. President Eisenhower apparently envisioned the ultimate rush hour, but he may never have imagined motorists dealing with daily morning and evening commutes using traffic reports from helicopters to guide them along these interstates to safe havens of home or work.

350 Healing Horses

Ahead 1 mile on the right, after crossing Mission Creek, you will spot the Arrow H Stables. For more than twenty years, Lee Hart has trained horses and taught riding to young and old alike. He boards about fifteen horses for other folks and has an additional fifteen that he uses for training. The most rewarding aspect of his job is teaching young people to ride and through riding to build confidence, self-control, self-esteem, and healthy lifestyles. Horse therapy, which includes not only riding but also on-the-ground activities such as feeding, grooming, and leading the horses, has been used successfully in addressing mental health issues such as depression, ADHD, post-traumatic stress disorder, eating disorders, and anxiety. It even has been used to treat children with Asperger's and autism. Clients call Lee "the horse whisperer" because he is so in tune with the needs of both horse and the rider.

352 Topeka: A "Capital" Place to Dig Potatoes

Just ahead is Topeka, the state's capital and fifth-largest city. Colonel Cyrus Holliday, who became the first mayor, wanted to name the town Webster after Daniel Webster, but others wanted a more colorful local name. *Topeka* comes from three Indian words that have the same meaning among the Otoes, Omahas, Iowas, and Kaws. *To* means "wild potato" (or other edible root), *pe* means "good," and *okae* means "to dig." Thus, *Topeka* means "a good place to dig potatoes."

Among the first settlers in the Topeka area were the French-Canadian Pappan brothers. They married three Kansa Indian sisters and established a ferry operation over the Kansas River in 1842. The Oregon Trail crossed the river at Topeka, and as a result, several ferryboat services were established here.

On December 5, 1854, nine antislavery men met on the banks of the Kansas River at what is now Kansas Avenue and Crane Street and drew up the first plans for establishing a town. Topeka was incorporated in 1857 and became the capital of Kansas in 1861. Mayor Holliday, a Pennsylvania native, became better known as the founder of the Atchison, Topeka and Santa Fe Railroad, which spawned further growth and made Topeka a prominent railroad town.

Topeka is the home of astronaut Ron Evans, commander of the pilot ship on the *Apollo 17* flight to the moon. It's also the home of the popular musical group Kansas. Other famous Topeka residents have included noted psychologist Dr. Karl Menninger and Charles Curtis, who served as vice president during Herbert Hoover's administration. Curtis is the only partial Native American to have served in this post.

Another interesting resident was Sergeant Boston Corbett, the man who shot John Wilkes Booth, assassin of President Lincoln. Corbett defied specific orders to take the assassin alive, claiming that God had told him to avenge the assassination. He later served as doorkeeper at the Kansas capitol building, which you will see shortly. While serving there, he became violent—shooting his pistol off in the building and threatening visitors and employees. He was arrested and sent to the State Hospital for the Insane. But Corbett stole a visitor's pony from a hospital hitching post and escaped. He lived in a dugout shelter in Concordia, Kansas, for a while and eventually escaped to Mexico.

354 Museum and Menninger (358W and 357W, p. 22)

The Kansas Museum of History can be reached by taking the Wanamaker Road, Exit 356. The museum is located on a branch of the Oregon Trail. The vast and rich history of Kansas is told through exhibits that make the experience of living in a log house or traveling in a covered wagon come to life. A nature trail provides an opportunity to stretch your legs and learn about the natural surroundings.

If the spire rising above the trees on the hill to the left beyond the exit looks familiar, it is because it is part of a replica of Independence Hall in Philadelphia. For many years, this building was the home of the Menninger Foundation, a world-famous center for the study of psychological disorders, founded by author and psychologist Karl Menninger.

357 Governor's Mansion

To the left, on a hill and set back in a parklike setting, is Cedar Crest, the Kansas governor's mansion. The land around the mansion is open as a public park and includes trails, as well as ponds for fishing and ice-skating.

Governor's mansion

358 Twisters

The wind turbine ahead at the Kanza Education and Science Park (360W, p. 22) reminds us of the power of wind. Sometimes, powerful Kansas winds are destructive. Ever since Dorothy and Toto were carried off from Kansas to the Land of Oz, the state has been associated with tornadoes. One of the most disastrous occurred right here in Topeka. That tornado came through shortly after 7:00 p.m. on June 9, 1966, claiming 16 lives and injuring more than 500 people. The F5 tornado (the most intense category) cut a 22-mile path through the heart of the city. According to the *Topeka Capital-Journal*, "Trees were ripped helter-skelter. Homes were wrecked, roofs blown away and residents, who had sought safety, were staring at the ruins of their homes, sobbing in disbelief." The capitol dome sustained damage from tremendous flying debris.

Bill Kurtis was a law student who was filling in for a friend at the local CBS station that evening. When it became apparent that the tornado was destroying parts of Topeka, he urged people to "for God's sake, take cover!" His was the only television station not damaged by the tornado, and he stayed on the air for twenty-four hours. This dramatic event led him to forgo his law career and start down the path that led to a thirty-year career at CBS; in the process, he became a household name as a broadcast journalist and documentary producer.

In spite of the threat of tornadoes, most Kansans believe, like Dorothy, there is no place like home.

360 The Capitol

Ahead, as you curve through downtown Topeka, you will see the capitol dome to the right of the interstate. The Kansas capitol, completed in 1903, was modeled after the Capitol in Washington, DC, but wings were added to the rotunda section to create the shape of a cross, emphasizing the strong role of religion in the state. Inside the rotunda are murals depicting the story of Kansas, painted by native Kansan artist John Steuart Curry. One mural depicting famed abolitionist John Brown is particularly impressive. Curry also painted the murals at the Wisconsin state capitol. The capitol in Topeka is considered the state's most important architectural treasure. The Kansas Capitol Visitor Center has a gift shop and interpretive exhibits. Dome tours give a bird's-eye view of Topeka. Read about the statue on top of the capitol dome at 364W (p. 20).

361 Twin Spires

From a certain angle, the two spires of St. Joseph's German Catholic Church appear to contain the faces of owls, with the clocks forming the eyes. This Romanesque-style church was built in 1899 to serve the large German community here. For many years, the notably long sermons were preached in German.

362 The Road to Justice

Exit 362B will take you to the Brown v. Board National Historic Site, which tells the story of the 1954 landmark Supreme Court ruling that declared that state laws establishing separate schools for black and white students were unconstitutional. The Supreme Court unanimously (9–0) decided that "separate educational facilities are inherently unequal." You can tour the historic Monroe School building and experience engaging galleries about the civil rights movement, as well as interact with exhibits depicting the road to justice in America.

364 Topeka Industry

You have continued to see grain elevators, which testify to the importance of the food industries in Topeka. Frito-Lay and Hill's Pet

St Joseph's German Catholic Church

Products have factories here. And on the left just before mile 365, you will see the tortilla and taco factory of Reser's Fine Foods. Other major industry employers include Goodyear Rubber and Tire; Burlington Northern Santa Fe Railway; Payless Shoes; and the Mars chocolate factory, which makes M&Ms and millions of candy bars each year, including Snickers.

365 Symbols of Kansas

As you leave the capital city, you might reflect on Kansas's official state symbols. If you have been traveling from western Kansas and reading along, you have already been introduced to our state flower (the wild native sunflower), our state tree (the cottonwood), and our state bird (the western meadowlark). Likewise, if you read the accounts from western stretches of I-70, you will not be surprised to learn that the American buffalo, or bison, is the state animal (really, they meant state *mammal* because birds are animals, too). However, you might not guess that Kansas's official state reptile is the ornate box turtle, the state amphibian is the barred tiger salamander, and the state insect is the honeybee.

366 Woodlawn Dairy Farm

The white board fences outline the Woodlawn Farm property ahead on the left. When the new toll plaza was built in 2001, much of the land came from Woodland Farm. Read about this farm at 186W (p. 18).

After mile 366, I-70 joins the Kansas Turnpike. Note that the mileage number system now reflects the distance along the turnpike from the Oklahoma border. (The mile markers to this point have indicated the distance from the Colorado line.) Thus, Woodland Farm is about 366 miles from Colorado and 183 miles from Oklahoma. The stories that follow continue to refer to mile markers as they appear on the roadside.

184 Kansas Turnpike

Construction of the Kansas Turnpike began on December 31, 1954. The state legislature had authorized the Turnpike Authority to sell bonds to private investors to pay for construction and the expenses of the Turnpike Division of the Kansas Highway Patrol. Motorists pay for the road only when they drive on it, since no tax dollars are used for the toll road.

The 236-mile Kansas Turnpike was completed in a record twenty-two months. After the interstate system was created in 1956, federal planners chose to incorporate the turnpike but with no reimbursement to the state. As you travel the turnpike, your car is one of more than 51,000 vehicles a day that make a trip on this road, each averaging more than 40 miles.

186 The Oregon Trail

At the crest of the hill, this modern trail crosses a historic trail. Specifically, the Oregon Trail intersects I-70, then follows the ridge to the right of the interstate for the next several miles. The Oregon Trail generally went along the ridgetops of rolling Kansas hills to avoid stream crossings and the ups and downs of the terrain, thereby reducing stress on the animals pulling the wagons. In a sense, the early travelers were taking care of their "engines" to improve their mileage and reduce maintenance.

What became the Oregon Trail was first used by fur traders returning from the mouth of the Columbia River in 1813. In 1830, William Sublette took the first wagons along this route to the Rocky

Mountains. Traffic increased dramatically in 1849 as a result of the California gold rush. Some things never change, as Kansas is still a state that is experienced mostly by people passing through along cross-country “trails.” But what a contrast it is to be traveling at 70 miles per hour along the I-70 trail, in the comfort of a smooth-riding, temperature-controlled vehicle, rather than being exposed to rain, snow, ice, heat, wind, and cold in a slow and bumpy ox cart for weeks on end.

188 Douglas County

This county is named for Senator Stephen A. Douglas of Illinois, who wrote the Kansas-Nebraska Bill that allowed the formation of Kansas and Nebraska and gave them the right to choose whether they would be free or proslavery states during the Civil War era. Many assumed that Nebraska would be a free state and Kansas a slave state. But shortly after President Franklin Pierce signed the antislavery bill, immigrants from New England and other antislavery states came to Kansas to tip the balance in favor of freedom. Clashes erupted between the proslavery and antislavery settlers, resulting in the new territory becoming known as Bleeding Kansas.

Many eastern Kansas towns from Manhattan to Lawrence trace their histories to people who migrated from eastern states to make Kansas a free state. These abolitionists were successful, and Kansas sided with the North during the Civil War.

189 Big Springs

South of the interstate is the small farming community of Big Springs. When William Harper and John Chamberlain established Big Springs in the fall of 1854, it was known as an excellent watering place along the Oregon Trail. The town became an important trading post as travelers immigrated west. The springs that gave the town its name have since dried up. Read about two noteworthy events that occurred in Big Springs at 191W (p. 16).

190 Numbered Signs

On the right along the fence row, you may have noticed yellow signs with three-digit black numbers on them. Oil and natural gas companies use these signs, which are angled so they can be seen from an airplane, to check for leaks, vegetation in need of removal, and other problems with buried pipelines or cables. Problems are reported to ground crews, which are then dispatched to make repairs. The orange signs on the white posts indicate a buried telephone communications line.

192 The Clock House (193W, p. 16)

The clock over the front porch on the house ahead on the right was added in 1985. The owners found the clockworks at the Catholic church in Fairbury, Nebraska. It was restored, but it occasionally needs adjustment—so don't correct the time on your car clock! The clock face came from a clock that was at the Harvey County Courthouse in Newton, Kansas.

The house was built in 1905 from a kit ordered from Sears, Roebuck. All the parts, including window glass and doors, were shipped by rail to Lecompton, then hauled the final 6 miles by horse and wagon. It was erected at the high point of a 640-acre farm as a summer home. In 1908, it was selected as the National Farmhouse of the Year.

The house originally was a square, two-story design. The first floor consisted of the kitchen, dining room, living room, and parlor with a fireplace. Upstairs were four bedrooms. This house had many amenities that were not generally found in rural homes of that time, such as a 5,000-gallon water cistern and an electric generator. A classic original bathtub is still in use.

194 Roadside Gardens

Ralph Waldo Emerson once said, "The earth laughs in flowers." During the summer, stretches of I-70 laugh in wildflowers. You may have noticed the native wildflower signs along the road back at Exit 366 just before the tollbooths. Between here and Kansas City, notice the wildflowers growing along the road. Because a variety of flowers grow here and because their blooming periods are short and varied, it is impossible to know what will be blooming when you drive by, but here are some possibilities in the roadside garden. Pinkish or purple flowers might be prairie phlox, purple prairie clover, bee balm, various gayfeathers and milkweeds, verbena, ironweed, or *Echinacea* (sometimes called purple coneflower, a popular medicinal plant). Blue flowers may be chicory, a plant whose roots can be used to make a coffee. White flowers might be Queen Anne's lace, white evening primrose, white prickly poppy, daisy fleabane, and the greenish and creamy white "snow-on-the-mountain." In autumn, heath aster may be blooming

Yellow flowers include black-eyed Susan, flannel mullein, Missouri evening primrose, compass plant, various kinds of coreopsis, goldenrod, and of course the ubiquitous sunflower. The most conspicuous orange flowers are those of the butterfly milkweed, which brighten roadsides and prairies in June and July.

195 Drink Up!

The large building to your left is Berry Plastic Corporation's half-million-square-foot warehuse and manufacturing plant. More than 200 employees work around the clock seven days a week, producing 2 million plastic cups a day! Logos of all the major fast food restaurants are added to the cups in an onsite print shop before they are shipped out. If you have stopped for a soft drink on your trip, you probably have drunk from a cup made at this plant. The facilty also makes containers for potato salad, coleslaw, and other such products.

196 Lecompton: "Bald Eagle, KS"

Ahead is the exit to Lecompton. The town, founded in 1855, was originally named Bald Eagle for the eagles that roosted in trees along the Kansas River. Later, it was renamed in honor of Judge Samuel Lecompte, who presided over the town company that surveyed the 600-acre site halfway between Topeka and Lawrence on the Kansas River.

The proslavery leaders made it their territorial capital, and workers began building the state capitol as well as the governor's house. However, three years later, when the Free-State forces were victorious in Kansas, Topeka became the capital and the booming town went bust. There is more about Lecompton at 198W (p. 14).

Today, bald eagles still roost along the Kansas River and nest at Clinton Lake just south of this location. Watch for eagles soaring overhead, especially during the winter months.

198 Lawrence

The city of Lawrence, ahead, traces its roots back to Eli Thayer of Worcester, Massachusetts, who organized the New England Emigrant Aid Company to resist proslavery powers in Kansas. The company's first settlers arrived in the Lawrence area in August 1854.

Soon after the pioneers arrived, they adopted the name of Lawrence in honor of Amos Lawrence, a Massachusetts financier of the New England Company. Interestingly, Lawrence deplored naming the Kansas town after him. He feared that it would give the appearance of self-promotion, which would lessen his personal influence in the Free-State cause.

Lawrence had a bloody beginning. The newly arrived New Englanders fought with proslavery forces from Missouri. Proslavery raiders attacked the antislavery Lawrence residents here on two occasions, first on May 21, 1856, and again on August 21, 1863.

In the 1863 raid, a posse of 450 men led by William Clarke Quantrill attacked Lawrence and its 2,000 surprised and terrified citizens. The first person killed was the Reverend S. S. Snyder, who was shot in his barnyard 2 miles outside of town. Quantrill and his band then rode into Lawrence and down the main street, Massachusetts Street, burning houses, destroying two newspaper presses, and setting fire to the Eldridge Hotel. After about four hours, Quantrill and his raiders withdrew, leaving more than 150 dead and more than 100 homes and businesses destroyed. Resis-

Quantrill's raid (Internet Archive)

tance by the townspeople was so weak that only one of Quantrill's men was killed in the raid.

200 Jayhawks

In 1866, Lawrence's significance to Kansas and the world changed forever. A solitary building was erected on Hogback Ridge. This building marked the start of the University of Kansas. Use Exit 202 to visit the beautiful campus. Hogback Ridge seemed to be an undignified name for the location of a dignified institution, so the name was changed to Mount Oread. Mount Oread also happened to be the name of a girls' seminary in Worcester, Massachusetts, home of the previously mentioned Eli Thayer. By looking right over the next few miles, you can glimpse red-roofed campus buildings perched high on Mount Oread.

Today, KU is a world-class university with more than 28,000 students from all 50 states and more than 100 countries. The jayhawk mascot is a familiar image throughout the state. The jayhawk is a mythical bird whose name combines the names of two groups of intelligent and aggressive birds, jays and hawks. Though the origin of the word *jayhawk* is unknown, one story tells of a pioneer who crossed Kansas with a bare minimum of provisions, saying he would survive the remainder of his journey by "jayhawking" his way. The term *jayhawk* was used to describe antislavery individuals who raided Missouri, and it has been applied to any particularly tough, resilient group of individuals.

KU has a long history of excellent basketball teams. In fact, the inventor of basketball, Dr. James Naismith, was a faculty member from 1898 to 1937. A coach here for thirty-nine years, Phog Allen was a driving force behind basketball becoming an Olympic sport in 1936, and he was also behind organizing the NCAA basketball tournament. Many KU basketball players have gone on to stardom in the NBA, including the great Wilt Chamberlain.

202 The Kaw (203W, p. 13)

You will be crossing the Kansas, or Kaw, River. As mentioned at 292E (p. 210), this river begins in Junction City where the Republican and Smoky Hill Rivers come together. It continues on to join the Missouri River in Kansas City.

203 Grass Farm

The Pine family produces sod at the farm ahead on the left. The Pines' grass crop is rolled up and delivered for new lawns. They also cover large areas with their sod, such as the infield at the Kansas Speedway (ahead near mile 226). Besides grass, the farm raises traditional crops—corn, soybeans, and potatoes. Since the early 1970s, sod has been sold as a way to stretch out the harvest season and to hedge against a failure of the weather-sensitive potato crop. Read more about the Pine farm at 205W (p. 12).

204 Sand Pit/Phosphorus Factory

The lake on the right was once a sand quarry. Because of its depth, waterfowl use its open waters during their fall and spring migrations.

Across the lake, the Astaris factory has the appearance of a chemical plant. It is. It's also a food industry facility. This plant is a major North American supplier of food-grade phosphates and phosphoric acids. Did you ever drink an effervescent "phosphate" at an ice cream parlor or soda fountain? You'll see phosphoric acid on the nutrition label of soft drinks.

Phosphate is an essential ingredient for baking powder. Products from this plant find their way into cereals, cakes, pancakes, and waffles. Phosphates for dentistry and for processed cheese and meat are made here as well. Phosphate is important for metabolism in both plants and animals. It is essential in plant food fertilizers and is added to cattle rations. People need phosphate for bone, nerve, and muscle health.

Phosphate rock is mined in Idaho and shipped here in rail gondola cars. After processing, rail tankcars and trucks take the phosphoric acid to food plants all across the country for use in the food we eat.

Astaris is a new company, organized in 2000, but the plant was first opened in 1951. Three generations of workers are employed here, many from families who have had a long affiliation with agriculture and the food industries.

206 Leavenworth County

At this point, you have entered Leavenworth County, established in 1855, one of the oldest counties in Kansas. Named after Fort Leavenworth, the first fort west of the Missouri River, this county was carved out of Delaware Trust Lands of the Delaware Indians.

207 Fort Leavenworth

Fort Leavenworth and the town of Leavenworth lie about 15 miles north of I-70 (Exit 224). Colonel Henry Leavenworth set up a fort to protect wagon trains from Native Americans who were angry at the intrusion of settlers. The fort was supposed to be located on the east bank of the Missouri River. However, upon arrival, Colonel Leavenworth noted that the east bank was an unsuitable, marshy area. He sent a message to the War Department, saying that, with its permission, he would build the fort upon the west bank's bluff overlooking the river. Permission was given, and on May 8, 1827, he established Fort Leavenworth on what would become the Kansas side of the river, rather than on the Missouri side.

The fort was used as an army headquarters during the Mexican War of 1846. Abraham Lincoln made a campaign stop here when he was running for president in 1859, and during the Civil War, the fort was used to muster volunteers into Union service. Fort Leavenworth was never attacked by Indians or Confederates.

Today, the 8,000-acre fort is the site for the army's Command and General Staff College. More than 80,000 US and international officers have passed through the army's senior tactical college since its inception in 1881. A US federal penitentiary is also located nearby. The fame of this prison and the infamy of its inmates have made *Leavenworth* synonymous with *prisons*.

The city of Leavenworth was created after the fort had been built. Politically, Leavenworth was proslavery early on, and it prospered because of its proximity to the fort and the Missouri River. Today, Leavenworth has more than 35,000 residents and still prospers by being adjacent to the fort and prison.

210 Kansas Forests

Notice how many more trees there are here than you saw west of Topeka. Less than 5 percent of Kansas is forested, but those 2.5 million acres of forests are important ecologically and economically. Most forests are here in the eastern third of the state, with 83 percent of them adjacent to rivers or streams. These riparian forests not only harbor wildlife, including endangered species, but also protect water quality in the streams by stabilizing the banks.

Kansas forest products—wood, lumber, paper—and related industries contribute $2.1 billion to the state economy annually, support over 9,000 jobs, and are responsible for about $169 million in taxes each year. The state has more than fifty sawmills that harvest over 20 million board feet of timber annually, enough wood to construct an estimated 1,700 average-sized homes. However, most Kansas timber is not used for home construction but ends up as furniture, veneer, pallets, and gun stocks. In fact, much of the walnut harvested here goes into making gun stocks, establishing Kansas as a leading supplier for this industry. Black walnut accounts for most of the timber harvested. Other important species are bur oak, red oak, and ash.

Although forests are scarce, they make a vital contribution to the quality of life in Kansas. As you drive east from here, you will see more and more trees.

213 Ice Age Kansas

The gentle rolling hills indicate that you are traveling in the Glaciated Region of Kansas, which is bounded roughly by the Kansas River on the south and the Blue River (near Manhattan) on the west. Read more about the effects of glaciers in this eleven-county area of northeast Kansas at 214W (p. 9).

214 Woodland Wildlife

The deer crossing sign reminds us that the woodlands of eastern Kansas, interspersed with farm fields and pastures, provide ideal habitats for many kinds of wildlife. White-tailed deer and wild turkey are conspicuous from the interstate as they stand in the fields. Bobcat and badger populations are increasing here. The red-tailed hawks mentioned previously are abundant in this area. Look for a white object in the trees. It may well be the white breast of a red-tailed hawk.

216 Silo Collection (218W, p. 7)

Just past the tollbooths on the left is a large group of grain storage bins. Bill Theno collects them to store grain—100,000 bushels of grain. The buildings are equipped to house cattle or hogs. So, depending on market conditions, there may be 7,000 to 8,000 head of hogs being fed, or the grain may be shifted to feed beef cattle. The long, horizontal buildings (180 feet by 70 feet) at the rear of the farmstead hold 150 head of beef cows and calves.

221 Welcome to Wyandotte (418W, p. 2)

You'll soon enter Wyandotte County—the last county you will cross before leaving Kansas. It is named for the Wyandot Indians, who were relocated here from their lands in Ohio in 1843.

222 Agriculture Hall of Fame

This next exit can take you north to historic Fort Leavenworth. Also, you may want to visit the National Agricultural Center and Hall of Fame just off the interstate. The Hall of Fame was chartered by Congress to honor America's farmers. It contains a collection of thousands of historic relics and pieces of farm equipment, including Harry Truman's plow. Interesting tales celebrating the achievements of farmers are told on this 172-acre site.

223 Marbles and Memories

If you've lost your marbles, you can replace them at Moon Marble Company south of Exit 224 in Bonner Springs. Moon Marble Company is one of the "8 Wonders of Kansas Commerce" because it is the only store in the country where you can buy handmade marbles and watch them being made. Read more about this company and the old-fashioned games that are sold there at 224W (p. 5).

224 Trail's End

You are nearing the end of the trail—at least in Kansas. If you have been using this guide since western Kansas, you will recall reading about locations along the Butterfield Overland Despatch stage line and the Smoky Hill Trail, the quickest but most dangerous route to the Denver goldfields. North of here in Atchison, the Smoky Hill Trail began. You may recall that David Butterfield's stage line traveled the Smoky Hill Trail from near here three times a week. Early pioneers followed the major river systems westward from Kansas City because they provided water for people and livestock and because the river valleys were relatively flat compared with the surrounding hills. Later, state and federal highways followed these same routes. As you have traveled across Kansas, you, too, have been following trails used by both Native Americans and pioneers many years ago.

At mile 226, the Kansas Turnpike ends. There is no indicator of this other than that the mile is now 410—the distance from Colorado.

226 The Kansas Speedway (411W, p. 4)

The large complex on the left is the Kansas Speedway motor sports complex. Since it opened in June 2001, it has hosted Indy Racing League and NASCAR races, including the Winston Cup Series and Craftsman Truck Series. The stands seat about 64,000 people, a crowd larger than the population of all but six Kansas towns. Only Wichita, Overland Park, Kansas City, Olathe, Topeka, and Lawrence have more people than would fit into these grandstands. In fact, the entire populations of most Kansas *counties* could watch a race together and not fill the stands!

North of the Speedway is the Legends shopping and entertainment complex. More than eighty Kansans are honored among the shops and restaurants. A free audio walking tour is available.

412 Kansas City, Kansas

Kansas City, Kansas, is not the biggest or most populated city in the state. Many people think it *is* because they consider the whole metropolitan area, most of which is in Kansas City, Missouri. The skyscrapers you see on the horizon are in Missouri.

Lewis and Clark passed by here in 1804 and 1806 and reported that the site had potential for commerce; it would be a perfect place to construct a trading house. But it was not until 1868 that businessmen organized the Kansas City, Kansas, Town Company.

Kansas City has always benefited from being centrally located on the continent. Originally, it attracted meat-processing companies because of its proximity to the railroads and the prairie pastures where beef cattle were raised. The meat-processing business was so good in the beginning that there were labor shortages in the city. Demand for labor caused wages to skyrocket. The high wages attracted many immigrants with the promise of a good job and a better way of life. From 1890 until the start of World War I, Kansas City, Kansas, became home for thousands of European immigrants, with members of each nationality settling in certain areas of the city. This made Kansas City a culturally diverse urban center.

Eventually, meat processing lost its position as the leading economic force in Kansas City because of the development of feedlots in the western part of the state. However, other industries took over. Kansas City developed the first planned industrial park in the United States. A B-25 aircraft bomber plant was opened in 1940, and after World War II, General Motors purchased the plant and used it for a new car assembly facility. From that point on, Kansas City never looked back as more manufacturers located or relocated to the area because of the ample supply of labor and the central location.

414 Grinter House and Ferry

Two miles south of I-70 at Exit 414 lies the Grinter Place Museum. The Grinter House was built by Moses Grinter in 1857. This two-story home is the oldest unaltered building in Wyandotte County. Grinter maintained the first ferry to cross the Kansas River. For a time, it was the only ferry serving an important military road between Oklahoma and Fort Leavenworth. See 415W (p. 3).

415 Another Indian Battle

North of this location is the Huron Indian Cemetery. Although this site is not significant for bloody battles fought between the US Army and the native Indians, a battle of a different sort was fought here nonetheless. After the Wyandots had been manipulated into ceding their Ohio lands to the US government, they decided to set up camp on a government-owned strip of land near the junction of the Missouri and Kansas Rivers. The Delaware tribe, distant relatives of the Wyandots, owned land on the north side of the Kansas River. They sold the Wyandots 36 square miles of land between the fork of the two rivers so they could have a home.

The Wyandots liked their new home but soon encountered difficulties. The tribe had come to the area 700 members strong, but an influenza epidemic swept through, killing 60 tribe members. Then a flood killed 40 more because the dead vegetation left behind by the floodwaters decomposed in the summer heat and spread a disease through the tribe.

The Wyandots designated an area, now known as the Huron Cemetery, as a burying ground for tribe members who had died as a result of the flood or the flu. Between the years 1844 and 1855, at least 400 people were buried there, including famous chiefs such as Warpole, Tauromee, Squeendehtee, Serrahas, and Big Tree. However, none of the graves were marked.

As the years passed, the land became neglected. Businesspeople from Kansas City thought the area was an eyesore and slipped through Congress an item in an Indian appropriation bill authorizing the secretary of the interior to sell the land. The item, buried in the sixty-five-page bill, allowed the secretary to relocate the remains of persons buried at the Huron Cemetery to another site.

Helena and Lyda Conley, descendants of Wyandot tribe members, learned of the bill and determined to save their ancestors' graves. The two women padlocked the cemetery gate, constructed a small fort, and placed signs that said "Trespass at Your Peril." The women vowed to kill anyone who tried to enter the cemetery or remove its contents.

The women also filed suit against the secretary of the interior to restrain him from selling the cemetery. A federal judge threatened to incarcerate the women for contempt. Later, the two were charged with disturbing the peace. Their small fort was even burned. But the women persevered and eventually aroused public sentiment in their favor.

Seven years later, Congress repealed the statute. The women had won the battle. In 1918, the government agreed to maintain the site forever. The cemetery remains as a monument to the Indians buried there and the sisters who kept them in their resting place.

419 Railroads

In 1802, Thomas Jefferson predicted, "The introduction of so powerful an agent as steam to a carriage on wheels will make a great change in the situation of man." As you have seen, nowhere was his prediction more correct than in Kansas. Railroads changed everything! The train yards to the right of I-70 for the next 2 miles are another reminder of the impact of railroads in shaping the Kansas landscape. Railroads determined which towns lived and which towns died. They brought people to Kansas. They transported the state's resources and products. Kansas City's central location has made it a transfer and consolidation point for numerous items shipped by rail. Today, the rail yard is primarily a railcar repair yard for Union Pacific cars, like the ones you see waiting to be fixed or refurbished.

The importance of the railroad cannot be overstated. For fifty years, up until the 1920s when autos and paved highways crossed the country, every facet of life was affected by the railroad. Union Pacific alone has 2,335 miles of track in Kansas and employs more than 1,700 people. It is fitting that we find a major rail yard near the end of our journey through Kansas.

421 Kaw Point Park

Take Exit 423B (James Street) ahead and follow the brown signs to visit the location of Lewis and Clark's campsite at the junction of the Kansas and Missouri Rivers. Their expedition arrived on June 26, 1804, and spent three days here resting, repairing their boats, and exploring the surrounding area. While here, they saw deer, elk, bear, and their first buffalo. They also noted many "Parrot queets," the now-extinct Carolina parakeet—a brilliant green, yellow, and orange bird that moved about in fast-flying flocks up and down the river bottoms. This park offers a great view of downtown Kansas City and a statue titled *Preceding On,* which honors the perseverance of Lewis and Clark. You will also find woodland trails, wildflowers, and several interpretive signs about their visit and about the Native Americans who lived here.

422 Modifying the Missouri

The junction of the Kansas and Missouri Rivers is just north of the spot where you will cross into Missouri at Kansas City. This river

Lewis and Clark statue, Preceding On

junction looks much different than it did when the Lewis and Clark expedition poled upstream. The river has lost its natural meander, wide marshes, and sandbars. Instead, it looks like a big ditch with clean, well-defined banks that allow for barge traffic and help the area to cope with major floods that come about every fifty years. The most destructive flood was in July 1951, when floodwaters 30 feet deep spread throughout neighborhoods, killing forty-one people and causing $900 million in damages. To counter this history of flooding, the river has been diked and channelized to cause the water to flow more quickly away from the city, and levees have been built to keep the water confined to the river channel. Ironically, though, these structures actually can contribute to flooding downstream. It is very expensive and often impossible to fight the forces of nature.

423 Low Point of Your Trip

As you approach the Kansas River ahead, you will be near the lowest elevation along I-70 in Kansas—760 feet above sea level. If you have been traveling from the Colorado line, you have dropped more than 3,000 feet in elevation as you drove east across Kansas. Traveling more than 400 miles to drop 3,000 feet is not the sort of elevation change that makes your ears pop, but it does mean there is a more moderate climate here in eastern Kansas. And for one last time, it reminds you that much of Kansas is not flat!

Happy Trails!

When Lewis and Clark camped along the river near here during their famous expedition, they reported that the area was "by no means bad." We trust that you feel the same way as you leave Kansas. Our hope is that as you traveled across our state, you were pleasantly surprised by our topography, history, natural beauty, prosperity, and productivity. Most of all, we hope that you will return soon to travel more Kansas trails.

References

The information presented in this book came from publications, personal interviews, and websites. We used the publications listed here for background information. Four books published by the University Press of Kansas were particularly useful: *The WPA Guide to 1930s Kansas*; *1001 Kansas Place Names*; *Ghost Towns of Kansas: A Traveler's Guide*; and *Roadside Kansas: A Traveler's Guide to Its Geology and Landmarks.*

We formally interviewed individuals at sites along I-70, as well as knowledgeable personnel at museums and universities in Kansas. On occasion, people shared a few comments to identify a particular sight or provide directions. Those whose names we have and who offered helpful information are listed here as well.

We also made use of selected websites for specialized information. These, too, are listed here.

Publications

ASABE Standards, Engineering Practices, and Data. St. Joseph, MI: American Society of Agricultural and Biological Engineers, 2001.

Bird, Roy. *Heartland History: Stories and Facts from Kansas.* New York: Cummings and Hathaway, 1990.

Buchanan, Rex C., and James R. McCauley. *Roadside Kansas: A Traveler's Guide to Its Geology and Landmarks.* Lawrence: University Press of Kansas, 1987.

Carter, Deane G. "The Unit Space Method of Barn Planning." *Agricultural Engineering* 9, no. 9 (September 1928): 271–273.

Chiras, Daniel, and John Reganold. *Natural Resource Conservation: Management for a Sustainable Future.* Upper Saddle River, NJ: Pearson Prentice Hall, 2010.

Federal Writers' Project. *The WPA Guide to 1930s Kansas.* Lawrence: University Press of Kansas, 1984.

Fitzgerald, Daniel C. *Ghost Towns of Kansas: A Traveler's Guide.* Lawrence: University Press of Kansas, 1988.

Frazier, Ian. *Great Plains.* New York: Farrar, Straus Giroux, 1989.

Harrington, Grant. *Historic Spots or Milestones in the Progress of Wyandotte County, Kansas.* Merriam, KS: Mission Press, 1935.

Harvey, Ethel M. "History of Collyer, Kansas." Unpublished manuscript, 1976. Archived at Trego County Historical Society.

Least Heat Moon, William. *Blue Highways: A Journey into America*. New York: Fawcett Crest, 1982.

Leland, Charles G. *The Union Pacific Railroad: Or, Three Thousand Miles in a Railway Car.* Altenmünster, Germany: Jazzybee Verlag, 2012.
Muilenburg, Grace, and Ada Swineford. *Land of the Post Rock.* Lawrence: University Press of Kansas, 1975.
Quayle, William A. *The Prairie and the Sea*. New York: Jennings and Graham, 1905.
Richmond, Robert. *Kansas: A Land of Contrast.* Arlington Heights, IL: Forum Press, 1979.
Schirmer, Sherry L., and Theodore A. Wilson. *Milestones: A History of the Kansas Highway Commission and the Department of Transportation.* Topeka: Kansas Department of Transportation, 1986.
Self, Huber. *Geography of Kansas.* Oklahoma City, OK: Harlow Publishing, 1959.
Van Meter McCoy, Sondra, and Jan Hults. *1001 Kansas Place Names.* Lawrence: University Press of Kansas, 1989.

Interviews

Janice Alfers, Edson SIGCO elevators, Goodland
Bob Atchison, Kansas Forest Service, Manhattan
Steve Boshoff, ADM, Goodland
Ben Brandvik, Pioneer Ag Grain Division, Goodland
Albert J. Brown, resident, Walker
Doug Burr, EnerSys, Inc., Hays
Don Cranston, rancher, Colby
George and Deb Davis, Clock House Antiques, Lawrence
Ken Deering, Astaris LLC, Lawrence
Marjean Dienes, Trego County Historical Society, WaKeeney
Frank Draney, Astaris LLC, Lawrence
Ron Eberle, Grainfield Lions Club, Grainfield
Linda Frederick, EnerSys, Inc., Hays
Gordon Fry, Astaris LLC, Lawrence
Frank Georgiana, Enel, Inc., Lincoln
Gary Gilbert, Woodlawn Farms, Topeka
Josh Gilliland, Mingo Location Manager, Frontier Ag, Inc., Mingo
Justin Gilpin, Kansas Wheat Commission, Manhattan
Brian Green, Armour Swift-Eckrich, Junction City
Lori Hall, Rolling Hills Wildlife Conservation Center, Salina
Lee Hart, Arrow H Stables, Topeka
Dan and Josh Helvey, farmers, Ellsworth
Kelly Hill, Kansas Speedway, Kansas City
Dan Holt, director, Eisenhower Center, Abilene
John Ingham, Abilene Elevator, Abilene
Janet Johannes, Ellis County Historical Society, Hays
Darnelle Keith, Grainfield Elevator, Grainfield
Tom Kinderknecht, Midwest Coop, Ogallah
Judy Kleinsorge, Prairie Museum of Art and History, Colby
Gerry Klema, resident, Wilson
Ron Koehn, Midwest Coop, Quinter
Norbert Korte, Red River Commodities, Rexford
Betty Lipp, rancher, Collyer
Cheryl Madison, rancher, Oakley
Ron Majors, resident, Wilson

Jason Morton, Berry Plastics, Lawrence
Derek Peine, Western Plains Energy, LLC, Oakley
Sue Pine, Pine Sod Farm, Lawrence
Todd Plummer, Western Plains Energy, LLC, Oakley
Dale Reynolds, Abilene Elevator, Abilene
Evea Rumple, Register of Deeds, Trego County, WaKeeney
David Shapland, Russell Stover, Abilene
Steve Tate, farmer, Bonner Springs
Susie Theno, farmer, Tonganoxie
Steve Wise, Cargill, Salina

Websites

Alma Creamery, www.kansastravel.org/almacreamery.htm
The Austin Company—Russell Stovers, www.theaustin.com
Brown v. Board National Historic Site, www.nps.gov/brvb
Buckeye Wind Energy Center, www.invenergyllc.com
City of WaKeeney, www.wakeeney.org
Ellsworth Area, www.kansasprairie.net
Engineering America, www.engamerica.com
Ethanol Plant, www.growthenergy.org
Frontier Ag, Inc., www.frontieraginc.com
Hays Visitor and Convention Bureau, www.haysusa.net
Iron Crosses, http://library.ndsu.edu/grhc/articles/magazines/articles/winistorfer.html
Kansas Beef Council, www.kansasbeef.org
Kansas Corn Growers Association, www.ksgrains.com/corn
Kansas Forest Service, www.kansasforests.org
Kansas Geological Survey, www.kgs.ku.edu
Kansas Grain Sorghum Producers Association, www.ksgrainsorghum.org
Kansas State University, www.ksu.edu
Kansas Turnpike Authority, www.ksturnpike.com
Kansas Wheat Commission, www.kswheat.com
Kanza Education and Science Park, www.westarenergy.com
Kaw Point Park, www.lewisandclarkwyco.org
Konza Prairie, www.konza.ksu.edu
Plumlee Bison Ranch, www.plumleeranch.com
Russell County Historical Society, www.russellkshistory.com
State of Kansas, www.kansas.gov
Sternberg Museum, http://sternberg.fhsu.edu
Sunflower, www.canadasunflower.com
Union Pacific Railroad, www.up.com
United States Department of Agriculture, www.usda.gov

United States Department of Agriculture Census of Agriculture, www.agcensus.usda.gov/
University of Kansas, www.ku.edu
Wamego Convention and Visitors Bureau, http://www.visitwamego.com

Index

COUNTIES

EVENTS, HISTORICAL

INDIAN TRIBES

PEOPLE

PLACES TO VISIT

RIVERS, CREEKS, AND LAKES

WILDLIFE AND PLANTS

Birds

Flowers

Mammals

Trees